Teamwork

Teamwork

Multi-Disciplinary Perspectives

Edited by

Natalie Gold

palgrave
macmillan

First published 2005 by
PALGRAVE MACMILLAN
Houndmills, Basingstoke, Hampshire RG21 6XS and
175 Fifth Avenue, New York, N. Y. 10010
Companies and representatives throughout the world

PALGRAVE MACMILLAN is the global academic imprint of the
Palgrave Macmillan division of St. Martin's Press, LLC and of Palgrave
Macmillan Ltd. Macmillan® is a registered trademark in the United
States, United Kingdom and other countries. Palgrave is a registered
trademark in the European Union and other countries.

ISBN 1–4039–3390–1

This book is printed on paper suitable for recycling and made from
fully managed and sustained forest sources.

A catalogue record for this book is available from the British Library.

Library of Congress Cataloging-in-Publication Data
Teamwork : multi-disciplinary perspectives / edited by Natalie Gold.
      p. cm.
  Includes bibliographical references and index.
    ISBN 1–4039–3390–1 (alk. paper)
      1. Teams in the workplace–Psychological aspects. 2. Interpersonal
relations. 3. Interpersonal communication. 4. Group problem solving.
5. Cooperation. 6. Decision making. I. Gold, Natalie, 1976–

HD66.T4384 2005
302.3'5–dc22   2004052229

10   9   8   7   6   5   4   3   2   1
14   13   12   11   10   09   08   07   06   05

Printed and bound in Great Britain by
Antony Rowe Ltd, Chippenham and Eastbourne

To the memory of Michael Bacharach

Contents

Preface

This volume results from the discussions at 'Teamwork: a Multi-Professional Workshop', held in Oxford on April 9th–10th, 2003. The workshop was originally conceived of by Michael Bacharach and, after his suddenly and untimely death in August 2002, it was organized as a tribute to him and the importance of his research programme. The workshop aimed to bring together researchers and practitioners from a wide range of fields to report both research findings and practical experiences, and to open new dialogues between them. This reflected Michael's view that teamwork needs to be studied both as a general human and animal faculty, defining a high-level topic in the theory of decision making, and at a practical level, in order to empower groups of actors in many specific fields including industry, the arts and entertainment to achieve their goals more fully. His background paper for the workshop appears as the foreword to this collection. It was appropriate to print only a selection of the academic presentations delivered at the workshop, plus some additional papers that have been commissioned, but I hope that our work has been informed by our discussions with the non-academic participants and that the resulting volume will be of interest to academics and non-academics alike. I would like to thank the Economic and Social Research Council and the Bounded Rationality in Economic Behaviour Unit at the University of Oxford for their sponsorship of the workshop; Abigail Barr, Ann Gibson and James Walmsley for invaluable help and advice on its organization; and Andrew Colman and John Rayneux for their help and advice on the editing of this book.

Natalie Gold

List of Tables

List of Figures

Acknowledgements

Sugden's contribution was first published in *Philosophical Explorations*, Vol. 6(3), pp. 165–181 and is reprinted with permission from the editors.

Wilson, Timmel and Miller's contribution was first published in Human Nature 15(3). Copyright © 2004 by Transaction Publishers. Reprinted with permission of the publishers, Transaction Publishers, Rutgers University, 35 Berrue Circle, Piscataway, NJ 08854.

The screen shots in the chapter by Wyatt, Matsumura and Todd are reprinted from www-2.cs.cmu.edu/~robosoccer/image-gallery/simulator/screenshot3.png courtesy of Brett Browning, Patrick Riley and Manuela Veloso of the Computer Science Department, Carnegie Mellon University.

Notes on Contributors

Peter Andras is a Lecturer in the School of Computing Science at the University of Newcastle. His research is focused on the study of complex systems. Previously he was the director of the non-profit Civitas Foundation in Romania working in the fields of local governmental development and civil society.

Cristina Bicchieri is Professor of Philosophy and Decision Sciences and Director of the Philosophy, Politics and Economics Program at the University of Pennsylvania. She has published widely in philosophy, sociology, political science and economics journals. She is the author of *Rationality and Coordination* (1993, 1997) and *The Grammar of Society: The Nature and Dynamics of Social Norms* (forthcoming), and co-author of *The Dynamics of Norms* (1997) and *The Logic of Strategy* (1999). Her current research interests are the emergence and dynamics of norms, social learning, and the foundations of game theory.

Carol Borrill is a senior lecturer in work and organizational psychology, based at the Aston University in Birmingham, UK. She has been involved in a range of major research projects in the NHS, including investigating causes of stress among staff working in the NHS, the effectiveness of multi-disciplinary team working, the relationship between people management practices and hospital performance, and the implementation of employee involvement practices in the NHS. She is also involved in a range of 'Research into Practice' projects, funded by the NHS Modernisation Agency that ensure that the major findings from health service research are disseminated and used within the service.

Andrew M. Colman is Professor of Psychology at the University of Leicester. Before moving to Leicester, he taught at Rhodes University and Cape Town University in South Africa. He has published numerous research articles and books including *Game Theory and its Applications in the Social and Biological Sciences* (2nd edn, 1995) and an edited volume entitled *Cooperation and Competition in Humans and Animals* (1982). His current research focuses primarily on interactive reasoning in games.

Margaret Gilbert is Professor of Philosophy at the University of Connecticut, Storrs. She has been a visiting teacher and researcher at many institutions including Princeton University and King's College London. Her current work focuses on applications within social and political philosophy of the theory of social phenomena first advanced in her book *On Social Facts* (1989).

Natalie Gold has a doctorate in economics from Oxford University. She investigates individual and collective decision making, using methods from a variety of disciplines including economics, philosophy and psychology. In particular, she is interested in the incorporation of developments in cognitive science into social scientific theories.

Wiebe van der Hoek is Professor in Computer Science at the University of Liverpool, where he heads the Agent ART group. He did his PhD thesis on Epistemic Logic at the Free University of Amsterdam. From 1993–2002 he was a member of the Intelligent Systems group in Utrecht, working on modal logics for agent systems. His current interests are Knowledge, Rationality and Action in a broad sense; he is also editor-in-chief of a journal carrying that name.

Susan Hurley is Professor at the University of Warwick and a Fellow of All Souls College Oxford. She is author of *Natural Reasons* (1989), *Consciousness in Action* (1998), and *Justice, Luck, and Knowledge* (2003), and editor of *Foundations of Decision Theory* (1991), On *Human Rights* (1993), *Perspectives on Imitation: From Neuroscience to Social Science* (in press), and *Rational Animals?* (forthcoming). She is currently working primarily in philosophy of psychology and neuroscience, and is interested in linking the cognitive sciences to social and political issues.

John Lazarus is Reader in Animal Behaviour in the Psychology, Brain and Behaviour division of the School of Biology at the University of Newcastle. His research has involved empirical and theoretical studies in the evolution of social behaviour, and in information gathering. He has edited the journals *Animal Behaviour* and *Ethology*. Currently he is working on human sex ratios and cooperation. His interest in cooperation centres on evolutionary origins, human psychology and ethics.

Yoshiyuki Matsumura is a Lecturer in the Faculty of Textile Science and Technology at the Shinshu University in Japan. He obtained his PhD from Kobe University in 2002, and was a research fellow of the Japan Society for the Promotion of Science from 2000 to 2003. His interests include evolutionary learning, neural networks and robotics.

Ralph R. Miller is a Distinguished Professor of Psychology at SUNY-Binghamton who studies basic information processing in rodents and humans cognition. His research has focused largely on rules for retrieval and expression of acquired information. In recent years, he has extended his studies to human contingency learning and causal judgement.

David P. Myatt is the Oxford University Lecturer in Economic Theory and Mathematical Economics, and the John Thomson Fellow and Tutor in Economics at St Catherine's College. He specializes in game theory –

the analysis of strategic decision-making – and its application to the fields of microeconomics, industrial organization, and political science.

Mark Pauly is a researcher for the national scientific research centre of France (CNRS) at the institute for computer science in Toulouse (IRIT). His general research interests are logic, game theory and the study of social mechanisms through formal models of interaction. His research on teamwork investigates the axioms of coalitional power in games and their complexity.

Robert Sugden is Professor of Economics at the University of East Anglia, Norwich. His research uses a combination of theoretical, experimental and philosophical methods to investigate issues in welfare economics, social choice, choice under uncertainty, the foundations of decision and game theory, the methodology of economics, and the evolution of social conventions.

John J. Timmel, Jr. is an evolutionary biologist who investigated human decision making and problem solving while earning his Ph.D. at Binghamton University.

Matthew Todd graduated in artificial intelligence and computer science from the University of Birmingham. He co-founded Iizuka Software in 2002.

Chris Wallace is Oxford University Lecturer in Economics and Fellow in Economics at Trinity College. He is mainly interested in game theory and, in particular, evolutionary game theory, and its application to economics, the social sciences, and theoretical population biology.

Michael West is a professor of Organizational Psychology, and the Research Director for Aston Business School. He has directed research projects in the NHS and private sector on the relationship between people management practices and organizational performance, and has researched and written extensively on creativity and innovation in organizations, team effectiveness, and how to create team-based organizations.

Michael Wooldridge is a Professor and Head of Department of Computer Science at the University of Liverpool. His research interests lie in the area of multiagent systems, and in particular, in the use of formal methods for reasoning about multiagent systems. He has authored three books in this area (most recently *An Introduction to Multiagent Systems*, 2002), and edited a further 12. He is editor-in-chief of the Kluwer journal *Autonomous Agents & Multiagent Systems*.

Jeremy Wyatt is director of the Intelligent Robotics Lab in the School of Computer Science, at the University of Birmingham. He works on machine learning, artificial intelligence and robots.

David Sloan Wilson is an evolutionary biologist who studies humans along with other species. He is best known for championing the theory of multilevel selection, in which adaptation and natural selection can occur at all levels of the biological hierarchy. Additional interests include the nature of individual differences and evolutionary processes that involve non-genetic inheritance mechanisms. He publishes in psychology, anthropology, and philosophy journals in addition to his mainstream biological research. His books include *The Natural Selection of Populations and Communities* (1980), *Unto Others: the evolution and psychology of unselfish behavior* (with Elliott Sober; 1998), and *Darwin's Cathedral: evolution, religion, and the nature of society* (2002).

Foreword: Teamwork

Michael Bacharach

A team is a group of agents with a common goal which can only be achieved by appropriate combinations of individual activities. Thus teamwork is a species of *cooperation*. Teams in the human world are of vastly different scales: couples, families, workgroups, platoons, sports teams and street gangs, bodies of supporters of political parties, groups of petitioners, nations in time of war, international military alliances. Teamwork is not confined to modern man; the hunting groups of chimpanzees bear most of the marks of teams, and early man was a team player in predation, foraging and defence. Teams may be long-lived institutions like terrorist cells, or ephemeral products of circumstances like three passers-by giving a motorist a push start. Communication may be minimal, as in the case of a platoon in a jungle or a partnership in bridge, or there may be a rich communicative structure. We ask: what makes all these be teams, what makes teams tick, what makes the more successful ones successful?

1 Background

There have been major developments in thinking about teams in recent years. Three prominent ones have been: new theories of cooperative group behaviour in anthropology, biology, psychology, and game theory, which seek non-individualistic explanations of successful group action in which groups are attributed one or more characteristics of teams; the description and design of goal-directed *multiagent systems* in AI, robotics, and other branches of computer science, which are groups of linked computers or robots which either model human agents for theoretical purposes, or substitute for human agents for practical ones; and the increasing use of teams of the form of *self-organizing workgroups* and *management teams* in management, due to a growing belief that teamwork raises productivity.

The phenomenon of teamwork has aspects that appear to evade explanation in terms of rational individual choice, and to be best explained by a propensity of individual humans to identify themselves at certain times as members of supra-individual agencies, such as teams. The faculty of group identification in general often arouses deep suspicion and hostility because it is associated with irrationality, hatred of outsiders, and a loss of autonomy. Yet it may be precisely this phenomenon that is also responsible for the universally applauded virtues and capacities that we call 'teamwork'. If so, then the easy association of human progress with individual choice may need to re-examined.

Much has been written about what teams are, how they operate, and what they can achieve. It is fair to say that, although this literature is rich and illuminating, it is essentially descriptive and there is as yet no comprehensive theory of teams. A major objective of this workshop is enable the several disciplines that study teams themselves to come together, team-like, to initiate the development of such a theory.

2   Dimensions of team theory

In addressing the basic questions above one can distinguish five different dimensions of teams – members' *motivations* and *competences*, and team *architecture*, *activity*, and *formation*. These give rise to different, though intimately connected, sets of questions.

Motivations

First, there are questions about motivations. Even if the very concept of a team involves a common goal, in real teams individual members often have private interests as well. Some individuals may be better motivated than others to 'play for the team' rather than for themselves. So questions arise for members about whether other members can be trusted to try to do what is best for the team. Here team theory meets *trust* theory, and the currently hot topic of when and why it is rational to trust. Organizational psychology studies how motivations in teams are determined in part by aspects of personality, such as leadership qualities, and by phenomena belonging to the affective dimension, such as mood and 'emotional contagion'.

Competences

Next there are questions about competences. Just as a member may be suspicious of others' motives, so she may also have concerns about others' abilities to perform their parts. A footballer may be concerned that if he passes the ball to X in the goal-mouth, X may go for glory and so fail to pass to a better-placed striker (a motivational failure), but also that X will fail to gather the ball (a physical skill failure) or fail to anticipate – to see where he is expected to be to receive it (a cognitive skill failure).

Under the heading of competences we may include the ability to solve the game-theoretic problems involved in coordination. There are usually several or many different ways in which groups of agents with a common goal can achieve it – different 'coordination points'. When communication is not possible, it is far from obvious how agents will manage to identify the same coordination point as each other; and if they go for different ones there will be a 'coordination failure'. Part of the answer is provided by humans' ability to choose the same point in virtue of its *salience* but for a long time it has been unclear how salience could weigh with rational agents. Recent theoretical and experimental work points towards a solution of the residual mystery based on the idea that group identifying agents do not reason about what to do in the ordinary way because they ask themselves not 'What should I do?' but 'What should *we* do?'. This leads them to 'team reason'. In philosophy, team reasoning provides a new account of 'collective intentions' and, in its 'circumspect' variety which allows for possible 'lapsing' by some team members, a game theoretic foundation for 'cooperative utilitarianism'.

While the paradigm setting for decision making studied in game theory has agents reasoning in complete isolation but with plenty of time, this is not the only sort of competence required for successful coordination. In music, dance and sport, team members often get fragmentary perceptual cues from each other, and can fall in with others' initiatives by very quick revision of their plans (called 'split second cuing'), or by anticipation. Improvised initiatives and their anticipation (called 'vision' in football) call for *creativity*, which has been ignored in the formal decision sciences for too long because game theory has taken her menu of options to be given for each player. One aim of the workshop is to enable theorists to learn from practitioners just what is needed for successful coordination in performances of these kinds.

Architecture

The term 'architecture' refers here to the organizational form of the team. At one extreme there is no communication: everyone works out the best team plan (as best she can given her information) and carries out her part in that plan. In another benchmark case, information is pooled, a director computes the best plan and informs everyone of it. There are many architectures in reality, with more or less communication and less or more distributed computation. For team success the architecture must respond to the initial distribution of interests. If personal goals differ from the team goal, it will include some 'incentive-compatible' mechanism which motivates the members to work for the team goal.

Activity

Next, 'activity'. In any team architecture there is room for different possible values of activity variables – ordinary actions such as kicking balls and fleeing from predators, but also the activities of computing and communicating. These are often the main focus in decision theory and in game theory, which deals with the choices by actors of values of the activities they control, given (typically) an architecture in which decision making is completely decentralized. Both for architecture and activity, the study of teams raises questions both about the description and explanation of actual behaviour, and about optimal design. The optimum architecture is the one best calculated to further the team's goal, taking into account the costs of communication and computation. A typical example of a theory concerned with optimizing activity is the 'theory of teams', which sets out to determine optimal decision rules for members, telling each member of a decentralized team what to do in response to each possible observation she may make of the environment.

Formation

'Formation' issues arise when we step back and consider the processes by which teams come into existence: the deliberate search for partners whose skills and other resources are well adapted to the achievement of the team goal; spontaneous formation of the sort that can occur in perceived emergencies and in general when there is perceived positive interdependence, perhaps mediated by group identification. Stepping back even further, we find that as yet little is known about the evolution in mankind of the disposition to work – and play – in teams, and of the capacities needed for successful teamwork. Just as the evolution of cooperativeness in Prisoner's Dilemmas has been a puzzle, so is the evolution of successful working together in the groups with common goals we call teams. Group selection now seems likely to be part of the explanation of both.

3 Applications

The potential applications of the theory of teams and teamwork are too numerous to list. There are many walks of life – domestic, social, political, diplomatic, military, economic, the workplace, entertainment and the arts – in which teamwork is found and in which, by general consent, it could be better. Better teamwork can help car drivers avoid accidents and dissolve traffic jams, football clubs win trophies, and nations win wars. In schools we teach our children teamwork skills, largely by applying educational theories and practices based on common sense and experience. If processes of group identification generate team motivation, using known stimuli for group identity can be used to improve performance of teams of any sort. Discoveries about the cognitive processes at work in improvised coordination, such as split-second cuing and team reasoning, can improve performance in sports and the arts. If team reasoning is a natural way to reason in teams, then inducing team identity can help produce efficient outcomes in the vast array of coordination problems and collective action problems, from unblocking traffic jams to attending to the environment, that characterize modern society. It offers us new ways of thinking about old problems, such as why and how people vote in elections and how to solve principle-agent problems in the workplace. In domains such as industry, government and the military world multiagent system theory may enable us to construct viable systems of connected teams of greater complexity than heretofore. As we discover more about the nature of teams and the processes that underlie successful teamwork, we will be able to design more effective methods for educating our children to be good and effective team players. Perhaps most important of all, studying the upside of group activity – teamwork – may help to right the balance in the debate between those who believe there is not and those who believe there is such a thing as society.

The Teamwork Workshop is intended to initiate a multidisciplinary scientific study of the nature of teamwork. Simply putting together the heads of specialists from many disciplines and professions for the first time may yield immediate new insights. Beyond that, the sheer scale of the phenomenon of teamwork, the deficiencies of real teams, and the scantiness of past research into many issues raised at this workshop, mean that new research on them is likely to yield a continuing stream of theoretical advances and practical benefits.

Introduction: Teamwork in Theory and in Practice

Natalie Gold

Teamwork is studied in many disciplines, but there is as yet no comprehensive theory of teams. This book brings together perspectives on teamwork from evolutionary biology, psychology, economics, robotics, philosophy, management and artificial intelligence. They provide a wide-ranging survey of current research on teams, using methodologies as diverse as laboratory experiments and evolutionary modelling, epistemic logic and the programming of robots. But teamwork is not only of theoretical, academic interest. It is also of practical application in our everyday lives. Obvious examples are found in the workplace and on the sports field but, if we allow that a team is a group of agents with a common goal which can only be achieved by appropriate combinations of individual activities, then it becomes clear that teamwork is a phenomenon which occurs in a wide variety of forms. Teamwork is commonly found when people engage in any type of joint activity. Professionals such as managers and coaches may have a specialist expertise but we all have some experience of teamwork.

In the professional arena, it is not uncommon to start with a task that is defined as needing teamwork, or a group that is defined as a team, and to ask how their goal can best be achieved, bypassing scholarly questions of what these have in common that makes them be teamwork or teams. In the academic arena, one legacy of previous fragmented, multidisciplinary research on teams is that we do not even have a common terminology, let alone a single answer to such questions. A first step towards this would be to relate the diverse disciplinary perspectives to a single framework. In this introductory chapter, I begin by outlining the rational choice perspective, which informs virtually all the chapters in this book, and may provide such a frame of reference. The rational choice approach models the making of choices and, like all models, it makes various simplifications of the real life phenomena it seeks to explain. I use it to present the core theoretical problems that researchers look to teamwork to resolve, but these by no means encompass all the problems that are important regarding teamwork. I identify some of the stylized features of the rational choice paradigm and compare them with the sort of conditions that may be found in teams in practice, in order to explore how these contrasting conditions affect the research questions that the contributors to this volume seek to answer.

1   Rational choice and the need for teamwork

The rational choice approach models *agents* – which could be any decision-making entity, such as individuals, households or firms – who optimize their actions given their beliefs and desires. It is used both to make normative claims, about what a rational agent should do, and also descriptively, as a basis for predictions about how agents actually behave. A distinction may be made between *decision theory*, where single agents make choices subject to constraints, and *game theory*, where an agent's outcomes may depend not only on her own actions but also on the actions of other *players*. Each player chooses a *strategy* and their *payoffs* depend on the combination of strategies, or *strategy profile*. The payoffs represent the desirability of the outcomes to the players. The basic theory only needs to assume that players have an ordinal ranking of the outcomes (Von Neumann and Morgenstern, 1944), but in many applications it is usual to insert numerical payoffs. Depending on the discipline and the researchers, these numbers could represent monetary or other tangible payoffs, utility payoffs (which include non-pecuniary reasons for acting and intangible payoffs, such as hedonic states) or Darwinian fitness.

The solution concept used in game theory is that rational players would play their parts in a *Nash equilibrium*, where each player makes her best response to the strategy of the other player(s).[1] But, in some games, this solution concept delivers results that are problematic: that are counter to some people's intuitions about what constitutes rational play or that fail to describe what people do when confronted with such games in practice. The most notorious of these games is the Prisoner's Dilemma, which has inspired research on cooperation and teamwork in many academic disciplines. The structure of the game is given in the matrix of Figure 1. There are two players, who each have a choice between two strategies, *C* and *D*. The numbers in the matrix, from one to four, could either be cardinal payoffs or an ordinal ranking of the outcomes, from least to most favourable. The Prisoner's Dilemma is named for the following anecdote, which explains the ordering of the payoffs. Two prisoners are in custody, having committed a serious crime, which carries a long prison sentence. However, there is only enough evidence to convict them of a minor charge, with a correspondingly more lenient punishment. The authorities offer each prisoner the following deal. If she will provide incriminating evidence, enabling them to secure a conviction for the major crime, then she will go free while her compatriot will face a long prison sentence with no parole. But if they both incriminate each other then they will both be con-

Player 2

		Deny	Confess
Player 1	Deny	3, 3	4, 1
	Confess	1, 4	2, 2

Figure 1   The Prisoner's Dilemma

victed of the crime, though they may get early parole in view of their com-
pliant behaviour. Consider the position of one of the prisoners. If her co-
conspirator provides incriminating evidence (strategy D), then she is better
off also providing such evidence (strategy D), as she will get early parole
rather than no parole on her lengthy prison sentence. If her co-conspirator
does not provide such evidence (strategy C), then she is better off incriminating her compatriot (strategy D), as she goes free rather than getting a
lenient sentence. The game is symmetric, anything that is true of one
player is true of both, so the Nash equilibrium is for both to play D.[2] This
results in them both going to prison for a long time (a payoff of two). But if
neither of them had given evidence then they would each have had a more
lenient sentence (a payoff of three). Although each did what was 'individually rational', each would have been better off if neither had provided
incriminating evidence, hence the strategy profile (C, C) is sometimes
referred to as 'collectively rational' and the strategies as 'Cooperate' and
'Defect'.

   This is the paradigm problem of cooperation, which might be said to occur
where there is *scope for common gain*, when there is some strategy profile that
is a Pareto improvement on (i.e. that leaves some players better off and no
players worse off than) the strategy profiles in the solution set (Bacharach,
1999).[3] The incentive structure is not limited to two-player games. The multi-
player version is sometimes called an 'n-person prisoners' dilemma' or a
'social dilemma'. One example of these are public good problems, where each
individual has the opportunity to make a (costly) contribution to a scheme
from which is it not possible to exclude non-contributors from benefiting,
such as street lighting. Another example is common pool resource problems,
where each individual has the opportunity to take resources for themselves
but doing so has a negative effect on others, such as Atlantic cod stocks,
which are being depleted faster than they can replicate themselves. In these
instances, although everyone may agree that we are better off if the public
good is provided or if the resource is not decimated, the individual incentives
are to take the action that leads to the opposite outcome.

One reason for studying teams is to explain how people solve such problems of cooperation, where there is a combination of actions that would be beneficial but also some incentive not to do them. However, standard game theory cannot even provide a full explanation of the seemingly simpler question of how people solve coordination problems, where there is no such incentive to deviate. (The distinction between cooperation and coordination is similar but not identical to that made by biologists between altruism and cooperation, which is discussed further below.) In a classic coordination game, the players get a positive payoff if they both choose the same action and nothing otherwise. Every strategy profile that has all players choosing the same strategy is a Nash equilibrium, so the solution concept is indeterminate. In practice, people do manage to coordinate, but standard game theory cannot explain how. Further, we sometimes have strong intuitions about which strategy profile rational players will play and standard game theory cannot be used to support these intuitions without making further assumptions. Consider the game of Hi-Lo, discussed by Robert Sugden and Susan Hurley in this volume, whose payoff structure is represented in the matrix of Figure 2. There are two Nash equilibria (*Hi*, *Hi*) and (*Lo*, *Lo*). Given the strategy of the other player, each is better off if the two choices match, so it is a coordination game. In fact, they are better off if both choose *Hi*. Many people have the intuition that rational players would do so, but game theory cannot explain why this is rational or how they can do this without introducing further principles of rationality. One suggestion is that standard game theory, in which each agent asks 'what should *I* do?', poses the wrong question and that *team reasoning*, where the players ask 'what should *we* do?', is a valid mode of reasoning that can explain this fundamental problem of coordination (Sugden, 1993; Bacharach, 1999) and that it provides the key to understanding problems of cooperation as well (Bacharach, 2005).

Player 2

		Hi	Lo
Player 1	Hi	2, 2	0, 0
	Lo	0, 0	1, 1

Figure 2   Hi-Lo

In both problems of cooperation and coordination individual agents could realize gains but standard game theory cannot explain why they should or how they would do so. It is in order to solve such problems that we look to teamwork.

2 Teams outside the rational choice model

These paradigm examples of the rational choice model have a number of stylized features: there are two symmetrical agents, who individually compute their best strategy and may decide to act together towards a common goal. These simplifying assumptions contrast with the circumstances that may be faced by teams in practice, both in their size and on the dimensions of motivation, competence, architecture, activity and formation. (The results of the following comparison are summarized in Table 1).

Team size
The paradigm examples of the rational choice approach are two-player games. There is no theoretical restriction on the number of players, witness the study of social dilemmas. But even a social dilemma, when investigated in a laboratory experiment, may have as few as four players. In the practical application of teamwork, team size may vary. Sometimes, in personnel management, it is claimed that a team is restricted by definition to be a certain size, so a group becomes a team when they number, say, between five and nine members (Campion et al., 1993). This may be partly due to a tendency by such practitioners to define teams in a way that is specific to management, where a team may be treated as synonymous with a 'self-organizing workgroup', which is defined by a number of criteria above and beyond a common goal (Goodman et al., 1988). However, whilst it seems correct to say that the number of team members may be related to the task they need to accomplish, if a theory of teams is to be comprehensive it cannot restrict the definition of teams in such a domain specific manner. (It may be the case that these definitions are not supposed to be used outside of the domain of work groups, or such practitioners may simply argue that teams as they occur in other domains are, in fact, not teams at all to the extent that they do not share the features of self-organizing workgroups.) It might be arguable that size is a proxy for some characteristic that distinguishes between a group and a team, but the size of the team itself is not a good basis for restricting what counts as teamwork. In some practical applications that are arguably teamwork, the number of people involved may be very large, for instance in armies or political parties or real world public goods and common pool resource problems.

Motivation

The rational choice model is behaviourist, in the sense that it is concerned with the actions that people take and the outcomes that they achieve, but not their intentions or the reasons for which they take the actions. Agents are modelled as maximizing payoffs, there is no explicit attention given to the heterogeneous motives they may have. If the payoffs are interpreted as pecuniary, this enables prediction of behaviour based on publicly observable parameters. If the payoffs are interpreted as utility, then any difference in motivation may be already be taken account of in the payoffs. However, we might be unwilling to define a group of individuals as a team unless there are corresponding intentions to work together. Further, it might be thought that a team would be characterized by a sense of belonging, or a group identity. In practice, these things might be important for improving the performance of teams. The motivations of team members may affect what incentives will encourage people to work for the team's goals and, if a sense of group identity is associated with successful teamwork, understanding its role and how to generate it will help us to promote effective teamwork.

Competence

In the paradigm examples of the rational choice approach, agents are symmetrical. They have the same strategies available to them and the same payoffs. In practice, the individuals on the team will all be different. In particular, they may have different competences and abilities. In business and management, heterogeneity is seen as a key, and even a defining, feature of teams (Magjuka and Baldwin, 1991). Teams are said to be characterized by 'cooperative role differentiation' (Belbin, 2000) and a lot of attention is given to making typologies, classifying people within these schema and identifying what types work best together (e.g. Beddoes-Jones, 1999; Belbin, 1981). Some of this is based on academic personality psychology (although that places more emphasis on identifying a parsimonious set of underlying dimensions which together capture all personality differences, reducing these from 16 (Cattell, 1947) to five (McCrae and John, 1992) to three factors (Eysenck, 1991), rather than on the classification of people) but such individual differences have yet to be widely incorporated into the academic study of teamwork. Even in robot football (e.g. Wyatt et al., this volume), where each member of the team must learn different skills in order for the team to be successful, before the learning process starts the team members are homogeneous, whereas in practice different team roles are based in pre-existing individual differences.

Architecture

The paradigm architecture in the rational choice model involves distributed decision making, where every agent computes her own action and there is no communication. As well as different competences, another type of asymmetry that may exist between agents is that one of the members is the team leader. One role a leader may perform is to work out the best team plan and then communicate to each member what she should do. Even without a leader, there may be communication between team members and good communication may be an important part of effective teamwork.[4] (In particular, intuition suggests that it is part of the solution of coordination problems.) One reason for the comparative neglect of communication in rational choice theory is that, if sending messages is costless, or *cheap talk*, then people may say anything and, if commitments are not costly to break, then they are not credible. For instance, in the Prisoner's Dilemma if the players could communicate before choosing their strategies and if they agreed to both play *C*, when it was time to play they would still face an incentive to play *D*. So even a player who would play *C* if she could be sure that the other player would too, and hence faces a problem of trust or 'assurance', has no guarantee that her co-player will cooperate when the time comes to make her move. Thus, for instance, in economic models of teams where each individual agent has only partial knowledge of circumstances, the problem is to design rules which tell each agent what action to take for each possible observation she may make (Marschak and Radner, 1972), not how best to communicate that knowledge. Often, in the experimental laboratory, there is an attempt to mimic the conditions of the theory and not to allow communication but, when the effect of communication in social dilemmas has been investigated, it is found that pre-play communication about the dilemma increases cooperation (this literature is surveyed by Mackie, 1997), in particular where this involves the unanimous exchange of promises (Dawes et al., 1990).[5] The importance of extending rational choice assumptions about communication is recognized, both to consider the mechanisms by which it promotes teamwork (e.g. Bicchieri, this volume) and to investigate the properties of the different architectures that it opens up (e.g. van der Hoeck et al., this volume).

Activity

In the rational choice framework, there tend to be a limited number of strategies chosen from a pre-existing menu, as represented in the matrix. In practice there may be a continuous rather than a binary strategy variable, i.e. there may be a wide variety of possible actions with nuanced differences between them, and agents may have to create these strategies themselves, as well as or instead of choosing between them. Further, in the paradigm examples, teamwork is a one-off decision. In practice, some teams have sustained interactions over time. As part of the simplification, what is modelled as one strategy in rational choice may consist of what, in fact, are a number of separate decisions. For instance, models may not differentiate between the choice to form a team and the choice of activity variable once in it (e.g. Myatt and Wallace, this volume). One theoretical justification for this is that a strategy is defined as a contingency plan, covering counterfactual scenarios, and an agent could make all decisions at the start of the game. Even if the agent will receive new information during the course of the game, a complete strategy specifies what she would do for every possible value the information variable could take. However the cognitive complexity of this increases with the number of possible moves, the amount of new information and the number of possible values that information can take. Further to this, in practice, it is often the case that people do not know that they are going to get new information until they receive it. Also, even if there is no new information during the game, it is recognized as a problem in intertemporal decision theory that, when an agent must make a sequence of decisions, when the time comes to make each choice she may deviate from her original plans (Strotz, 1955–6).

Formation

In rational choice theory, agents voluntarily form teams (this is another reason why it is not completely implausible that they make their joining decision and their activity decision at the same time) but, in practice, people may be assigned to teams and only get to choose the level of the activity variable. The decision to leave may not be costless, or even may not be possible. This leads to the possibility that there are unwilling members, who are assigned to the team but do not want to be on it and may even not consider themselves to be a part of it. This situation is one where the team members do not have the option of *exit*, although they may be able to express their dissatisfaction through *voice* (Hirschman, 1970). This relates to the issue of communication discussed above. In fact, those teams that are silent tend to be unsuccessful. West (2002) argues that 'constructive controversy', or disagreement about task related issues, is the sign of a successful team. Members must feel that they can raise problems if they are to collectively solve them.

3 Research questions

There are five main research themes that can be identified in this book:

(1) What is a team?
(2) How did we evolve to be team players?
(3) What factors make teamwork work?
(4) When their team memberships conflict, how do agents decide which team to play for?
(5) Can we learn to be team players?

Dimension	Paradigm Example	In Practice
Team Size	• Small– 2 players	• Variable – may be large
Motivations	• Payoff maximizing (though what payoffs consist of may vary)	• Heterogeneous motives
Competences	• Symmetrical agents	• Heterogeneous agents, different types with different skills
Architecture	• No communication • No hierarchy	• Communication • Leaders
Activity	• Limited strategy space (often binary variable) • Strategies given	• Many nuanced strategies • Creativity
Formation	• Voluntary team formation	• Assignment to team

Table 1   Teams in theory and in practice

The chapters, insofar as they can be categorized, are presented roughly in that order. Most of them make one or more of the simplifying assumptions of the rational choice model. In this section, I look at each of these questions in turn and consider how the questions and the answers might be affected by consideration of some of the contrasting features of the practical applications of teamwork.

3.1   What is a team?

Michael Bacharach (this volume) defined a team as 'a group of agents with a common goal which can only be achieved by appropriate combinations of individual activities'. This is behaviourist in the same way as the rational choice perspective. That is to say, teamwork is defined in terms of achieving certain outcomes and not with reference to the motivations of the agents. Indeed, Bacharach's definition could be read very weakly. Two people can have the same goal without being aware of it and, arguably, even this is teamwork (Colman, this volume). Before considering some ways we might extend his definition, it is worth noting one sense in which a common goal itself might be considered quite a strong requirement. In the rational choice perspective, formation of teams tends to be voluntary.

Where team membership is assigned, rather than chosen, there may be unwilling team members who do not share the common goal. In particular, this may be the case where there is some pool of agents who must all be assigned to a group. For instance, pupils being divided into teams for a PE lesson (where some may not want to participate at all) or a workplace where employees must be divided amongst tasks (and some prefer to be in a different workgroup from the one they are assigned to, or not want to be in a group at all). If we insist that a common goal is a requirement for a group to be a team, then either these groups are not, in fact, teams or these laggards are not, in fact, team members. This latter suggestion has some plausibility but, equally, we might want to say that the whole group is a team despite the presence of one member who does not want to be a part of it. Although it is not clear how we should treat the problem of unwilling members, who simply do not share the common goal, amongst those who do share a common goal, this requirement can still accommodate *disagreement*, about the actions that should be taken to reach it or about the sub-goals to be achieved along the way, and *circumspectness*, when a player 'lapses' and takes an action that is not optimal in achieving that goal (for instance, if a midfielder in a football team has the ball, passing it to the strikers may give the best chance of scoring a goal but the midfielder may lapse and keep the ball, going for glory herself).

We might extend Bacharach's definition, to make reference to the intentions of the team members to act together. One possibility is to specify that there be common knowledge of individual intentions (of the form 'I intend') to further the team goal. Another is that the common goal should be reached by a collective intention (of the form 'we intend') to act together. Both these formulations seem to share an assumption of the paradigm examples, namely that everyone knows who is in the team. This may not always be the case. For instance, there may be a leader who directs the team members and individual team members may not have contact with each other, particularly if tasks are not synchronized either in time or in location, or if the team is a subunit of a larger organization where the subunits function separately (for instance as a revolutionary cell is part of a larger team, the revolutionary organization). Or there may just be very large numbers, such as voters in an election. If you do not know who is in the team, you cannot have common knowledge of the members' intentions to work together. Equally, it requires further explanation how such a group could have a collective intention.

Margaret Gilbert (this volume) suggests that teams are characterized by a stronger condition still, a joint commitment that involves both a collective intention and *joint responsibility*, or obligations to other members of the team. Her examples follow the rational choice paradigm in that the individuals voluntarily choose to form an association. Where members are assigned to the team, it is less obvious that they incur a joint commitment. As discussed above, assignment may result in unwilling members and an unwilling member is unlikely to be part of a collective intention. Regarding joint responsibility, it is arguable that the fact of assignment to the team alone, whether the member is amenable to this or not, might be enough to create joint responsibility. Not all obligations are chosen. A team member who refuses to play, saying that she never wanted to be a part of the team, may still be characterized as letting the side down. So it may be the case that joint responsibility is a necessary condition for a group to become a team, but not a collective intention.

3.2 What is the evolutionary basis of teamwork?

We might wonder how we evolved to be team players. It turns out that, for similar reasons that cooperation and coordination pose an explanatory problem for rational choice theory, there are questions about how we could have evolved to have the capacity for successful teamwork. Natural selection occurs under the conditions of *variation* and *replication*, where there is some element or unit that varies in the population and some selection mechanism that causes differential replication, at a rate that is positively correlated with fitness (or payoffs). We might ask what traits will develop as a result of this evolutionary process or, in a population of players, what population mix will result at the *Evolutionary Stable State*, the equilibrium where the process comes to rest. It turns out that every Evolutionary Stable State is a Nash equilibrium (though not every Nash equilibrium is an Evolutionary Stable State) (Vega-Redondo, 1996). In the one-shot Prisoner's Dilemma, we might expect that the population would evolve to play *D*, as individual defectors have greater relative fitness than cooperators. In coordination games such as Hi-Lo, both the Nash equilibria may be the result of an evolutionary process. Even though the population as a whole may be better off if everyone played *Hi*, in a population where most agents play *Lo*, playing *Lo* will confer more fitness on an individual agent than playing *Hi*. Although there is a higher chance of reaching the equilibrium where everyone plays *Hi* than *Lo* in Hi-Lo,[6] this simple evolutionary process does not guarantee that the population will get there.

The essential features of natural selection are variation and differential replication, the element that evolves and the method of its replication may vary, nor do these need to be biological, hence we can talk of cultural evolution. (Non-biological evolutionary models will be taken up in section 3.5.) Even within biology, evolutionary explanations may be useful at different levels, to explain different features. At a very basic level, we may be interested in the evolution of genes, which are the replicators of our DNA, and the simplest form of replication is represented by *replicator dynamics*, where the element being selected (in this case, the gene) is reproduced in proportion to its current relative fitness (payoff). This may be an accurate depiction of biological evolution in very primitive creatures, such as amoeba, where (because the organism is only one cell) there is no particular need to distinguish between the gene and the organism's behaviour, and where replication occurs by meiosis (division into two exact replicas of the original). However, in more complex creatures there is a clear distinction between the gene and the organism itself, which is the *vehicle of selection* (Dawkin, 1976), and sexual reproduction means that there is no automatic guarantee that a fitness conferring gene will appear in the next generation.[7] At the level of genetics, one explanation why people endowed with such 'selfish genes' would become team players is *kin selection*, where the vehicle of selection will act to promote the interests of other vehicles that (probably) share the same genes (Hamilton, 1964).

At the opposite extreme, we may be interested in the evolution of an organism's behavioural traits, rather than its genetics. Biologists define *altruism* as an act that benefits the recipient at a cost to the actor and *cooperation* as an act that benefits both the actor and the recipient. Playing *C* in the Prisoner's Dilemma might be thought of as altruism (e.g. Sober and Wilson, 1998) because someone who chooses this strategy will get a lower payoff than she would have done if she had played *D*, given the choice of the other player. Since the altruist will be less fit than the non-altruist, there is a puzzle about how altruism would evolve. But the definition of playing *C* in the Prisoner's Dilemma as altruism depends on what is chosen as the baseline against which playing *C* is compared. Although the individual is worse off compared to what she would have got if she played *D*, the players taken together are better off than they would have been if both played *D*, so it might be considered cooperation (e.g. Andras and Lazarus, this volume). This is the key to one explanation of why we might have evolved to play *C*. At the level of the individual (within the group), the evolutionary pressure is to play *D*. At the level of the group (between groups), the evolutionary pressure is to play *C*. Which trait evolves will depend on which level exerts the strongest evolutionary pressure. To be precise, the agent will evolve to play *C* if there is variation between groups and *assortative re-grouping*, or a mechanism whereby those who play *C* can congregate together (Sober and Wilson, 1998). Under these conditions, we can also be sure that, in Hi-Lo, a population of *Hi* players will evolve (Bacharach, 2005).

Explanation at the level of behavioural traits using replicator dynamics is *functionalist*: behaviour that brings relative fitness benefits is reproduced in the next generation, but there is no explicit consideration of how this behaviour is produced.[8] This might be thought of as the analogue of the assumptions made about motivations and behaviour in the paradigm rational choice model. We can distinguish between the *ultimate* and the *proximate* causes of behaviour (Sober and Wilson, 1998). Ultimately, behaviour evolves because it is functionally adaptive but there must also evolve a proximate mechanism, that allows the organism to produce the behaviour. In humans, behaviour is brought about by intentional action so, at an intermediate level between genetics and behaviour, we may want to explain how we evolved to have the cognitive capacities for teamwork. One argument in favour of any proximate mechanism is that it could have been the result of an evolutionary process. In evolutionary psychology, the mind is seen as a collection of adaptations to the problems of survival and reproduction in our ancestral environments. For instance, Caporael (1997) postulates that we are adapted to live in certain 'core configurations' that originally corresponded to the 'modal tasks' that our Pleistocene ancestors had to do: dyad (two people, to make and rear babies), task group (five, for hunting and gathering), band (25, for general living and moving around together) and macroband (300, for exchange of individuals for mating at a seasonal gathering).[9] She argues that the psychological correlates of these are social identities, which have since been extended to other types of interaction. If correct, this provides an evolutionary basis for our cognitive capacity to group identify, which predisposes us to be team players. Evidence to support the plausibility of a particular proximate mechanism may be provided by ethnographic data on modern hunter-gatherer societies (for instance this strategy is used by Wilson et al., this volume, as part of their argument for the existence of cognitive cooperation).

3.3   What makes teamwork work?

Most of the chapters in this book are concerned, if only indirectly, with the question of what makes teamwork work. A number of factors are identified that are important for effective teamwork, using a variety of methodologies. Rather than reviewing them, in this section I explore the relationship between the causes and effects of successful teamwork. In the paradigm examples, the activity variable is a one-off decision about teamwork. In practice, at least some teams have sustained interactions over a period of time. In this case, it may be ambiguous what is a cause and what is an effect of good teamwork. In particular, this raises two questions: a metaphysical question, about the relationship between effective teamworking and the continued existence of the team, and a more general methodological question, of how we can identify whether a particular characteristic of a successful team is a cause or an effect of teamwork.

Where the team does not exist separately from the fact that agents choose to act together, as in our paradigm examples, there is no clear theoretical distinction between an ineffective team and a non-existent team. In practice, we might expect that ineffective teams will not survive indefinitely. Where teams are assembled to perform a specific task, badly functioning teams may be disbanded, so teams that operate below a certain level of effectiveness will cease to exist. For a particular task, we may be able to identify factors that are associated with increased team effectiveness, such as the size of the team or certain types of diversity amongst the members. However, we saw above that sometimes these optimum conditions are incorporated into the definition of a team. One reason that this occurs may be precisely the fact that teams which lack these characteristics will not be enduring.

Studies of teams allow us to identify factors that are associated with successful teamwork (e.g. Borrill and West, this volume). When we discover a characteristic that is correlated with effective teamworking, it might be either the cause or the effect of successful teamwork. We may not know the direction of causality without further theory or evidence. Group identity, or the definition of 'self' in terms of shared group membership (Brewer, 1991; Turner et al., 1987), is one such a characteristic of successful teams. It is associated with certain judgments, attitudes and behaviour that tend to favour other, in-group members and discriminate against non- or out-group members (Brewer and Miller, 1996; Oakes et al., 1994). In social dilemma experiments stimulating group identity is associated with an increase in cooperation. This may be done by making people be subject to a common fate (e.g. Brewer and Kramer, 1986; Rabbie and Horwitz, 1969), by emphasizing their common interests (e.g. Cookson, 2000), by making pre-existing group identities salient (e.g. Kramer, De Cremer and Van Vugt, 1999; Brewer, 1984; Dion 1973; Wilson and Katayani, 1968), or by giving them an out-group to define themselves against (e.g. Bornstein et al., 2001; Kramer and Brewer, 1984). Group identity theorists suggest that it is inducing group identity that produces good treatment of the in-group and the resulting teamwork. In the 'minimal group paradigm' the classification into in-group and out-group members is induced by the experimenter, for instance by saying that everyone in the group has under- or over-estimated of the number of dots on a screen in a previous task, and this is associated with positive treatment of in-group members (Tajfel, 1970). However, interdependence theorists argue that common perceived individual interests are essential in the explanation of these effects. They suggest that if you block a subject's expectations of fair or good treatment from the in-group, then there is no in-group effect as typically measured by identity theorists (e.g. Rabbie et al., 1989). So, if there is no successful teamwork, then they claim there will be none of the classic effects of group identity. The two sides dispute whether the various experimental designs properly contrast the two sides. Another plausible hypothesis is that it is both a cause and an effect: that group identity may cause teamwork but that successful teamwork may also enhance group identity, so there is feedback between the two. If teamwork, by definition, involves interdependence then it may be difficult to discriminate whether group identity is a cause of teamwork, an effect of teamwork or both.

3.4   Which is my team?

Individuals have more than one team membership and, sometimes, the objectives of the different teams that they are members of will conflict. (The individual agent being the limiting case of a team with only one member.[10]) At any point in time, it may be important which team the agent is playing for. When team memberships conflict, there are two types of question we could ask: a normative one, 'which team should the agent play for?', and a descriptive one, 'what determines why people play for one team rather than another?' In fact, these questions are not so easy to separate.

We might be concerned with which team we ought, morally, to play for or with which we ought, rationally, to play for. (A further question is whether it is rational to be moral and, hence, the answers to these questions coincide.[11]) It is not clear that there is necessarily a definitive answer to either of these questions. On the question of which team it is rational to play for, the two opposite points of view are represented in the papers of this volume. Susan Hurley thinks that the choice of team (or which unit of agency should be operative) would be part of a complete theory of rationality. Robert Sugden thinks that the unit of agency cannot be endogenized in this way, but remains as a primitive, so we can only conclude that some action would be rational *given* a particular team membership. However, even for Sugden, for team reasoning to be rational there must be the 'right kind of assurance about the motivation, reasoning or behaviour of other team members'. So, for both authors there are requirements that must be met if it is to be rational to play for a particular team. Each makes a suggestion as to when or why their requirements will be met. Hurley argues that the capacity to identify with others as part of a collective unit of agency requires mind-reading, or the ability to understand other agents in terms of their mental states. Sugden suggests that one way we can get rational assurance is by observing peoples' behaviour and making inferences about their motivations.

Each of these suggestions seems to rely on assumptions regarding the team architecture: both seem to require contact with the other members of the team and, in Sugden's case, assurance is based on previous observations of behaviour. Two phenomena that we see in the real world that may not fulfil these requirements are large teams and temporary teams. One might ask how either of these rationality requirements would operate in cases where there are large teams, whose members do not know each other. Take the example of voters in an election. This is a social dilemma because the chances of any individual voter being decisive in an election are very small so, if there is a cost to voting, maybe in terms of time, effort or travel costs, then it would seem not to be rational for an individual to vote. Team reasoning may solve this dilemma as, if one team reasons, then going to vote may be playing one's part in the optimal team plan of the supporters of a particular party. However, it may well be the case that you do not know all the other voters, so it is not clear that it helps to be a mind reader or that there can be assurance based on observations of behaviour. Even where teams are small, sometimes for effective teamwork it is necessary to generate assurance without prior observations of behaviour, so we may need to supplement Sugden's account. In *temporary teams* with a finite lifespan, such as film crews, theatre and architectural groups, presidential commissions, senate select committees and cockpit crews, there may need to be *swift trust* (Meyerson et al., 1996). This involves the willingness to trust strangers and a positive expectation that the group activity will be beneficial before it even starts. This generates teamwork, so the trust is self-fulfilling. If such trust is rational, then it is not so because of any basis in past observations of behaviour, but it may be essential for successful teamwork in temporary teams. One way to get assurance about what others are going to do, in both large and temporary teams, is to have a leader announcing the plan. But this just pushes the problem of rational assurance one step back, to why we should trust the leader or believe that other people will be doing what the leader says; there is a regress.

A psychological mechanism that might both explain why people play for a team and also why it is rational to do so is group identity. If group identity is correlated with the positive treatment of ingroup members, either because it causes the positive treatment or because it is a signal that such behaviour will occur, then this may make it rational to play for the team in circumstances that elicit group identity. For the same reason that it affects people's behaviour, it may affect our expectations of their behaviour and, hence, our actions. Group identity may be also be a psychological mechanism that causes us to play for a particular team for non-rational reasons. Bicchieri (this volume) argues that group identity triggers particular social norms, which are not the object of rational reflection, that cause us to cooperate. But even here there may be a connection to rationality. If social norms are enforced by sanctions, then there is also a rational reason to follow then, namely to avoid such sanctions. Group identity is a psychological mechanism that may lead to improved outcomes in situations of coordination and cooperation. How far group identity can be incorporated into a theory of rationality, rather than remaining as a primitive, is related to the question of the extent to which our identities are 'discovered' rather than 'chosen' (Sandel, 1982). Even if we cannot choose to be group identifiers, if we know that group identity is generated under certain conditions, we may be able to adjust the conditions we find ourselves in accordingly.[12]

3.5   Can we learn to be team players?

One can make a distinction between explicit and implicit learning (Berry, 1997). Whilst explicit learning is done consciously and with full awareness of the learning process, implicit learning occurs without the intention to learn and the resulting knowledge is difficult to express. It appears that many things we learn about, such as language, are learnt without concomitant awareness of the relevant information. The chapters in this volume that study the learning of teamwork use an implicit learning approach. They also both use evolutionary methodologies. It was noted above that evolutionary models of selection are specified by the element that is evolving and the method of its replication. In biological applications, the method of replication involves reproduction in future generations. But, in non-biological applications, the unit being selected is behaviour and the method of replication some crude from of learning, whose reproduction may be intra-generational. For instance, these may include: imitation, or the copying of behaviour that has yielded higher payoffs to others; reinforcement learning, or the adoption of actions that yielded high payoffs to oneself in the past; or a limited form of best-response, where the agent optimizes her expected payoff given some expectation about others' play. The chapters in this volume that study the learning of teamwork use such an approach, where the unit being selected is behaviour and the method of replication is re-enforcement learning. Such an approach can illuminate questions other than the learning of teamwork but also leaves questions of explicit learning untouched.

Re-enforcement learning, as utilized in the chapters in this volume, is connected to the use of rewards to encourage the learning of teamwork. In a similar manner to which pressure for selection at the level of the group may lead to the biological evolution of teamwork, reward at the level of the group may lead to the learning of teamwork (Wyatt et al., this volume). This has implications for the study of incentive payments for teamworkers. The standard assumption in economics is that the closer we can tie an individual's payments to her own performance, the better we can incentivize her to work for the team objective. In the economic analysis of teams, the team is a set of employees on whose effort the output of the firm depends (Rasmussen, 1987; Holmstrom, 1982). Because individuals' efforts cannot be observed, any payment scheme has to be based on the workers' joint output and the scheme is treated as a 'principle-agent problem', where the management has to give each team member a financial incentive to make an effort. The research reported here suggests that, in some situations, the most effective reward system may involve incentives at the level of the group, not the individual. Another factor that is not included in these learning models, which might also support this conclusion, is that payment at the level of the team may re-enforce group identity, a further mechanism that can induce individuals to work for the team goal over their individual interests.

There are questions we might want to ask about explicit learning, on each of the five dimensions of teamwork. On the dimension of motivation, we may wonder how taking into account agents' heterogeneous motivations affects the processes described above. For instance, although it may seem natural to assume that paying someone to do a task can only increase their motivation to do it, the theory of motivation crowding suggests that payment may in fact substitute for other, intrinsic, motivations (Frey and Jegen, 2001). This suggests that we need to carefully consider the method of reward we use.[13] On the dimension of competences, teamwork may require skills that are above and beyond those required for successful performance of the role allotted. It may require particular types of reasoning, such as team reasoning, or skills necessitated by deviation from the paradigm example on the other dimensions. For instance, more complicated architectures may require the learning of communication skills, leadership skills and the flexibility to balance working alone and being directed. Regarding activity, it may be possible to learn some forms of creativity, such as how to improvise, or to improve these skills with practice. When formation is not voluntary, we may be able to learn how to encourage unwilling members to participate or how to achieve the team goal despite their presence.

4 Further questions

Having briefly surveyed the main questions that we cover, I will even more briefly note some areas of importance that are not covered. This is a book about individuals in teams. (That may be unsurprising, given the underlying individualist rational choice perspective). One major area that is not covered is the interaction of different teams. In business, practitioners may be interested in how teams fit into wider organizations. Nor does this book cover optimal team building. It was noted above that, in practical applications, the task that needs teamwork may be identified before the team is formed and, given this task, it is asked how best to structure the team or who are the optimal team members. The questions addressed here are more general ones, where insights from different disciplines are more readily transferable. Finally, the contributions raise a philosophical issue. Michael Bacharach's definition of teamwork is activity done by teams, but his definition of a team is fairly broad. Given the debate about the definition of a team, and the possibility that it should be more restrictive, we might ask whether it is possible to have teamwork without teams. Practitioners sometimes talk of synergy, where the team achieves more than any individual could alone. In both these questions that we do not tackle here and those that we do, there is scope for future research. They also call for further teamwork, between the several disciplines that study teams and between researchers and practitioners, if we are to achieve a synergy of our own.

Notes

1. For a discussion of why we might expect agents to play a Nash equilibrium, see Kreps (1990).
2. In fact, each prisoner has a *dominant strategy* to confess, as whatever the other prisoner does each is better off confessing.

3. Note that Bacharach's definition of scope for common gain does not insist that the solution set is coterminous with the set of Nash equilibria but, in the context of rational choice theory, this is an obvious way to specify it.
4. In fact, there may be an interaction between leadership and communication. Bicchieri (this volume) reports that in an experiment with a discussion period, in groups where a leader did not emerge, subjects found it difficult to reach an agreement and often opted to end their discussion period early.
5. One theory is that emotions, such as guilt and shame, act as devices that make it costly to break such commitments and hence make them credible (Elster, 2000).
6. In a deterministic process, which equilibrium is reached will depend on the original population proportions. It is more likely that this will be the one where everyone plays *Hi* because a larger proportion of the initial distributions lead to it. In a stochastic process, where errors or random variations are introduced, the population will move between equilibria but it will spend more time at the *Hi*-playing one for the same reason that the deterministic process is more likely to end up there.
7. So there is a mystery why sexual reproduction should have evolved, for which we do not have a definitive explanation (Ridley, 2000).
8. Or, indeed, why it is reproduced. As noted above, in models involving sexual reproduction the replicator dynamic is a simplification. There are also non-biological methods of replication, both within and between generations. Replication within generations is considered in section 3.5.
9. Though it is not clear what the direction of causation is here. The group sizes we lived in may have influenced our cognitive development or our cognitive structures may have influenced the size of the groups we formed.
10. When an individual has to make a sequence of decisions, the agent is sometimes analyzed as a succession of transient agents, each of which exists in a distinct period of time and is in control of the person's decisions in that period. A central problem in the literature of dynamic choice is to investigate the conditions under which the separate decisions of a person's transient agents are consistent with a single rational plan for the person as a whole. In this case, the person may be seen as a team composed of that person at different times (Bacharach, 2005).
11. Donald Regan's theory of cooperative utilitarianism might be interpreted as one where it is sometimes both moral and rational to act as a member of a team (Regan, 1980).
12. There may be an analogy with the emotions, which are characterized by cognitive, physical and behavioural aspects, but which may be to some extent within our control (and which are discussed in Elster, 1999).
13. An analogous argument may apply to the use of sanctions against non-teamworkers (Orr, 2001).

References

Bacharach, M. (1999) 'A Contribution to the Theory of Cooperation', *Research in Economics* 53, 117–47.

Bacharach, M. (2005) *Beyond Individual Choice*, N. Gold and R. Sugden (eds) (Princeton: Princeton University Press).

Beddoes-Jones, F. (1999) *Thinking Styles: Relationship strategies that work!* (Stainby: BJA Associates).

Belbin, R. M. (2000) *Beyond the Team* (Oxford: Butterworth Heinemann).

Belbin, M. (1981) *Management Teams: Why they succeed or fail* (London: Butterworth Heinemann).

Berry, D. (1997) *How Implicit is Implicit Learning* (Oxford: Oxford University Press).

Bornstein, G., Gneezy, U., and Nagel, R. (2002) 'The effect of intergroup competition on group coordination: An experimental study,' *Games and Economic Behavior*, 41(1), 1–25.

Brewer, M. (1991) 'The social self: on being the same and different at the same time', *Personality and Social Psychology Bulletin* 17: 475–482.

Brewer, M. B. and Kramer, R. M. (1986) 'Choice behavior in social dilemmas: Effects of social identity, group size and decision framing', *Journal of Personality and Social Psychology*, 3, 543–549.

Brewer, M. and Miller, N. (1996), *Intergroup Relationships* (Open University Press: Buckingham).

Frey, B. and Jegen, R. (2001) 'Motivation Crowding Theory: A Survey of Empirical Evidence', *Journal of Economic Surveys* 15(5), 589–611.

Goodman J. P. Campbell and R. J. Campbell (1988) *Productivity in organizations*. San Francisco, CA: Jossey-Bass.

Campion, M. A., Medsker, G. J. and Higgs, A. C. (1993) 'Relations between work group characteristics and effectiveness: Implications for designing effective work groups', *Personnel Psychology*, 46, 823–850.

Caporael, L. R. (1997). 'The evolution of truly social cognition: The core configuration model', *Personality and Social Psychology Review*, 1, 276–298.

Cattell, R. (1947) 'Confirmation and Clarification of Personality Factors', *Psychometrica* 12, 197–220.

Cookson, R. (2000) 'Framing Effects in Public Goods Games', *Experimental Economics*, 3, 55–79.

Dawes, R. M. Orbell, J. and van der Kragt, A. (1990) 'The Limits of Multilateral Promising', *Ethics* 100, 616–627.

Dawkins, R. (1976) *The Selfish Gene* (New York: Oxford University Press).

De Cremer, D. and Van Vugt, M. (1999) 'Social Identification Effects in Social Dilemmas: a Transformation of Motives', *European Journal of Social Psychology* 29, 871–893.

Dennett, D. (1995) *Darwin's Dangerous Idea* (London: Penguin).

Dion, K. L. (1973) 'Cohesiveness as a Determinant of Ingroup-Outgroup Bias', *Journal of Personality and Social Psychology* 28(2), 163–171.

Elster, J. (2000) *Ulysses Unbound* (Cambridge: Cambridge University Press).

Elster, J. (1999) *Alchemies of the Mind* (Cambridge: Cambridge University Press).

Eysenck, H. J. (1991) 'Dimensions of Personality 16, 5, or 3? Criteria for a Taxonomic Paradigm', *Personality and Individual Differences* 12, 773–90.

Hamilton, W. (1964) 'The genetical evolution of social behaviour I & II', *Journal of Theoretical Biology* 7, 1–16, 17–52.

Hirschman, A. (1970) *Loyalty, Voice and Loyalty: Responses to Decline in Firms, Organizations, and States* (Cambridge Ma.: Harvard University Press).

Holmstrom, B. (1982) 'Moral hazard in teams', *Bell Journal of Economics* 13, 324–340.

Kramer, R. M. and Brewer, M. B. (1984) 'Effects of Group Identity on Resource Use in a Simulated Commons Dilemma', *Journal of Personality and Social Psychology*, 46(5), 1044–1057.

Kreps, D. (1990) *A Course in Micro-economic Theory* (New York: Harvester Wheatsheaf).

Mackie, G. (1997) 'The Intrinsic Credibility of Social Contracts: Communication and Commitment in Social Dilemma Experiments', Paper delivered at the Cooperative Reasoning Seminar, University of Oxford *mimeo*.

Magjuka, R. and Baldwin, T. (1991) 'Team-based employee involvement programs: Effects of design and administration', *Personnel Psychology* 44(4), 793–812.

Marschak, J. and Radner, R. (1972) *Economic Theory of Teams* (Yale Univ Press, New Haven).

McCrae, R. R. and John, O. P. (1992) 'An Introduction to the Five Factor Model and its Applications', *Journal of Personality* 60, 175–215.

Meyerson, D., Weick, K. E., and Kramer, R. M. (1996) Swift trust and temporary groups. In R. M. Kramer and T. R. Tyler (eds), *Trust in organizations: Frontiers of theory and research* (pp. 166–195). Thousand Oaks, CA: Sage Publications.

Oakes, P., Haslam, A., and Turner, J. (1994) *Stereotyping and Social Reality* (Blackwell: Oxford).

Orr, S. (2001) 'The economics of shame in work groups: How mutual monitoring can decrease cooperation in teams', *Kyklos* 54, 49–66.

Rabbie, J. and Horwitz, M. (1969) 'Arousal of Ingroup-Outgroup Bias by a Chance Win or Loss', *Journal of Personality and Social Psychology* 13(3), 269–177.

Rabbie, J. M., Schot, J. C. and Visser, L. (1989) 'Social identity theory: A conceptual and empirical critique from the perspective of a behavioural interaction model', *Advances in group processes, 11,* 139–174.

Rasmusen, E. (1987) 'Moral Hazard in Risk-Averse Teams', *RAND Journal of Economics,* Vol. 18 (3) pp. 428–435.

Regan, D. (1980) *Utilitarianism and Co-operation* (Oxford University Press: Oxford).

Ridley, M. (2000) *The Red Queen: Sex and the Evolution of Human Nature* (London: Penguin).

Sandel, M. (1982) *Liberalism and the Limits of Justice* (Cambridge: Cambridge University Press).

Sober, E. and Wilson, D. (1998) *Unto Others: The Evolution and Psychology of Unselfish Behavior* (Cambridge Ma.: Harvard University Press).

Sugden, R. (1993) 'Thinking as a Team: Towards an Explanation of Nonselfish Behavior', *Social Philosophy and Policy* 10, 69–89.

Strotz, R. H. (1955–6) 'Myopia and Inconsistency in Dynamic Utility Maximization', *Review of Economic Studies* 23, 165–180.

Tajfel, H. (1970) 'Experiments in intergroup discrimination', *Scientific American* 223, 96–102.

Turner, J. C., Hogg, M., Oakes, P. J., Reicher, S., and Wetherell, M. (1987) *Rediscovering the Social Group: A Self-Categorization Theory* (Blackwell, Oxford).

Vega-Redondo, F. (1996) *Evolution, Games and Economic Behaviour* (Oxford: Oxford University Press).

Von Neuman, J. and Morgenstern, O. (1944) *Theory of Games and Economic Behavior* (Princeton: Princeton University Press).

West, M. A. (2002) 'Sparkling fountains or stagnant ponds: An integrative model of creativity and innovation implementation in work groups', *Applied Psychology: An International Review,* 51, 355–424.

Wilson, W. and Katayani, M. (1968) 'Intergroup Attitudes and Strategies in Games Between Opponents of the Same or of a Different Race', *Journal of Personality and Social Psychology* 9, 24–30.

1
A Theoretical Framework for the Understanding of Teams

Margaret Gilbert

In his description of the aims of a projected workshop on teamwork the distinguished economist Michael Bacharach included the following examples of *teams* in the human world: couples, families; workgroups, platoons, sports teams and street gangs; nations in times of war, international military alliances, terrorist cells.[1] This list makes it clear how vital it is to understand the nature and functioning of teams if one is to understand and, one might add, cope with the human situation.

In my book *On Social Facts* (1989) and a number of subsequent publications I have proposed, in effect, that what I call *joint commitment* is crucial for the understanding of teams.[2] There I spoke of *social groups*. A team in Michael Bacharach's sense seems to be much the same as a social group in the standard sense I had in mind. Certainly, his examples of teams are all at the same time canonical examples of social groups in this sense. Broader understandings of what a social group is are sometimes in evidence. I shall here I refer to 'social groups' without qualification, intending the sense indicated above.

In this paper I attempt, in a short presentation, to explain to what I mean by joint commitment and why I think it is crucial to a proper understanding of teams in the sense of Bacharach and other authors.[3] I conclude by attempting to defuse some concerns about the invocation of other authors joint commitment. Before launching into this material I sketch how I came to believe that social theory and in particular the theory of social groups and their features needs the idea of a joint commitment.

1.1   A note on the word 'team'

The term 'team' tends to evoke, for me, the idea of a social group dedicated to the pursuit of a particular, persisting goal: the sports team to winning, perhaps with some proviso as to how this comes about, the terrorist cell to carrying out terrorist acts, the workgroup to achieving a particular target.[4] Insofar as 'team' is thus interpreted, it is not clear to me that we do best to think of some of Michael Bacharach's examples as teams.

It is not clear, for instance, that families, as such, need be dedicated to the pursuit of a particular, persisting goal. The life of a family, meanwhile, tends to be structured by a set of rules, beliefs and values that are, in a sense, its own. These things alone may be what make us think of it as akin to other items in Bacharach's list of kinds of team or, in my terms, as social groups.

This is not to say, of course, that no families are dedicated to persisting goals or that families never engage in goal-directed activity. Obviously many families engage in such activity from time to time. The family may plan a holiday, for instance, its members sitting down to discuss where to go and what to do, different members researching different routes, and so on. Nonetheless, it surely does not count against the idea that certain people form a family that there is no persisting goal to which they are dedicated. To say that they are a team, meanwhile, suggests to me at least that they are dedicated to such a goal.[5]

There is no need to quibble about the use of words here. My position is that the idea of joint commitment is fundamental for the understanding of teams in both of the senses just noted. That is, it is fundamental for the understanding of teams in both the broad sense adopted by Michael Bacharach – a sense allowing that couples and families in general are properly referred to as teams, as are workgroups and sports teams – and in a narrower sense that would restrict teams to sets of people dedicated to the pursuit of a persisting goal.

1.2 Some background

My belief in the importance of joint commitment was the result of extended reflection on the nature of a number of social phenomena referred to in everyday discourse.[6] These phenomena included social conventions and rules, the so-called beliefs of groups, group languages, collective or shared actions, and social groups themselves.

Some of these phenomena had barely received prior attention. Perhaps the most carefully discussed was social convention, on which David Lewis focused in Lewis, 1969. On careful examination, Lewis's game-theoretical account appeared to be inadequate.[7]

For one thing, it did not appear to provide social conventions with a specific normative dimension they were commonly understood to have. Both social conventions and the other phenomena mentioned were commonly understood to carry with them a set of rights and correlative obligations. To put this more precisely: absent special circumstances, at least, when the phenomenon in question was present – when there was a social convention, for instance – such rights and obligations were inevitably present. Such rights and obligations were not necessarily present, however, when the conditions posited by Lewis's account were present.

I saw that if one introduces the idea of a joint commitment into one's accounts of these phenomena one can explain their normative dimension. It was not clear that this idea could adequately be captured without an appeal to joint commitment.

It is common in philosophy to argue, following the great philosopher David Hume, that one cannot 'will an obligation' into being. I would argue that this is wrong, if 'obligation' is understood in a particular way. Obligation of the relevant sort is, I would argue, part of the normative dimension of the central social phenomena I listed above, and of others as well, including collective or in that sense 'shared' values and collective emotions.[8]

Such obligation is not the creature of any one individual's will or commitment. It is, however, an inevitable aspect of joint commitment, the product of more than one will. Having said this much in preamble, I now explain what I mean by 'joint commitment'.[9]

1.3   What is joint commitment?

As a way of introducing joint commitment it will be useful to say something about a type of commitment I refer to as a personal commitment. Suppose that Terri decides to have lunch at 12 p.m. today. I take it that she is now in some sense committed to having lunch at 12 p.m. today. She can, of course, change her mind. But as long as she does not do so, she is committed. A personal decision creates what I call a personal commitment. By this I mean a commitment of a person A, such that A is in a position unilaterally to make and unilaterally to unmake or rescind it.

I take the following, at least, to be true of any commitment in the sense in question. If one violates a commitment to which one is subject, one has done what in some sense one was not supposed to do. One is in some way at fault. Personal decisions are one source of commitment; mere inclinations, desires, even compelling urges, are not.

One last point with respect to personal commitments. Suppose Terri decides to lunch at 12 p.m., does not change her mind about this, but absent-mindedly finds herself still at her desk at one. Failing special circumstances, she will understand herself to be answerable to no one but herself for this lapse.

What, then, is a *joint* commitment? And how does such a commitment come about? Simply put, a joint commitment is the commitment of two or more people.

Some important aspects of any joint commitment so conceived are as follows:

(1) A joint commitment is not constituted by nor does it entail a set of personal commitments as I have characterized these above.

(2) Nonetheless, it has implications for the individual participants: *each is committed through it.*

(3) Each party is *answerable to all of the parties* for any action that fails to conform to the joint commitment. This is a function of its *jointness*. In the case of failure each can say to the other: you have not simply failed to conform to a commitment of your own. You have failed to conform to *our* commitment, a commitment in which I, as well as you, have an integral stake.

(4) People jointly commit to *doing something as a body*, where 'doing something' is construed broadly so as to include, for instance, intending and believing. I say more, below, about what it is to intend (and so on) *as a body*.

The next two points relate to the creation and dissolution of joint commitments:

(5) All of the parties must play a role in the creation of a given joint commitment. Given special *'authority-creating' side understandings,* some particular person or body consisting of fewer than all may create a joint commitment for all the parties.

(6) *Without* special side understandings, no individual party to a joint commitment can rescind a joint commitment unilaterally.

As just indicated, joint commitments come about in two ways. In the *primary* case, each party must express to the others *his or her readiness to be jointly committed with them in the relevant way,* in conditions of 'common knowledge'.[10] Roughly, these expressions must be 'entirely out in the open' from the point of view of the parties. When and only when all the expressions are made, the joint commitment exists.

In the *secondary*, or *authority-involving* case, the parties jointly commit to allowing some person or body to create new joint commitments for them in some relevant domain, possibly without their knowledge. For example, the parties may jointly commit to accepting as a body that a certain person or body may make decisions for them, in effect jointly committing them to intend as a body to perform certain actions.

Any set of jointly committed persons, whatever the content of the particular joint commitment in question constitute, by definition, a *plural subject*. My use of this technical phrase for the sake of a label is not intended to have any particular metaphysical implications.

1.4 Sketch of a joint commitment account of team action

Teams dedicated to a particular persisting goal will likely perform many actions on the way to that goal. Teams in what I take to be the broader sense of Bacharach and others may also perform many actions in the course of their existence.

Here is a rough account of *team action* in terms of joint commitment. It can be set out in two stages.

First, there is an account of collective (or team) intention.[11]

> *Persons A and B (and so on) collectively intend to do X (e.g. get the car up the hill)* if and only if A and B (and so on) are jointly committed to intend as a body to do X.

Before moving on from this, something should be said about what it is for A and B to be jointly committed to intend *as a body* to do X. One aspect of this is that there need be no commitment on any one individual's part *personally to intend* to do X. It might be quite unreasonable, in the case of getting a car up a hill, for any of the individual parties personally to intend to get the car up the hill, though it was perfectly reasonable for several people collectively to intend to do so. A given individual might more pointfully intend to *see to it* that the car got up the hill. I take it that it is not an implication of the account that anyone is committed personally to intend this either.

What the parties are jointly committed to, rather, is *to constitute, as far as is possible, a single body with the intention to (for instance) get the car up the hill*. In practical terms, this means that each is to behave appropriately to a constituent of such a body where the other parties are the other constituents. This will mean coordinating his behaviour with that of the other parties to the commitment so that *an observer might think they together constituted a single body with the intention in question*. Similar things can be said about the corresponding ideas of believing as a body, accepting a particular goal as a body, and so on.

A given party to the joint commitment may or may not initially have personal intentions, beliefs, and so on that accord with the intention, belief, or what have you specified in the joint commitment.[12] Meanwhile, that member's participation in a joint commitment to intend such-and-such or to believe that such-and-such – which is, if you like, his fundamental contribution to the existence of the collective intention or belief in question – is apt to affect his behaviour. It gives him reason to act as the member of a body with the relevant intention or belief. Insofar as he acts in accordance with this reason, he will likely form a range of personal intentions that accord with the intention specified in the joint commitment.

Next, there is an account of collective (or team) action that assumes the previous account of collective intention.

> *Persons A and B (and so on) are doing X together (or collectively, or as a team)* if and only if A and B (and so on) collectively intend to do X (where this

is understood according to (1)) and each acts in light of this collective intention. More precisely, each acts in light of the joint commitment to intend as a body to do X.

1.5 Why invoke joint commitment?

Here I first briefly list four things that an underlying joint commitment would explain. Taken together the points on this list make a good case for understanding teams in terms of joint commitments.

An understanding of team action in terms of joint commitment would satisfactorily explain at least:

(1) an intuitive logical independence of what are said to be *our – team – intentions* on the one hand, and what are said to be *my* intentions, *your* intentions, *his* and *her* intentions, on the other. Thus one can say '*We are trying to win this game*' – perhaps in a rebuking tone, to a straggler – without logically implying that any particular individual in the team personally intends to bring it about that we win.

(2) the apparent force of reasoning from '*We are doing A*' to '*I – being one of us – have reason to do X, where X is the best I can do in the circumstances to promote our doing A*'; in other words, the *motivational relevance* of team intentions, given the logical independence noted above. Note that something can be *motivationally relevant* without being *motivationally conclusive*. If, traitorously, I prefer that we lose the game, I might decide to act according to my personal preference.

(3) salient aspects of the *phenomenology* of team membership, such as a 'sense of unity' or 'fusion', or 'belonging together' between the parties. Clearly for people to be jointly committed in some way with others is for them to be *unified* or *bound together* in a clear way.

(4) important *normative phenomena* intrinsic to team action.

I now elaborate on this fourth point with an example. Suppose five women have agreed to push the car of one of them up the hill. They now understand themselves to form a team engaged in getting the car up the hill by pushing it.

Absent special background circumstances, I suggest that in such situations each participant understands the following: each needs the permission of the others to act contrary to the team action if they are to be without fault; each has a right in some sense against the other to action appropriate to the team intention. Correspondingly, each is obligated to the others to perform such action; each therefore has the standing to rebuke the others for contravention without permission or for purposing to do so. Such understandings are manifest in the kinds of ways people react to contraventions.

If there is a joint commitment to intend as a body to do such-and-such, then each of these understandings will be explained. Each needs the permission of the others to act contrary to the joint commitment. Such permission, if granted, amounts to a rescission or amendment of the original commitment. As noted earlier, if we are jointly committed in some way each of us is answerable to the others for any non-conformity to the commitment. In addition, one can argue that each has a right against every other to conformity, and each has a corresponding obligation to every other to conform to a standing joint commitment unless someone has received special permission not to conform. Each will then have the standing to rebuke others for non-conformity.

I do not say that each necessarily has a specifically *moral* right or a moral obligation. That depends precisely on what moral rights and obligations are thought to be. Nonetheless the language of rights and correlative obligations seems to be well in place here.[13]

My reasons for preferring an account of team action in terms of joint commitment can be summed up as follows. I do not believe that any theory that does not invoke a joint commitment can do as well on all four of the above counts.

1.6   Team phenomena other than team action: goals, beliefs, emotions, values

Team phenomena other than team intention and action can plausibly be explained in joint commitment (plural subject) terms. These will include team goals, beliefs, emotions, and values.

I cannot fully discuss these cases individually here, but will elaborate a little on the case of collective or in that sense 'shared' values. One reason for doing so is this. Those who have more 'hands on' concerns about teams than most philosophers – those in management science, for instance – often appeal to shared values as an important factor in the success of a team with a specific task. Political philosophers also appeal to shared values in the context of a concern with what has come to be known as nation building.

What, then, are shared values? Different people may give different accounts of them. The point I want to make is that when what is at stake is something we might want to call the values of a team as such, a plural subject account is attractive.

Such an account would run along similar lines to the account of collective intention given above. It would say people share a value if they collectively value something in accordance with the following definition.

Persons A and B (and so on) collectively value such-and-such if and only if they are jointly committed to value such-and-such as a body.

An important practical consequence of collective values in the sense just defined is this. When the members of a team collectively value something in this sense, they will understand that each has the standing to rebuke the others for speaking and acting in ways that do not accord with such valuing. This provides an important incentive for adherence to collective, as opposed to personal, values.

One practical suggestion for the success of teams, then, is that one should encourage the growth of pertinent collective values in the sense just adumbrated. This means to worry less about what individuals personally value, and more about what is happening at the collective level. More concretely, conversation should be encouraged on the topic of what is valuable, and about what we, as a team, value – promptness, efficiency, kindness, whatever – as opposed to what one or another particular individual among us values.

Similar things can be said, *pari ratione*, of collective beliefs and emotions. If we are to succeed as a team, our collective beliefs should be well founded and our collective emotions appropriate to the situation. Otherwise what we collectively do is likely to be misguided.

1.7   Are there good reasons not to invoke joint commitment?

Since I began writing on the topic various people, formally and informally, have expressed doubts about the idea of a joint commitment. These doubts are usually not very well articulated. The idea might be referred to as 'mysterious' for instance. Unless one is told what precisely the mystery is, this is not a very helpful criticism. (It is, one might say, quite mysterious itself.)

Why might one not wish to invoke the notion of a joint commitment in one's theory of team action, for instance? Here I list three possible reasons that might be offered and attempt brief rebuttals of them.

(1) *Theoretical parsimony*: if we need to invoke personal commitments elsewhere in our accounts of human action, it would be nice not to have to introduce another type of commitment as well.

Rebuttal: perhaps so, but if one wants adequately to characterize the phenomena one may have to introduce another type of commitment. Theoretical adequacy is presumably more important than theoretical parsimony.

(2) *One may not 'wish to be bound'* (Bittner, 2002). In other words, one may be emotionally averse to being jointly committed, with particular reference to the need (in the basic case) for mutual rescinding.

Rebuttal 1 (*ad personam*): maybe so, but one may then have to choose between becoming a team member (according to our everyday understanding of what this is) and not doing so. Or one must at least sue for special terms.

Rebuttal 2 (methodological): one's descriptive, analytical theorizing about teams should not be infected by one's personal desires or aversions.[14]

(3) *It smacks of a pernicious 'holism', or 'supraindividualism', or 'reification' of teams.*

Rebuttal 1 (query): please define these terms, say why the 'ism' or 'ation' in question is pernicious, and explain how invoking joint commitments involves it.

Rebuttal 2 (alternative query): please explain what, if anything, is pernicious about the invocation of joint commitments in the theory of teams.

Rebuttal 3 (observation): my proposal is that human beings routinely if inexplicitly understand themselves to be creating joint commitments and to be jointly committed in the course of their lives. The conditions for the creation of these commitments are relatively simple and easily satisfiable. Is there really a problem here?

1.8   Concluding remarks

I am, I confess, somewhat puzzled by the preference of so many other contemporary philosophical theorists – such as Bratman, Searle, and more recently, Kutz – to prefer accounts of team action that invoke only personal commitments or subjective 'team thoughts' as opposed to robust joint commitments.[15]

One can speculate that this is a matter of the 'singularist' assumption that there is nothing in the human world that is not understandable in terms of the thoughts, attitudes, commitments, and so on of individual human beings.[16] This assumption may seem to be simple common sense. Or it may be the only congenial assumption for people raised in a culture that focuses on 'individualist' values such as autonomy, self-reliance, and the pursuit and achievement of personal goals. If there are joint commitments, however, this assumption is simply not true.

If I am right, those who theorize about teams need to take on board the concept of a joint commitment and to understand fully the various features of such commitments. If, as I suggest, this concept is incorporated in the thought of team members, their action is unlikely to be fully comprehensible without an appeal to it.

Notes

1. I dedicate this paper to the memory of Michael Bacharach. I am grateful for his supportive interest in my work dating from the time we met in the late 1980s. Michael's text can be found at the beginning of this book. The projected workshop took place in April 2003.

2. See in particular Gilbert, 1989, ch. 4. Also, more briefly, Gilbert, 1990, reprinted with some revisions in Gilbert, 1996.

3. I have in mind here, in particular, Robert Sugden, another distinguished economic theorist who has worked on these matters. In his paper 'Team Preferences', 2000, he gives as an example of a team preference his family's preference for a certain kind of activity. I responded to some of the arguments in 'Team Preferences' in Gilbert, 2001.

4. The personal goals of the individual members of the group need not be the same as the group's goal. To cite an example suggested to me by Natalie Gold, individual members of a sports team may play in it with the primary purpose of increasing their physical fitness. This does not negate the idea that the team, as such, has the primary goal of winning. How these things can be needs to be spelled out. This will I hope become clearer later in the text.

5. This paragraph was added in response to a query from Natalie Gold.

6. These reflections are incorporated in Gilbert, 1989 and further developed in numerous articles focusing on specific topics. For some methodological discussion see Gilbert, 1989.

7. See Gilbert, 1989, Chapter 5 (on Lewis on social convention). An account of social institutions similar to Lewis's account of social convention is to be found in Shotter, 1981. This account may not have been intended to capture an everyday concept in the way Lewis's was, but rather to articulate a model useful for economic analysis.

8. I discuss the case of values in 'Shared Values, Social Unity, and Liberty' 2005 forthcoming. For a brief discussion see the text below. On collective emotions see my discussion of collective remorse in Gilbert, 2000; also Gilbert, in press.

9. Other theorists have used this term in different senses, or without making clear the sense of the term. Suffice it to say that I explicate only the sense in which I personally use this (technical) term here.

10. See Lewis, 1969; Schiffer, 1972.

11. Action theorists tend to give accounts of action in terms of intentions rather than goals. In the vernacular the term 'goal' or 'aim' may tend to be used for something more or less 'ultimate' in terms of a given sequence of movements. For present purposes this distinction is not important. In any case I present my rough account of team action in the text in terms of intention. My account of a team goal is exactly parallel, *mutatis mutandis.*

12. In principle he need never have corresponding personal intentions. See Gilbert, 1997, on the matter of corresponding personal intentions, and the text, below.

13. This point is argued at some length in Gilbert, 1999. See also Gilbert, 1993. The focus there is on the obligations rather than the rights, but the obligations and rights, in this case, are but two sides of the same coin. The relationship of rights of joint commitment and moral rights according to a common understanding of these is discussed in Gilbert, forthcoming.

14. I discuss the suggestions of Bittner, 2002 (who speaks for many) in Gilbert, 2002 and 2003.

15. See, for instance, Searle, 1990; Bratman, 1993; Kutz, 2000. The idea of 'group-identification' that has also been appealed to appears to fall on the 'subjective "team thoughts"' side of this divide.

16. I introduced the label 'singularism' in Gilbert, 1989. The more standard term 'individualism' is susceptible of diverse interpretations.

References

Bittner, Rudiger (2002) 'An Action for Two' in Georg Meggle (ed.) *Social Facts and Collective Intentionally* (Deutsche Bibliothek der Wissenschaften, Dr. Hansel-Hohenhausen Ag: New York).

Bratman, Michael (1993) 'Shared Intention', *Ethics* (104), 97–113.

Gilbert, Margaret (1989) *On Social Facts* (Princeton University Press: Princeton).

Gilbert, Margaret (1990) 'Walking Together: A Paradigmatic Social Phenomenon' in *Midwest Studies in Philosophy* (15) P. A. French, T. E. Uehling Jr. and H. K. Wettstein (eds) reprinted in Gilbert, 1996.

Gilbert, Margaret (1993) 'Agreements, Coercion, and Obligation', *Ethics* (103), 679–706, reprinted in Gilbert (1996).

Gilbert, Margaret (1996) *Living Together: Rationality, Sociality, and Obligation* (Rowman and Littlefield: Lanham, MD).

Gilbert, Margaret (1997) 'What is it for us to Intend?' in G. Holmstrom-Hintikka and R. Tuomela (eds) *Contemporary Action Theory*, vol. 2., *The Philosophy and Logic of Social Action* (Kluwer Academic Publishers: Dordrecht), reprinted in Gilbert, 2000.

Gilbert, Margaret (1999) 'Obligation and Joint Commitment', *Utilitas* (11), 143–163, reprinted in Gilbert (2000).

Gilbert, Margaret (2000) *Sociality and Responsibility: New Essays in Plural Subject Theory* (Rowman and Littlefield: Lanham, MD).

Gilbert, Margaret (2001) 'Collective Preferences, Obligations, and Rational Choice', *Economics and Philosophy* (17), 109–119.

Gilbert, Margaret (2002) 'Considerations on Joint Commitment: Responses to Various Comments' in Georg Meggle (ed.) *Social Facts and Collective Intentionally* (Deutsche Bibliothek der Wissenschaften, Dr. Hansel-Hohenhausen Ag: New York).

Gilbert, Margaret (2003) 'The Structure of the Social Atom: Joint Commitment as the Foundation of Human Social Behaviour', in Frederick Schmitt (ed.) *Social Metaphysics* (Rowman and Littlefield: Lanham, MD).

Gilbert, Margaret (in press) 'After Atrocity: the Possibility and Pointfulness of Collective Feelings of Guilt' in Charles Jones (ed.) *War Crimes* (McGill University Press: Montreal).

Gilbert, Margaret (2005, forthcoming) 'Shared values, Social Unity, and Liberty', *Public Affairs Quarterly*.

Gilbert, Margaret (forthcoming) *Rights Reconsidered* (Oxford University Press: Oxford).

Kutz, Christopher (2000) *Complicity: Ethics and Law for a Collective Age* (Cambridge University Press: Cambridge).

Lewis, David (1969) *Convention: A Philosophical Study* (Harvard University Press: Cambridge, MA).

Schiffer, Stephen (1972) *Meaning* (Oxford: Oxford University Press).

Searle, John (1990) 'Collective Intentions and Actions' in P. R. Cohen, J. Morgan, M. E. Pollack (eds) *Intentions in Communication* (MIT Press: Cambridge, MA).

Shotter, Andrew (1981) *Economic Theory of Social Institutions* (Cambridge University Press: Cambridge).

Sugden, Robert (2000) 'Team Preferences', *Economics and Philosophy* (16), 175–204.

2
Cognitive Cooperation: When the Going Gets Tough, Think as a Group

David Sloan Wilson, John J. Timmel and Ralph R. Miller

Cooperation is found throughout the animal kingdom and is especially common in our own species. For cooperation to evolve, there must first be a task that requires the coordinated action of more than one individual. Then it must be possible to solve the problems of cheating that often accompany coordinated action. Sometimes there is little incentive to cheat because cooperation produces large benefits for everyone at trivial individual cost. At other times cooperation is more costly and evolves only in groups where genetic relatedness is high or social control mechanisms are in place. Social insect colonies are one pinnacle of cooperation in the animal kingdom. Human social groups are another pinnacle, although the evolutionary pathways were not necessarily the same in the two cases (Sober and Wilson, 1998).

Cooperation is usually studied in the context of physical activities such as hunting, gathering, warfare, or childcare. However, cooperation can also take place in the context of cognitive activities such as perception, attention, memory, and decision making. All of these cognitive processes can potentially benefit from the coordinated action of more than one individual, just as physical activities do. Thus, we should expect to see animals merging their minds in addition to their muscles – perhaps even more so if the benefits of cooperation are greater and the problems of cheating less for cognitive than for physical activities.

The idea of cognitive cooperation in addition to physical cooperation is well understood by social insect biologists. For, example a honeybee colony monitors and adaptively responds to its resource environment over an area of several square kilometers. When the quality of a nectar source is artificially raised and lowered, the hive responds within hours with an appropriate allocation of workers (Seeley, 1995). Similarly, when a colony splits and a new nest site must be found, scouts that have investigated single sites integrate their information and the swarm moves directly to the best site (Seeley and Buhrman, 1999). Just as individual cognition requires neuronal interactions in which each neuron plays a small role in the process, group cognition in social insect colonies requires social interactions in which each insect plays a small role. The idea of a 'group mind' might sound like science fiction, but it has been firmly established for the social insects by the meticulous experiments of Seeley and many others (e.g. Camazine et al., 2001).

If social insects can merge their minds in addition to their muscles, how about humans? Strangely, cognitive cooperation is not well studied in our own species. The first social scientists imagined human societies as organic units, complete with 'group minds', but this holistic perspective was largely rejected during the middle of the twentieth century (Wegner, 1986). The modern psychological literature includes hundreds of papers that employ terms such as 'group problem solving' and 'group decision making', consisting of numerous specific research programs on various cognitive tasks. It is difficult to summarize such a diverse literature, but the verdict often appears to be that human groups do *not* function well as cognitive units. Two outstanding examples are the concepts of 'groupthink' and 'brainstorming'. Janis (1972, 1982) claimed that groups are prone to faulty decision making and that these deficits were responsible for foreign policy disasters such as the Bay of Pigs and the Vietnam war. His term 'groupthink' became a household word and invokes an image of groups as greatly inferior to individuals as cognitive units. The term 'brainstorming' was coined by an advertising executive who claimed that people generate more and better ideas in groups than alone (Osborne, 1957). Dozens of studies attempted to confirm this claim by comparing the performance of groups composed of interacting individuals with the performance of an equal number of individuals thinking by themselves (nominal groups) on a variety of tasks. The results were so uniformly negative that Mullen, Johnson, and Salas (1991) concluded their meta-analysis with the following strong statement: 'It appears to be particularly difficult to justify brainstorming techniques in terms of any performance outcomes, and the long-lived popularity of brainstorming techniques is unequivocally and substantively misguided.' Current research on brainstorming has largely stopped looking for performance advantages of groups and instead attempts to explain the performance deficits (Brown and Paulus, 2002; Stroebe and Diehl, 1994).

Wilson (1997) has reviewed the traditional psychological literature on group decision making from an evolutionary perspective. His assessment will be summarized in the discussion section of this paper, but first it is necessary to ask what the newer field of evolutionary psychology has to say on the subject. Evolutionary psychology has had much to say about cognition at the individual level, such as the existence of innate specialized adaptations to solve problems encountered in the ancestral environment (Cosmides and Tooby, 1992), the need to receive information as frequencies rather than percentages (Gigerenzer and Hoffrage, 1995), and the use of simple heuristics that make us efficiently smart rather than trying to comprehensively solve problems (Gigerenzer et al., 1999). However, the possibilities that groups might engage in coordinated cognitive processes, and that some of the insights just listed for individual cognition might also apply to group cognition, have not been considered.

To summarize, the idea of cognitive cooperation in humans is in a highly unsettled state. We are known to be a cooperative species, and cognitive tasks are as amenable to cooperation as physical tasks. The other pinnacle of sociality (the social insects) is known to engage in cognitive cooperation, yet traditional psychologists appear to find little evidence for it in humans and evolutionary psychologists haven't even started looking.

In this paper we show that cognitive cooperation can be demonstrated in humans, even in brainstorming experiments where it has previously been notoriously difficult to find. Furthermore, cognitive cooperation might operate beneath conscious awareness and without the need for learning, much as evolutionary psychologists have emphasized for individual-level cognition. Our experiments only begin to address a very large subject, but they suggest that cognitive cooperation should occupy center stage in human evolutionary psychology, as it already does in the study of social insects.

2.1 The experiments

Cooperation is most useful for tasks that exceed the ability of individuals acting alone. Most people can lift a glass of water by themselves and efforts to help would only get in the way. Most people cannot lift a piano by themselves and coordinated action is absolutely essential. This point is obvious in the context of physical activities, but it has not been sufficiently appreciated in the context of cognitive activities. For example, we cannot find a single brainstorming experiment that manipulates task difficulty as an independent variable.

We therefore made task difficulty the focus of our research. We chose the game of Twenty Questions because it is familiar, can be played by either individuals or groups, and has a number of advantages for studying task difficulty (Taylor and Faust, 1952). The object of the game is to guess a word by asking no more than 20 questions that can be answered with 'yes,' 'no,' or 'ambiguous'. Determining the word out of a set of many possibilities can easily tax the ability of an individual thinker, as anyone who has played the game knows. Task difficulty can be manipulated by altering the obscurity of the word to be guessed. In addition, task difficulty increases during the course of a single game as the amount of information that must be managed accumulates. We therefore predicted that groups would solve a higher proportion of games than individuals, that the relative advantage of groups would increase for obscure words relative to simple words, and would increase during the later part of the game relative to the early part of the game.

All complex tasks – physical or cognitive – consist of a number of subtasks that must ultimately be isolated and studied in relation to each other for more complete understanding. We therefore conducted a second experiment in which part of what is required to solve the game of Twenty Questions was presented in the format of a brainstorming experiment. Using the brainstorming format enabled us to relate our findings to a large body of previous research and to compare real groups with nominal groups in addition to single individuals.

2.1.1   Experiment 1: The standard game of Twenty Questions
Methods

The experiment was part of a semester-long course in which 36 undergraduate students first acted as participants and then helped to analyze the results while learning about decision making in a seminar format. Prior to the experiment, 40 students from the Binghamton University Psychology Department's human subject pool were asked to write as many job titles as possible (defined as any activity that is done for payment and can be described in a single word) over a 40-minute period. These lists were merged and redundancies were removed to yield a master list of 442 job titles. The number of lists upon which a given job title appeared served as an index of its availability for recall in our subject population. For example, 'doctor' appeared on all 40 lists while 'bricklayer' appeared on only one list, even though 'bricklayer' can easily be recognized as a job title once it is recalled. We deliberately chose the category of job titles for our experiment because it was familiar but presumably did not exist as an already organized category in the minds of our subjects, in contrast to a category such as mammals.

The experiment was divided into two phases. During Phase 1, half the participants were randomly assigned to same-sex groups of three people while the other half functioned as individuals. The groups and individuals played the game of Twenty Questions for five one-hour sessions in which the job titles to be guessed were drawn randomly from the master list. They were told that the object was to guess the word using no more than 20 questions and without regard to time. Games that were in progress at the end of a session were discarded from the analysis. The games were conducted in two rooms similar to each other and with a minimum of objects present, to avoid cueing effects. Participants were instructed not to talk about the experiment with anyone outside their groups. Individuals and groups were read the same set of instructions at the beginning of each session, and groups were allowed to conduct their interactions as they saw fit. Writing was prohibited during the games. Phase 2 of the experiment consisted of four one-hour sessions in which the Phase 1 groups were split into individuals and the Phase 1 individuals were formed into same-sex groups of three individuals. The experiment was conducted during a period of five weeks with two sessions/week.

Analysis

Our main dependent variable was the proportion of games solved by an individual or group during a single session. This unit of analysis avoids certain statistical biases by providing a single score per individual (or group) per session, regardless of how many games were played in a session. In addition to the final outcome of winning or losing, performance during the course of a single game was analyzed in the following manner. Consider an actual game in which the job title to be guessed is 'bricklayer' and the first question asked is, 'Does the job require a college degree?' This question can be answered, not only for the job title of bricklayer but for all job titles on the master list, allowing the fraction of job titles excluded by the question to be determined. The second question – such as, 'Is the job performed outdoors?' – can similarly be answered for all the job titles on the master list that were not excluded by the first question. In this fashion, a single game can be represented as a decay curve for the number of job titles on the master list remaining for consideration. The decay curve is steep for a well-played game and shallow for a poorly played game, regardless of whether the job title is actually guessed by the end of the game. This analysis required the construction of a large file in which all the questions asked by either individuals or groups for a number of games (more than 800 questions) were answered for all 442 job titles on the master list. This job was accomplished with the help of the students in the course after the experiment was over, and the decay curves for individual games were calculated with a computer program written for the purpose.

Results

Figure 2.1 shows the mean proportion of games solved by groups and individuals for both phases of the experiment. Analysis of variance (2 conditions × 2 phases, with sessions nested within phases) detected a main effect of group vs. individual (ANOVA, $F_{1,212} = 16.56$, $p < 0.001$), but no significant main effect for Phase 1 vs. Phase 2 ($p = 0.94$), and no significant interaction ($p = 0.73$). There was also no difference between sessions within a phase ($p = 0.69$). Thus, groups performed roughly twice as well as individuals, but neither condition increased in performance over the course of the experiment. In addition, the experience of playing as a group during Phase 1 did not increase the performance of group members when they played as individuals in Phase 2. The advantages of thinking as a group evidently required actually being in a group.

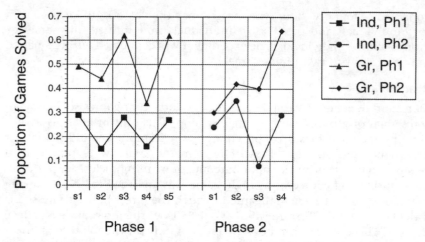

Figure 2.1   Mean proportion of games solved by individuals (Ind) and three-person groups (Gr) as a function of session number and phase. The members of groups during Phase 1 played as individuals during Phase 2 and vice versa. Phase 1 consisted of five 1-hour sessions (s) and Phase 2 consisted of four 1-hour sessions.

Because there were no significant differences between phases or sessions, they were combined for subsequent analysis. Figure 2.2 ranks the performance of the 12 groups, from best to worst, along with performance of the best group member and the average performance of the three group members when playing as individuals. There is not even a hint of a correlation between group and individual performance ($n = 12$, $r^2 = 0.014$, $p = 0.63$ for group vs. average member; $n = 12$, $r^2 = 0.020$, $p = 0.66$ for group vs. best member). Some of the best groups were composed of members who were mediocre as individuals and vice versa.

Figure 2.3 shows the mean decay curves for the first game of Phase 1, Session 1 and the first game of Phase 1, Session 5. The curves for individuals and groups are similar for the first five questions of the game but then diverge, with the groups exhibiting steeper curves than the individuals. There was a significant difference in number of job titles remaining prior to questions 6–12 and 18–20 (Kruskal-Wallace one-way ANOVA, $0.004 < p < 0.032$). Note that differences necessarily became smaller toward the end of the game owing to a 'floor effect' in which the number of remaining job titles converges upon zero. Our interpretation of Figure 2.3 is that a certain degree of task difficulty is required for groups to outperform individuals. By its nature, the game of Twenty Questions becomes more difficult with every question because an accumulating amount of information must be remembered and evaluated to intelligently parse the remaining possibilities in framing the next question. Individuals were evidently as good as groups at asking the first few

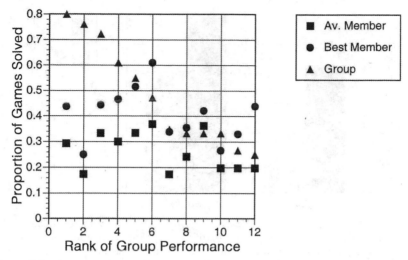

Figure 2.2 A comparison of group performance with the performance of the members playing as individuals. The groups are ranked according to group performance for convenience. There is no correlation between group performance (triangles) and the individual performance of either the average member (squares) or the best member (circles) of that group.

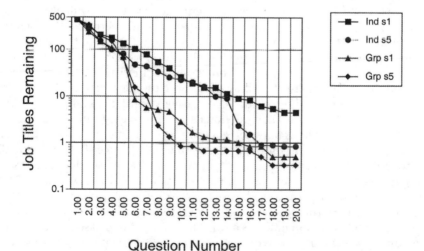

Question Number

Figure 2.3 Mean number of job titles remaining as a function of the number of questions asked during a game of Twenty Questions. Squares and circles represent individual performance during Phase 1, Session 1 and Phase 1, Session 5, respectively. Triangles and diamonds represent group performance during Phase 1, Session 1 and Phase 1, Session 5, respectively.

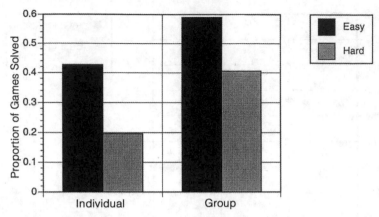

Figure 2.4   Performance of individuals and groups for job titles that could be recalled with ease ('easy') or with difficulty ('hard'). Groups surpassed individuals and experienced a performance decrease of only 32 per cent for hard words, compared with 55 per cent performance decrease for individuals.

questions but then began to falter under the weight of the accumulating information load.

The obscurity of the job titles to be guessed affords another way to measure task complexity. In principle it would have been possible to make obscurity a third factor of the experiment, along with individual vs. group and Phase 1 vs. Phase 2, but sample sizes did not permit a three-factor experiment. Instead, job titles were drawn at random from the master list for all games. To analyze the effect of obscurity, we split the job titles into two groups, those that appeared on 11–40 of the lists used to create the master list (relatively easy to recall) and those that appeared on 1–10 of the lists used to create the master list (relatively hard to recall). Figure 2.4 shows that groups surpass individuals for both easy and hard games. Groups and individuals both solve a lower proportion of hard games than easy games, but the performance decrease was 55 per cent for individuals and only 32 per cent for groups (all relevant pair-wise comparisons in Figure 2.4 are statistically significant: $X^2 = 4.32–19.30$, $p = 0.04–0.001$). This analysis does not permit us to attach statistical significance to the difference in the performance decrease (in contrast to an analysis of variance if obscurity had been included as a third factor, in which case the difference would appear as an interaction effect). Nevertheless, it qualitatively supports the conclusion that the advantages of cognitive cooperation increase with task difficulty.

Individuals may not think *better* than groups, but it seems likely that they usually think *faster* than groups. Surprisingly, this reasonable expectation was confirmed for Phase 1 of our experiment but not for Phase 2, as

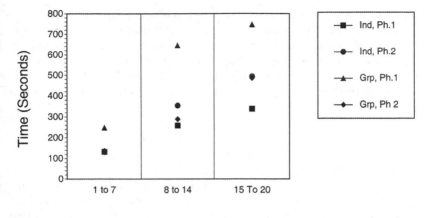

Question Blocks

Figure 2.5 Mean time required to ask a question for individuals and groups during Phase 1 and Phase 2 of the experiment. The amount of time required to ask a question increased during the course of the game for both individuals and groups. Groups required more time than individuals for Phase 1 but not for Phase 2.

shown in Figure 2.5. The difference in the amount of time spent on each question disappeared (perhaps because the participants were growing tired of playing the game of Twenty Questions) while the performance difference between groups and individuals remained.

2.1.2 Experiment 2: Partial Twenty Questions game in a brainstorming format

We originally chose the game of Twenty Questions because we wanted to present individuals and groups with a challenging cognitive task. Not only did groups outperform individuals overall, but the details of their performance, as revealed in Figures 2.3 and 2.4, pointed to task difficulty as a critical variable for demonstrating the advantages of thinking in groups. However, the very complexity and multifaceted nature of the game made it difficult to identify the exact mechanisms that enhanced group performance. In addition, the most stringent test of group cognition is to compare the performance of real groups, not with single individuals, but with the same number of individuals thinking alone (nominal groups), as in brainstorming experiments. The game of Twenty Questions does not lend itself to the formation of nominal groups.

We therefore conducted another experiment to address these issues. Real groups and nominal groups composed of two people were asked to perform one of two tasks: (1) to think of as many job titles as possible, or (2) to think of as many job titles as possible that satisfy the criteria of a partially completed game of Twenty Questions in which seven questions had already been asked and answered. The second task is clearly more challenging than the first, although simpler than a complete game of Twenty Questions. We predicted that the increase in task complexity would enhance the performance of real groups relative to nominal groups. We also included a condition in which the task was performed by friends rather than strangers, to see if familiarity of group members had an effect on task performance.

Methods

One hundred eighty students (108 females, 72 males) from psychology classes at Binghamton University participated as part of their course requirement. Students were requested to sign up with a friend of the same gender if possible. The ideal experimental design would have included only pairs of friends, who would be kept together or split to form individuals and pairs of strangers. Such a design was not possible because an insufficient number of pairs of friends signed up for the experiment. We therefore paired friends with each other for the 'friends' condition and used participants who signed up alone for the other conditions. This design leaves open the possibility that participants in the 'friends' condition were drawn from a different sample population, but it does not affect the comparison of nominal groups with real groups of strangers. Participants who signed up as individuals were randomly assigned to nominal or real same-sex groups.

The experiment had three participant conditions (pairs of friends, pairs of strangers, and nominal pairs) and two levels of task difficulty (all jobs [easy] and partial game [hard]). Each individual participated in only one condition. Table 2.1 shows the questions and answers given to participants in the partial game condition, which were obtained from an actual game played during the previous Twenty Questions experiment. After signing the informed consent form, participants were given typed copies of the instructions, they followed along as the experimenter read the instructions aloud, and they were then asked if they had any questions. Next, they were

1. Is it an office job?	No
2. Does the job involve contact with others?	Yes
3. Does the job require a college degree?	No
4. Does the job involve working with all ages?	Yes
5. Does the job involve working in a hospital?	No
6. Is it a government job?	No
7. Does the job involve working with food?	No

Table 2.1 A partial game of Twenty Questions used for the partial game condition of the brainstorming study (Experiment 2). Real and nominal groups were asked to generate a list of job titles that satisfy these criteria.

provided 45 minutes to generate as long a list of single-word job titles as possible, either without constraints or with the constraints provided by the questions and answers of the partial game, which were provided on a written sheet. The experiment was conducted in four identical cubicles; trials on real and nominal groups were run in parallel whenever possible. After a sample size of approximately 10 pairs had accumulated for each of the six conditions, a preliminary analysis was conducted, prompting us to discontinue the 'friends' and 'all jobs' conditions and to double the sample size to approximately 20 pairs for the remaining partial-game conditions (real groups of strangers vs. nominal groups; see Methods). During analysis it became evident that four participants clearly misunderstood the instructions (e.g., by writing a list of job titles that satisfied the first question, followed by a list of job titles that satisfied the second question, and so on) and their lists were removed from the analysis.

That the 'partial game' task is more difficult than the 'all jobs' task may seem self-evident and is supported by comparing the lists generated for the two task conditions, as described in more detail below. Nevertheless, it seemed desirable to have at least some participants perform both tasks and subjectively rate their relative difficulty. Accordingly, five additional participants (beyond the 180 within the core part of the experiment) performed both tasks in random order for ten-minute periods and were asked to rate their relative difficulty (e.g., a rating of .5 indicates that the partial game was thought to be half as difficult as the full list, a rating of 2 indicates that the partial game was thought to be twice as difficult as the full list, and so on). These participants typed the job titles into a computer that was programmed to record the time of entry, enabling the rate of recall to be measured on a second-by-second basis along with the final number at the end of the tasks.

Results

In the first analysis of the data, real groups of strangers, real groups of friends, and nominal groups were found to perform equally well on the relatively simple all-jobs task ($F_{2,31} = 1.17$, $p = 0.32$; see Table 2.2). Performance on the more difficult, partial-game task was ranked in the order real groups of strangers > real groups of friends > nominal groups, although the differences did not reach significance at the 0.05 level ($F_{2,26} = 2.13$, $p = 0.14$; restricting the comparison to real groups of strangers vs. nominal groups, $F_{1,18} = 4.02$, $p = 0.06$). For both tasks, groups of friends did not perform better than groups of strangers. These results prompted us to increase the sample size for the most important comparison, that between real groups of strangers and nominal groups for the difficult task. The additional data alone demonstrated a significant performance advantage for real groups over nominal groups ($F_{1,23} = 5.72$, $p = 0.025$). When the data for all participants were pooled, real groups of strangers had approximately a 50 per cent

| | First 63 pairs | | | | | | Last 25 pairs | | |
| | Full list | | | Partial game I | | | Partial game II | | |
	n	mean	s.e.	n	mean	s.e.	n	mean	s.e.
Strangers	11	187.0	13.3	10	96.7	16.6	11	93.1	13.74
Friends	11	177.4	10.2	9	77.8	11.9	–	–	–
Nominal	12	161.8	11.9	10	60.6	6.4	14	61.1	5.40

Table 2.2   Mean number of job titles and standard errors listed by pairs of strangers, friends, and nominal groups of two. The full-list condition involved guessing any one-word job title. The partial-game condition involved guessing one-word job titles that satisfied the conditions of the questions and answers shown in Table 2.1.

performance advantage over nominal groups on the partial game task, a difference that is highly significant (with means of 94.8 vs. 60.8 items recalled; $F_{1,43}$ =10.20, p = 0.003).

All types of groups (real and nominal) listed half or less as many job titles for the partial-game task than the all-jobs task. By itself this is not surprising because fewer job titles qualified for the partial-game task. However, the lists from individuals who constituted nominal groups were actually less redundant for the partial-game task than for the full-list task (17.4 per cent vs. 22.7 per cent, respectively; $F_{1,34}$ = 11.48, p = 0.002). In other words, participants were far from exhausting the set of possible job titles for either task, but the process of recalling job titles for the partial-game task was slower and presumably more difficult. This interpretation was supported by the five additional participants who performed both tasks and whose rate of recall was measured throughout their 10-minute test period (Figure 2.6). The ratio of the number of words recalled for the partial-game task divided by the number of words recalled for the all-jobs task provides an index of the relative difficulty of the two tasks as a function of time. The ratio is lowest at the beginning of the period, as participants struggled to assimilate the constraints imposed by the seven questions, and then rose to a plateau of approximately 0.30–0.35 after three minutes. The five participants subjectively rated the partial-game task as 2–5 times more difficult than the all-jobs task (mean = 2.6, s.e. = 0.6).

2.2   Discussion

Cooperation is most effective for tasks that exceed the capacity of individuals. This statement might seem so obvious that it doesn't need to be made. However, the 'unsettled state' of the literature that we described in the introduction requires a back-to-basics approach to cognitive cooperation in humans. We tested the most basic prediction for the game of Twenty Questions and found exactly what one might expect: Not only did groups

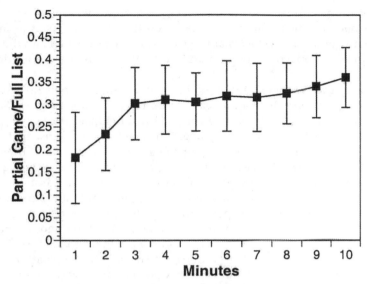

Figure 2.6   Ratio of the number of job titles recalled per minute for the partial game condition divided by the number of job titles recalled per minute for the all-jobs condition, providing an index of relative task difficulty. The ratio is lowest at the beginning of the recall period.

outperform individuals overall, but their relative advantage increased with task difficulty, both within single games and between games that differed in terms of the obscurity of the target word.

In addition to this basic result, some of our more detailed results are anything but obvious: It is reasonable to expect individuals and groups to improve their performance during the course of playing many games, but no learning effect was observed. Similarly, it is reasonable to expect that the experience of playing in a group during Phase 1 would increase individual performance during Phase 2, but this was not observed. Finally, it is reasonable to expect that whatever makes an individual good at playing the game alone would also contribute to group performance, but this was not observed. These results can be summarized as follows: performance is not based on learning (at least over the short term), the advantages of groups require being in a group, and the mechanisms that contribute to group performance are not just a sum of the mechanisms that contribute to individual performance.

Brainstorming is one task in which traditional psychologists have looked very hard for cognitive cooperation and generally failed to find it. However, the fact that task difficulty has not been recognized and manipulated as an independent variable in brainstorming experiments shows how much a back-to-basics approach is needed. We manipulated task difficulty in a brainstorming format and found exactly what one would expect: Real groups outperformed nominal groups when the cognitive task was made sufficiently difficult. The fact that the friendship of group members did not have an effect on group performance will be discussed in more detail below.

We do not wish to imply that task difficulty is a single variable. There are many kinds of tasks that can be easy or difficult in different ways. Some very difficult tasks are still best performed by individuals (e.g. playing the violin), while some tasks that require groups are easy in the sense that they require minimal coordination (e.g. lifting a table), even though they are difficult in the sense of exceeding the weight or dimensional lifting capacity of a single person. Every physical task must be examined on its own terms for the potential costs and benefits of cooperation, and the same is true of cognitive tasks. Our experiments merely demonstrate the performance advantage of groups for the game of Twenty Questions and the effects of increasing task difficulty in a crude and poorly understood sense. Much more work will be required to understand the cognitive operations that comprise the game in detail and why they are improved by cooperation.

It is clear – if only in retrospect – that cognitive cooperation should receive as much attention as physical cooperation in the study of our own species, no less than that of the social insects. For the rest of this paper we will consolidate our back-to-basics approach by addressing two questions: How can cognitive cooperation be incorporated into the field of evolutionary psychology? Why does the traditional psychological literature often give the impression that human groups function poorly as cognitive units?

2.3   Cognitive cooperation and evolutionary psychology

One hallmark of evolutionary psychology is to study the mind as a collection of adaptations to the problems of survival and reproduction in ancestral environments. Although the 'environment of evolutionary adaptedness' (EEA) is difficult to reconstruct, it is crudely approximated by modern hunter-gatherer societies. Timmel (2001) searched the electronic version of the Human Relations Area File (HRAF) using the key word 'decision' to see how often human decision making takes place in a solitary vs. group context in hunter-gatherer and other non-technological societies. The answer is that decision making almost invariably takes place in a group context, at least according to these ethnographic sources. The main exception is warfare, which sometimes places a premium on the speed of the decision. Similarly, Boehm (1996) searched the ethnographic literature for examples in which a group was faced with an important decision and an anthropologist was present to describe the decision making process in detail. One example involved a natural disaster and two others involved decisions about going to war. In all three cases, the decisions were made by a lengthy and well-orchestrated group-level process. We do not mean to imply that all decision making took place in groups in the EEA, much less that they were always made cooperatively. Clearly, individuals do make decisions by themselves, and those decisions are less likely to be noticed by ethnographers than decisions made by groups. Nevertheless, it is safe to say that decision making and other forms of cognition have taken place largely in a group setting throughout our evolutionary history. Put simply, when our ancestors were thinking, they were usually socializing at the same time. This is an important precondition for the evolution of cognitive cooperation.

A second hallmark of evolutionary psychology is its reliance on theoretical models to determine what adaptations are likely to evolve in a given environment. It might seem that cognitive cooperation is more likely to evolve in social insect groups than human groups because genetic relatedness is usually higher in the former. However, genetic relatedness is only one of many factors that influences the evolution of cooperation. Other factors include the costs and benefits of cooperation, probabilities of repeated interactions, conditional behaviors such as the 'Tit-for-Tat' strategy of game theory, social control mechanisms, and so on (Dugatkin, 1997; Sober and Wilson, 1998). When all of these factors are considered, the evolution of cognitive cooperation in humans becomes extremely likely theoretically. Cognitive cooperation often produces substantial gains for everyone at minimal individual cost. For example, in a group that must stay together, everyone gains from making a wise decision about where to move; the cost of the mental operations required to make the decision are energetically trivial and in any case are shared among the group members. This kind of low cost/high gain cooperation can evolve even in groups of unrelated individuals. In general, the cost/benefit ratio for cognitive cooperation might often be very low because the mental operations required for cooperation can be trivial in terms of time, energy, and risk, while the beneficial impact on behavior can be substantial.

We do not mean to imply that cognitive cooperation is invariably adaptive in human groups. Not only are many tasks performed best by individuals, as we have already stressed, but various kinds of free-riding and exploitation are possible, especially when there is a conflict of interest about the behavioral outcomes of cognition. Furthermore, even when cognitive cooperation is adaptive, the optimal group size might often be smaller than the actual size of the group. Just as some tasks are best performed by a single individual and a second would only get in the way, other tasks might best be performed by three individuals and a fourth would only get in the way. For all of these reasons, theoretically we should expect cognitive cooperation in humans to be richly context-sensitive and protected by social control mechanisms to eliminate the potential for exploitation. For example, pairs of friends did not perform better than pairs of strangers in our brainstorming experiment. However, the task was such that even strangers had everything to gain and nothing to lose by cooperating with each other (assuming that they were motivated to perform well at the task). If the task had been changed to provide an opportunity for exploitation, we predict that individuals might 'shut down' in the presence of a stranger and 'open up' in the presence of a friend, making friendship an important variable in cognitive cooperation. In general, context sensitivity provides many opportunities to formulate and test specific hypotheses about cognitive cooperation in humans based on theoretical models.

A third hallmark of evolutionary psychology is its emphasis on sophisticated, special-purpose adaptations that operate beneath conscious awareness (Barkow et al., 1992). Cognitive abilities such as vision and memory are 'simple', 'effortless', and 'natural' in the sense that we do them without conscious effort and without the need for instruction, but the cognitive mechanisms that make these abilities so effortless are highly complex. We suggest that these same insights might apply to cognitive cooperation. Individuals playing the game of Twenty Questions by themselves frequently became exasperated and even downright stressed when they were 'stumped', 'ran out of ideas', and so on. They clearly had depleted their own cognitive resources in some sense and seemingly were yearning for external input. Some even described the experience of playing by themselves as 'agonizing'. In contrast, the members of three-person groups simply seemed to 'click' into action, erupting into animated conversation, often with much gaiety and laughter. Individuals would impulsively barge into the conversation when they felt they had something to contribute, praise other members for ideas deemed valuable, and groan loudly when a promising idea proved to be wrong. Guessing the right word sometimes even resulted in cheers and the slapping of hands, as when a sports team scores a goal. These social dynamics are so familiar to us that we take them for granted, like sight and memory. However, the mechanisms that make them so effortless might be highly complex, as evolutionary psychologists already appreciate for individual-level cognitive adaptations (see Wilson et al., 2000 for a similar analysis of gossip as a group-level cognitive adaptation).

To summarize, there is every reason for cognitive cooperation to occupy center stage in human evolutionary psychology and to be integrated with the insights that are already being applied to the study of individual cognition.

2.4   Cognitive cooperation and traditional psychology

The traditional psychological literature on thinking in groups has been reviewed from an evolutionary perspective by Wilson (1997) and consists of dozens of research programs on different cognitive tasks. These programs are often highly sophisticated and informative within their own domains but poorly integrated with each other, and some of the most basic questions that need to be asked from an evolutionary perspective often are not addressed. Evolutionary psychologists will be unsurprised to learn this because it is typical for nearly every major subject in psychology. Here we will summarize a few points from Wilson (1997) to show that the traditional psychological literature offers much support for the concept of cognitive cooperation, even though appearances are often to the contrary.

In the first place, some research programs do ask the right questions from an evolutionary perspective and impressively show the advantages of thinking in groups, especially for difficult tasks. Two outstanding examples are the work of Edwin Hutchins (1995) on cognition in naturalistic situations and Daniel Wegner on what he calls 'transactive memory' (1986; Wegner et al. 1991). Hutchins uses navigation in both traditional and modern societies as a naturalistic setting for studying cognition. When a modern ship is a comfortable distance from shore, the task of sighting landmarks and marking the position of the ship on a chart can be accomplished by a single person. When the ship approaches the shore and its position needs to be determined at more frequent intervals and with less tolerance for error, this task is accomplished by a six-person team whose interactions have been refined over decades and even centuries of nautical history. Hutchins minutely analyzes these interactions in cognitive terms, much as social insect biologists examine the social cognition of bees and ants. Hutchins is one of the few to emphasize the transition from individual cognition to group cognition *as the task becomes more difficult,* which also forms the basis for our research. Wegner invites us to imagine how a computer engineer would connect a number of microcomputers, each with limited memory capacity, to form an integrated network with a larger memory capacity. That is how we should think about human memory according to Wegner, who supports his claim with a number of convincing laboratory studies. Wegner (1986) also reviews the history of thinking on group cognition in the social sciences, which should be read by everyone who wishes to integrate the psychological and evolutionary literatures for this subject.

Janis (1972, 1982) also studied group decision making in naturalistic situations, but he came to the opposite conclusion as Hutchins when he coined the word *groupthink:* 'I use the term "groupthink" as a quick and easy way to refer to a mode of thinking that people engage in when they are deeply involved in a cohesive in-group, when the members' strivings for unanimity override their motivation to realistically appraise alternative courses of action. Groupthink refers to a deterioration of mental efficiency, reality testing and moral judgement that results from in-group pressures' (Janis, 1972:9).

Janis based his assessment on a qualitative and retrospective analysis of foreign policy disasters, but his work stimulated a more rigorous literature based on both laboratory experiments and the quantitative analysis of historical events. There are, of course, examples of both good and bad decision making groups in American foreign policy history. For example, Lyndon Johnson was an overbearing leader who greeted dissenting views from his advisors with the ominous statement 'I'm afraid he's losing his effectiveness,' forcing many to leave his inner circle and those who remained to withhold their opinions. In essence, Johnson reduced the size of his decision making group to himself. In contrast, the Marshall plan was formulated in a period of three weeks by a leader (George Kennan) who deliberately encouraged discussion and disagreement among his advisors. These and other historical examples have been analyzed with methods that illustrate the best of traditional social science research. They show that the quality of a group decision depends very much on how the group is structured and that groups dominated by a single individual usually do not make the best decisions. By itself, this is an argument for cognitive cooperation, not against it. However, even if groups can be structured to make better decisions than individuals, it is important to ask whether human groups spontaneously adopt the right structure, as we would predict from an evolutionary perspective and as our own research seems to indicate. Janis disagreed; he thought that human groups spontaneously adopt structures that lead to maladaptive outcomes. Subsequent research has proven Janis wrong on this point. When groups are made more cohesive and tasks are made more salient in laboratory experiments and in naturalistic situations, they become better decision making units, not worse. As Aldag and Fuller (1993: 539) conclude, 'On the basis of our review, it seems clear that there is little support for the full groupthink model ... Furthermore, the central variable of cohesiveness has not been found to play a consistent role ... This suggestion is diametrically opposed to Janis's (1982) view that high cohesiveness and an accompanying concurrence-seeking tendency that interferes with critical thinking are "the central features of groupthink".'

It is easy to sympathize with the appeal of the groupthink concept, since so many efforts to think in groups do appear dysfunctional in modern life, as anyone who has attended committee meetings can attest. However, evolutionary theory does not predict that groups are invariably better than individuals as cognitive units. There are plenty of situations in which individuals function better than groups, small groups function better than large groups, groups structured one way function better than groups structured another way, or lack of interest in the task and bitter conflicts of interest about the outcome turn groups into slumber parties or battlefields rather than cooperative units. Part of studying cooperative cognition from an evolutionary perspective involves appreciating its richly context-sensitive nature, which makes simple generalizations impossible but provides the basis for many specific predictions. When we contemplate the efficacy of groups as cognitive units, we should think not only of boring committee meetings but also parties, scientific conferences, urgent councils of war, and hushed conversations with intimates. As we have already described, the participants in our experiment found the experience of playing the game of Twenty Questions far more enjoyable in groups than as individuals.

Groupthink is an outstanding example of a literature in traditional psychology that superficially portrays groups as dysfunctional cognitive units but upon closer examination does nothing of the sort. The brainstorming literature provides another example. Brainstorming researchers frequently lament that brainstorming techniques remain popular in business and industry even though experiments do not provide evidence for their efficacy. The implication is that the experience of business and industry is subjective and poorly controlled, and therefore wrong, while the psychological experiments are objective and carefully controlled, and therefore right. We agree that subjective experience is prone to a host of biases, but we also think that another difference separates brainstorming in the real world from brainstorming in laboratory experiments: the difficulty of the task. Until brainstorming researchers vary task difficulty as an independent variable, there is simply no way to relate the results of their experiments to the challenges of making decisions in the real world.

Another major problem concerns frames of comparison. From an evolutionary perspective, the most important comparison is an individual thinking alone vs. as a member of a socially interacting group. For brainstorming researchers, the most important comparison is between so-called real groups of interacting individuals and so-called nominal groups composed of the same number of individuals thinking by themselves. These two comparisons might seem the same, but a closer look reveals that 'nominal' groups are socially interacting groups in their own right in which the experimenter functions as a member. First the experimenter takes the ideas compiled by members of the nominal group and merges them into a single list, throwing out the redundancies along the way. The fact that this list is longer (and no less creative) than the list compiled by real groups is used as evidence that nominal groups are superior to real groups. However, the real groups do not require the services of the experimenter to compile their list, and the time spent by the experimenter is not added to the time spent by the nominal groups. In addition, actually using the list to make a decision requires examining all the items on the list. The real groups can do this while compiling the list, whereas the nominal groups can't even get started until after the experiment is over. When these factors are taken into account, it is not clear that a real group trying to make a real decision would want to emulate the structure of so-called nominal groups, even for the simple tasks employed in brainstorming experiments. Even if they did, they would be participating in a group-level cognitive process requiring social interactions between individuals in addition to neuronal interactions within individuals. The comparison of real vs. nominal groups is a comparison between two differently structured groups, not a comparison of individuals vs. groups. Individuals are so obviously inferior to either real or nominal groups in brainstorming experiments that the result seems unworthy of attention, yet it is exactly this 'obvious' comparison that needs to be made from an evolutionary perspective and that reveals the advantages of individuals joining their minds with others to make better decisions than they can by themselves.

It is interesting to compare the brainstorming literature with computer algorithms that employ groups of cooperating agents to solve very complex problems (such as the travelling salesman problem), and which sometimes are inspired by cooperation in nonhuman species such as social insects (e.g. Bonabeau, Dorigo, and Theraulaz, 2000). Typically these algorithms involve alternating between an autonomous phase in which the agents search the parameter space independently and an integrative phase in which the agents communicate to decide what to do next. The parallel processing that takes place during the autonomous phase is regarded as an advantage of group cognition that is unavailable to a single, sequentially processing unit. In brainstorming experiments, it is the members of nominal groups who enjoy the advantages of parallel processing while the members of real groups are forced into a sequential processing mode. Thus, what is properly regarded as an advantage of group cognition in one field of inquiry is associated with nominal groups (therefore an 'individual' property) that is somehow unavailable to real groups in brainstorming experiments. This bizarre state of affairs can be avoided in the future by first comparing the performance of individuals who truly function alone with the performance of groups that themselves can differ in their social organization, of which so-called real and nominal groups count as two examples.

We do not mean to imply that the comparison between real and nominal groups is uninteresting. Having found that groups often surpass individuals as cognitive units, it becomes important to know exactly how group cognition works, what makes some social structures better than others, and especially the kinds of social structures that people adopt spontaneously. The brainstorming literature has been exemplary in dissecting the so-called performance deficits of real groups in comparison to nominal groups, and this surgical approach will become even more interesting when applied to tasks that allow real groups to surpass nominal groups, as in our second experiment, and especially for social structures that emulate what people adopt spontaneously. In a recent review of brainstorming, Brown and Paulus (2002: 211) state: 'It is clear that unstructured groups left to their own devices will not be very effective in developing creative ideas.' We predict that the very opposite conclusion will be reached when brainstorming and other cognitive tasks are studied from an evolutionary perspective.

We will provide one other example of how even the most clear-cut demonstration of cognitive cooperation in the psychological literature can be made to appear 'individualistic' by altering the frame of comparison. Michaelsen, Watson, and Black (1989; see also Watson, Michaelsen, and Sharp, 1991) taught college courses in which students were organized into learning groups that lasted the entire semester. The majority of class time was spent on group problem-solving tasks, including six objective and at least two essay exams that accounted for more than 50 per cent of the course grade. Groups also met frequently outside of class to study and complete projects. This is one of the few research programs in which groups were presented with contextually relevant tasks and group dynamics had time to develop, as opposed to short-term laboratory experiments.

Exams were administered first to individuals and immediately afterward to groups (see Hill 1982 for a discussion of this and other experimental designs in group-decision research). In other words, after group members handed in their answer sheets, they were given an additional answer sheet for the same exam to fill out as a group. For a total of 222 groups from 25 courses taught over a five-year period, the mean individual test score was 74.2, the mean score of the best individual in each group was 82.6, and the mean group score was 89.9. A total of 215 groups (97 per cent) outperformed their best member, four groups (2 per cent) tied their best member, and three groups (1 per cent) scored lower than their best member.

These results provide overwhelming evidence that groups do not simply defer to their best member but scrutinize the questions on a case-by-case basis to decide which member is most likely to be correct. This is an impressive error-correcting capability that can take place only in groups. Nevertheless, the research was criticized by Tindale and Larson (1992a, 1992b), who claimed that groups must be able to answer a question right when every member answered it wrong to demonstrate a so-called 'assembly bonus effect'. Michaelsen, Watson, Schwartzkopf, and Black (1992) replied that their groups actually do display this effect, but our point is that the entire debate is peripheral from an evolutionary perspective. The ability to figure out which member is most likely to be correct by itself is an example of cognitive cooperation. The ability to figure out that no one was correct would be even more impressive, but is not necessary to show the basic advantage of thinking in groups.

These examples and others reviewed by Wilson (1997) show that the traditional psychological literature provides much evidence for cognitive cooperation, but only after it has been carefully reinterpreted from an evolutionary perspective.

We can summarize the results of our experiments, along with our review of the evolutionary psychology and traditional psychology literatures, as follows: The single human mind is adapted to function as a self-contained cognitive unit in some respects, but in others it is adapted to merge with other minds through social interactions to produce cooperative cognitive outcomes. This ability is surely a product of genetic evolution in addition to short-term learning and cultural processes. Cognitive co-operation needs to occupy center stage in evolutionary psychology, which in turn can provide a unifying conceptual framework for all research on group cognition.

Acknowledgements

We thank our 1996 decision making class for participating in this research. We also thank the ecology, evolution, and behaviour graduate group at Binghamton University for helpful discussion.

References

Aldag, R. J. and S. R. Fuller (1993) 'Beyond Fiasco: A Reappraisal of the Groupthink Phenomenon and a New Model of Group Decision Processes', *Psychological Bulletin*, 113, 533–552.

Barkow, J. H., L. Cosmides and J. Tooby (eds) (1992) *The Adapted Mind: Evolutionary Psychology and the Generation of Culture* (Oxford: Oxford University Press).

Boehm, C. (1996) 'Emergency Decisions, Cultural Selection Mechanics and Group Selection', *Current Anthropology*, 37, 763–793.

Bonabeau, E., M. Dorigo and G. Theraulaz (2000) 'Inspiration for Optimization from Social Insect Behavior', *Nature*, 406, 39–42.

Brown, V. R. and P. B. Paulus (2002) 'Making Group Brainstorming More Effective: Recommendations from an Associative Memory Perspective', *Current Directions in Psychological Science*, 11, 208–212.

Camazine, S., J.-L. Deneubourg, N. R. Franks, J. Sneyd, G. Theraulaz and E. Bonabeau (2001) *Self-organization in Biological Systems* (Princeton: Princeton University Press).

Cosmides, L. and J. Tooby (1992) 'Cognitive Adaptations for Social Exchange' In *The Adapted Mind,* J. Barkow, L. Cosmides, and J. Tooby (eds), pp. 163–225 (New York: Academic Press).

Dugatkin, L. A. (1997) *Cooperation among Animals* (Oxford: Oxford University Press).

Gigerenzer, G. and U. Hoffrage (1995) 'How to Improve Bayesian Reasoning without Instruction', *Psychological Review*, 102, 684–704.

Gigerenzer, G., P. M. Todd and A. R. Group (1999) *Simple Heuristics That Make Us Smart* (Oxford: Oxford University Press).

Hill, G. W. (1982) 'Group versus Individual Performance: Are N+1 Heads Better Than One?', *Psychological Bulletin*, 91, 517–539.

Hutchins, E. (1995) *Cognition in the Wild* (Cambridge, Massachusetts: MIT Press).

Janis, I. L. (1972) *Victims of Groupthink* (Boston: Houghton Mifflin).

Janis, I. L. (1982) *Groupthink*, 2nd edn (Boston: Houghton Mifflin).

Michaelsen, L. K., W. E. Watson and R. H. Black (1989) 'A Realistic Test of Individual versus Group Consensus Decision Making', *Journal of Applied Psychology*, 74, 834–839.

Michaelsen, L. K., W. E. Watson, A. Schwartzkopf and R. H. Black (1992) 'Group Decision Making: How You Frame the Question Determines What You Find', *Journal of Applied Psychology*, 77, 106–108.

Mullen, B., C. Johnson and E. Salas (1991) 'Productivity Loss in Brainstorming Groups: A Meta-analytic Integration', *Basic and Applied Social Psychology*, 12, 3–24.

Osborne, A. F. (1957) *Applied Imagination* (New York: Scribners).

Seeley, T. (1995) *The Wisdom of the Hive* (Cambridge: Harvard University Press).

Seeley, T. and S. C. Buhrman (1999) 'Group Decision Making in Swarms of Honey Bees', *Behavioral Ecology and Sociobiology*, 45, 19–31.

Sober, E. and D. S. Wilson (1998) *Unto Others: The Evolution and Psychology of Unselfish Behavior* (Cambridge: Harvard University Press).

Stroebe, W. and M. Diehl (1994) 'Why Groups Are less Effective Than Their Members: On Productivity Losses in Idea-Generating Groups', *European Review of Social Psychology*, 5, 271–303.

Taylor, D. W. and W. I. Faust (1952) 'Twenty Questions: Efficiency in Problem Solving as a Function of Size of Group', *Journal of Experimental Psychology*, 44, 360–368.

Timmel, J. J. (2001) *Group Cognition from a Multilevel Evolutionary Perspective*. Ph.D. dissertation, Binghamton University.

Tindale, R. S. and J. R. J. Larson (1992a) 'Assembly Bonus Effect or Typical Group Performance? A Comment on Michaelsen, Watson and Black (1989)', *Journal of Applied Psychology*, 77, 102–105.

Tindale, R. S. and J. R. J. Larson (1992b) 'It's Not How You Frame the Question, It's How You Interpret the Results', *Journal of Applied Psychology*, 77, 109–110.

Watson, W., L. K. Michaelsen and W. Sharp (1991) 'Member Competence, Group Interaction, and Group Decision Making: A Longitudinal Study', *Journal of Applied Psychology*, 76, 803–809.

Wegner, D. M. (1986) 'Transactive Memory: A Contemporary Analysis of the Group Mind' In *Theories of Group Behavior,* B. Mullen and G. R. Goethals (eds), pp. 185–208 (New York: Springer-Verlag).

Wegner, D. M., R. Erber and P. Raymond (1991) 'Transactive Memory in Close Relationships', *Journal of Personality and Social Psychology*, 61, 923–929.

Wilson, D. S. (1997) 'Incorporating Group Selection into the Adaptationist Program: A Case Study Involving Human Decision Making' In *Evolutionary Social Psychology*, J. Simpson and D. Kendricks (eds), pp. 345–386 (Mahwah, New Jersey: Erlbaum).

Wilson, D. S., C. Wilczynski, A. Wells and L. Weiser (2000) 'Gossip and Other Aspects of Language as Group-Level Adaptations' In *Cognition and Evolution,* C. Heyes and L. Huber (eds), pp. 347–365 (Cambridge, Massachusetts: MIT Press).

3

Cooperation, Risk and the Evolution of Teamwork

Peter Andras and John Lazarus

Our aims in this chapter are twofold. First, we place teamwork in the context of the evolutionary analysis of cooperation and altruism. This allows us to predict the evolutionary scenarios likely to have favoured the evolution of team work, the probable origins of human teamwork and the biases to be predicted in team thinking. Second, we examine the influences of environmental adversity and uncertainty (both conceptualized as 'risk') on cooperation in the organic world and describe a new model to explain these influences. We conclude by drawing conclusions about the role of environmental risk in the emergence of human cooperation and teamwork.

3.1   The evolution of teamwork and team reasoning

If teamwork is a strategy that follows from team reasoning (*sensu* Colman, 2003; Sugden, this volume) then the function of teamwork can be said to be to maximize utility for the team as a whole. This goal is reached by a particular combination of actions by members of the team. Since the goal of maximizing utility for the team may compromise utility for (at least some of) its constituent individuals, teamwork may require cooperative or altruistic acts by team members. In this section we examine the various selective mechanisms for cooperation and altruism distinguished by evolutionary biology and ask which of these mechanisms might result in teamwork as defined here. We ask, in other words: how does teamwork evolve?

We are concerned here largely with functional and evolutionary questions concerning teamwork, cooperation and altruism, and not with questions of motivation, development, intention or psychological mechanism (see Tinbergen, 1963, for a classic account of these distinctions). In evolutionary biology, functional questions about behaviour are concerned with the consequences of action and ask how action might be adaptive; how it might solve some problem important to the organism's survival or reproductive success, and thus to its Darwinian fitness. Adaptations inevitably have both benefits and costs, and natural selection results in changes in the

56

organism over time that hone its adaptations towards the optimal condition of maximum fitness, or net benefit (i.e. benefit minus cost), although Darwin (1872) himself appreciated that there is no guarantee that the optimal state will be reached. Consequently, the building blocks of functional analysis are the benefits and costs of action measured in the currency of fitness. Cooperation and altruism are defined functionally in evolutionary biology, therefore, simply in terms of their resultant benefit and cost. Cooperation is defined as a social action resulting in a benefit both to the actor and to the recipient of the act, while altruism is defined as an act that benefits the recipient at a cost to the actor. These are the definitions we use in discussing the evolution and function of cooperation and altruism.

We can distinguish, in principle, between two kinds of cooperation. In the first, sometimes called mutualism, all individuals involved in the interaction benefit but none benefits at the expense of others. A simple example is group-living, which reduces predation risk for all in the group by (with some simplification) 'diluting' the risk of capture by the number in the group. A second example is group hunting by wolves in which only by cooperative hunting is it possible to bring down a prey many times larger than an individual wolf. By not cooperating – not joining the group, or not joining the hunt – the individual loses out.

In the second kind of cooperation the payoff to each individual depends critically on the responses of others. In the Prisoner's Dilemma game, for example (see Sugden, this volume, for details), the alternative to cooperation is defection, which always gives the defector a greater payoff and the other player a worse payoff. However, if both players cooperate their individual and collective payoff is greater than if they both defect, and cooperation is therefore a form of teamwork. The second type of cooperation has been of greater interest to psychologists and economists since it seems more strategic – payoff depends on the choice made by the other party. It also invokes a range of phenomena in humans – such as cheating, trust, reciprocity, fairness, sanction, retribution, punishment, guilt, forgiveness and reconciliation – that raise complex questions concerned with social decision making, emotions and ethics.

This distinction is more apparent than real, however, since the first type of cooperation will often provide opportunities for differential benefit. Even in the simple case of gregariousness an individual may seek an advantage by attempting to gain a safer position in the centre of the group, protected from predatory attack by more peripheral individuals and increasing their risk by its move towards the centre. In the group hunt some may hang back and not pull their weight, but still take a share of the spoils, influencing the payoffs to those involved. And in both examples the payoffs of these actions – moving to the centre or shirking in the hunt – will be influenced by whether others do the same. Wherever there is room for strategic choice we expect to find it exploited, with effects on all players in the action.

3.1.1   How might teamwork evolve?

Group selection

Until the 1960s it was believed, with little formalism, that natural selection could act at the level of the group or species, as well as at the individual level. In this climate Wynne-Edwards (1962) argued that altruistic restraint would be selected if it aided population survival by preventing over-exploitation of resources. He drew the analogy of setting fishing limits to maintain fish stocks for the long-term benefit of all fishing fleets. Groups – rather than individuals – were seen as the unit of selection, with more successful groups surviving at the expense of the less successful. Since Wynne-Edwards' controversial work group selection has been much modelled and debated, and the concept of a group has shifted from isolated populations to 'trait-groups'. The trait-group is conceptualized as a set of interacting individuals. Altruists are reproductively outcompeted by selfish individuals in the same group but, because of the altruism, the group as a whole produces more offspring than groups with fewer altruists. If groups remain isolated this does the altruists no good since they are gradually swamped by the more successful egoists. For altruism to be favoured by selection the altruists must escape from the egoists and disperse. If they are to flourish in the long term, in the face of egoism, however, they must also recongregate selectively with other altruists to reproduce the advantageous conditions of the argument we started with: groups with more altruists produce more offspring (Dugatkin, 1997; Sober and Wilson, 1998).

In terms of how natural selection is working, between-group selection favours the altruists while within-group selection favours the egoists. The problem for the evolution of altruism by between-group selection is twofold. First, between-group selection must outweigh the strength of selection within groups at the individual level and, second, the pattern of dispersal must result in assortment so that altruists tend to congregate in the same groups (Maynard Smith, 1964, 1976). Whether group selection has been a significant force in evolution has been hotly debated, Sober and Wilson (1998, p. 194) proposing that it has been important in human evolution and that 'much of what people have evolved to do is *for the benefit of the group*' (their emphasis).

Group selection is therefore a candidate mechanism for the evolution of teamwork, the team being equivalent to the group whose fitness – rather than that of its constituent individuals – is the target of selection.

Kin selection

Relatives share genes by common descent. Genes influencing social behaviour between relatives (e.g. parental care, sibling rivalry) therefore have the chance of influencing the replication of those same genes in other individuals. In this case the evolutionary fate of the behaviour in question is determined by its consequences for the fitness of both parties, since both bear the relevant genetic material. The behaviour is favoured by natural selection as long as it results in the genes that influence it – *regardless of the body they are inhabiting* – collectively having a greater chance of replication into the next generation. The unit upon which natural selection acts in this case is therefore the gene rather than the individual and the pair of relatives concerned are a team, since selection is expected to result in actions whose consequences enhance their combined fitness. In the case of interactions between kin, natural selection therefore favours teamwork, since the team's optimal solution coincides with that of the gene, and the positive social relationships between kin are readily understood in evolutionary terms.

The argument can be quantified. The benefit arising from cooperative and altruistic behaviour relies on the beneficiary bearing the gene responsible for the cooperation or altruism. The probability of this occurring, for any gene, is readily calculated for different relatives from the knowledge that a particular parental allele (i.e. version of a gene) has a probability of 0.5 (i.e. a 50–50 chance) of being passed to an offspring, and that siblings have the same probability of sharing an allele by common descent from a parent (Hamilton, 1964). This probability reflects the closeness of kinship between the individuals and is termed the *coefficient of relatedness*, r.

Now, suppose an altruistic act produces a cost C to the actor and a benefit B to the recipient relative, and the coefficient of relatedness between them is r. The gene promoting altruism will be benefited if the relative contains it, which it does with probability r. So, on average, the benefit of such acts to the relevant gene is equal to Br. For natural selection to favour the altruistic act its benefit must outweigh its cost, so that the condition favouring altruism between relatives can be expressed as $Br > C$ (Hamilton, 1964), and the payoff to the team is $Br + C$. For altruism between full sibs ($r = 0.5$) to be favoured, for example, the benefit must be greater than twice the cost.

Individual selection and reciprocity

The first attempt to understand the evolution of cooperation and altruism between unrelated individuals by individual selection was based on reciprocity. Trivers (1971) pointed out that if altruistic acts were exchanged between two individuals, with benefits exceeding costs, then both parties would receive a net benefit after a pair of reciprocated interactions. Such an exchange would thus fit the definition of teamwork. The problem for the evolution of reciprocity by this means, as Trivers realized, is the same one that threatens to undermine the establishment of all cooperative relationships, that of cheating. The recipient of the first altruistic act gains a higher pay off by not reciprocating than by reciprocating.

Trivers' (1971) ideas were combined with games theory and evolutionary modelling (Maynard Smith, 1982) by Axelrod and Hamilton (Axelrod and Hamilton, 1981; Axelrod, 1984) to explore the evolutionary fate of various strategies in the iterated Prisoner's Dilemma. Axelrod and Hamilton sought an evolutionarily stable strategy or state (ESS); one in which a single strategy increases in frequency over generations in the simulated population until it becomes 'fixed' in the population as the sole strategy. Alternatively, a mixture of different strategies may remain stable at particular frequencies. Stable states are of interest for the obvious reason that, by definition, they are the states that endure and are expected to be seen in nature. An ESS that emerged in this and related work was 'Tit-for-Tat' (and similar strategies: Boyd and Lorberbaum, 1987), that started by cooperating and then matched the partner's last move (cooperation or defect), so that a population of Tit-for-Tat strategists would always cooperate. Given the payoff structure of the Prisoner's Dilemma Tit-for-Tat strategists are exhibiting teamwork (see also Sugden, this volume).

Beyond reciprocity

This work was just the start of two productive decades of theoretical and empirical work on the evolution of cooperation and altruism, with an increasing emphasis on attempting to understand the origins of human cooperative and altruistic acts when reciprocity is not expected (Fehr and Fischbacher, 2003). There is a current emphasis on explaining human altruism and trustworthiness as strategies for building the kind of reputation that brings rewards in the longer term (Frank, 1988; Milinski et al., 2001, 2002), so that ultimately altruism increases fitness. A closely related idea is that cooperation constitutes an honest signal of an individual's quality as a mate or coalition partner, and thus results in future rewarding alliances (Roberts, 1998; Gintis et al., 2001). Examples of the unilateral generosity that might arise from reputation building or honest signalling are charitable giving, tipping waiters and generous acts to strangers and others from whom reciprocation is unlikely. For a reputation to be enhanced by such acts they must be observed by others (and result in 'indirect reciprocity' by third parties) and, since they are sometimes performed without being observed, this may limit reputation building as a full explanation of them. However, adaptations do not have to be perfectly tuned to environmental contingencies to be favoured by selection so that if the trait of giving without expecting reciprocation increased fitness *on average* this would be sufficient for its evolutionary success. Of course, individuals who acted altruistically – and without the possibility of reciprocation – *only* when it was in their long-term interest to do so would be even fitter than the 'unconditional altruist' but it may be difficult to build a human psyche capable of such a precisely self-serving social calculus. The emotions, for example, seem to be somewhat uncontrollable causes of actions that may be far from self-serving in their consequences. Even Frank's (1988) commitment model (see section 3.1.2), if perfectly embodied, would not predict acts of generosity unobserved by potential future long-term partners. If unobserved, unreciprocated generosity is to be explicable in an evolutionary framework then either it must be of sufficiently low cost for reputation enhancement to maintain it, or some new explanation is required. It should also be remembered that selection on human unreciprocated cooperation has occurred, for most of our history, within small social groups of hunter-gatherers (section 3.1.2). In this context – in contrast to much of the contemporary and historical world – it would be far more likely that an unobserved and unreciprocated cooperative act would be reported by the recipient to others who were part of the actor's social world, and thus help to build that actor's reputation. And when third parties did observe unreciprocated cooperative acts it would be far more likely that they knew the actor and could therefore influence his reputation and modify their own future interactions with him. Consequently, unreciprocated generosity may be an evolved activity that is largely maladaptive in the loose social networks of the modern and historical world in which there are opportunities to help strangers who can have no direct or indirect influence on our future welfare.

Whether for reputation building or honest signalling such unilateral acts of giving would not seem to count as teamwork. Where human teamwork can emerge successfully, in a context that goes beyond simple reciprocity, is in real life common pool resource groups, such as fisheries and grazing commons (Ostrom, 1990), and in small group simulations of these same organizations (Ostrom et al., 1992), but these have not received direct evolutionary analysis. Trust and a belief in fairness (e.g. Fehr and Rockenbach, 2003) are important determinants of success.

3.1.2 The origins of human teamwork

Having examined how teamwork might evolve as a result of general selective processes applying to many types of organism we turn to the evolutionary origins of human teamwork. Humans have a particularly rich cooperative life (Fehr and Fischbacher, 2003), although before accepting this as a special human attribute we should consider whether our cooperative sophistication is any greater than that for, say, violence or sexual activity when we compare ourselves to other species. That aside, where should we look to understand the evolutionary origins of our own brand of teamwork, apart from the general evolutionary processes already described?

Important influences on the evolution of human teamwork are likely to have been the small social groups in which early humans lived, and our capacity for forming long-term relationships. Caporael et al. (1989, p. 683), for example, propose that behaviour, defined here as teamwork: 'evolved under selection pressures on small groups for developing and maintaining group membership and for predicting and controlling the behavior of other group members.' They and many other psychologists and economists have found, in experimental games, that individual decisions are less selfish, more fair, and closer to teamwork outcomes than predicted by rational egoism (e.g. Colman, 2003).

Frank (1988) argues that the rewards available from trusting, long-term, loving and commercial relationships have favoured the evolution of the kind of non-verbal commitment signals that are difficult to fake and that allow us to assess character and reliably predict, after a short interaction, whether another person will cooperate or defect in an experimental game (Frank et al., 1993). It is these cooperators, Frank argues, who are more likely to be selected as long-term partners.

3.1.3 From teamwork to team reasoning

How might evolutionary thinking help us to understand the kinds of reasoning that result in human teamwork (Lazarus, 2003)? Understanding the modes of reasoning employed is an interesting and unsolved issue precisely because they do not result in rationally selfish behaviour (Colman, 2003).

The above analysis of selection processes and evolutionary origins suggests the existence of the following biases in reasoning or emotional influence that would favour team thinking (together with their selective source):

• Consideration for welfare of the group as a whole (group selection); this is the most problematic proposal due to the uncertainties connected with group selection. Caporael et al.'s (1989) scenario described above seems to employ group selection.
• Consideration for kin (kin selection).
• Concern for reciprocity, extending to concerns with trust, fairness, punishment, forgiveness and reconciliation (reciprocal altruism).
• Concern for reputation.
• Concern to impress potential partners; correlated with personal quality.
• Concern for commitment.

This list provides some testable predictions of the reasoning biases involved in team thinking.

Decision making in real-life economic team contexts may reflect evolved predispositions, and may tap motivations that are also at work in the economically elementary scenarios of the psychological laboratory. For example, studies of the way in which communities govern their own use of common pool resources (CPRs), such as grazing pastures (Ostrom, 1990), may be revealing evolved influences on cooperative decision making, and even evolved modes of reasoning, since the hunting and gathering activities of early humans also have CPR properties. Successful CPR decisions – ones that are good for the group – are characterized by: a clear in-group/out-group distinction; resource provision in proportion to need and sharing of costs in proportion to ability to pay; and graded punishments for the greedy (Ostrom, 1990). Whether these characteristics apply to decision making in other kinds of cooperative relationship is open to evolutionary psychological and empirical analysis.

Finally, it falls within an evolutionary psychological view to accept that human teamwork results from the maladaptive application of reasoning in a novel environment that was adaptive in the 'environment of evolutionary adaptedness' of early humans (Barkow, Cosmides and Tooby, 1992).

3.2 Cooperation and environmental risk

In the remainder of the chapter we consider a single issue – risk – that has important impacts on cooperative behaviour and therefore on teamwork. An organism's environment can vary in two different ways that have both been conceptualized as risk (Daly and Wilson, 2002), and we term these adversity and uncertainty. First, we can describe an organism's environment as being more risky if something about it – some quality such as resources, physical structure, climate, competitors, parasites or predators – is more *adverse* in the sense of decreasing Darwinian fitness or some currency of human value. We talk of an animal 'taking a risk', for example, if it ventures into an area with more predators, or less food, since there is a greater risk – or chance or probability – of dying as a result. If this environmental quality is not fixed but has a distribution of values varying in time and space then adversity is taken to be the mean of this distribution of values. Second, risk can also refer to the *uncertainty* or unpredictability of some phenomenon (Gigerenzer, 2002). Playing roulette is risky because, while the probability (i.e. long-run frequency) of success of any bet is precisely known, the outcome of any single bet is not. Feeding in a 'patchy' area, where some places are rich in food and others barren, results in greater uncertainty of nutritional status compared to foraging where food density is the same in all places. Uncertainty can be operationalized as the variance of the distribution of the environmental quality in question. Adversity and uncertainty can therefore be measured as mean and variance respectively.

In this section we review natural examples of cooperation and altruism between various organisms that demonstrate what seems to be a widespread tendency for pro-social behaviour to be enhanced under conditions of increased adversity or uncertainty. In the following section we present a model that explores one way in which these effects might be explained. We end by drawing conclusions about the role of environmental risk in the emergence of human cooperation and teamwork.

3.2.1   Bacterial colonies

In response to certain environmental stressors bacteria form various multi-cellular structures such as biofilms and mushroom bodies (Greenberg, 2003) that develop as a result of cellular communication by, for example, the secretion or membrane expression of signalling molecules. For example, in the presence of antibiotics the bacterium *Pseudomonas aeruginosa* is likely to form a biofilm structure that boosts its antibiotic resistance (Drenkard and Ausubel, 2002) – presumably to the mutual benefit of all individuals – and is responsible for the development of antibiotic resistant lung infection in hospitalized patients (O'Toole, 2002). Biofilm formation can be prevented by triggering twitching behaviour, in which daughter cells move rapidly away from each other after cell division (Singh et al., 2002). The twitching behaviour can be switched on by environmental factors, like the presence of lactoferrin, a common constituent of human external secretions (Singh et al., 2002).

In the case of the amoeba *Dictyostelium discoideum* starvation results in the formation of a slug with the participation of tens of thousands of cells (Strassmann et al., 2000). Around 20 per cent of the slug formation altruistically develops into a non-viable stalk, supporting the rest of the cell colony. If starved cells are mixed with non-starved ones, the non-starved cells are likely to cheat during colony formation by participating less in the stalk component of the slug (Strassmann et al., 2000).

Unicellular organisms are thus able to form multicellular structures in the presence of environmental stress factors (e.g. antibiotics, lack of nutrients) by communicating about the nature of the environment. Such multicellular biofilms, mushroom bodies and slugs are cooperative structures, enhancing fitness in the presence of environmental stressors.

3.2.2   Cooperation among plants

A recent analysis of plant communities living at alpine and sub-alpine ranges in many parts of the world shows that competition for resources is more characteristic of sub-alpine plant communities, while cooperation is more typical in alpine habitats (Callaway et al., 2002). In alpine conditions the plants live under greater environmental stress, and thus adversity. Alpine plants produce significantly more biomass if they live close to other plants, receiving mutual protection from the wind, for example. Conversely, sub-alpine plants produce less biomass if they grow together with other plants, suffering relatively more from competitive interactions and benefiting less from cooperation.

3.2.3   Social feeding of worms

The roundworm *Caenorhabditis elegans* feeds on bacteria. When meeting lawns of bacteria the worms may slow down to increase their bacterial intake. Alternatively they may continue moving and occupy a position at the boundary of the bacterial lawn, letting other worms also feed. The behaviour of the worms depends on two neurons which play an important role in sensing nociceptive (tissue damage) signals (Sokolowski, 2002). If the worms live in a crowded environment the two neurons trigger the social response in the worms (de Bono et al., 2002) leading to the sharing of resources. If the neurons are destroyed the worm continues its solitary feeding behaviour, irrespective of crowding. Thus *C. elegans* worms form cooperative social structures in response to the environmental stress of increased competition (crowding). The control of the social behaviour by critical nociceptive neurons indicates that the perception of environmental stress is crucial for the triggering of social behaviour.

3.2.4   Cooperation in fish schools

Small fish subject to predation (e.g. guppies, *Poecilia reticulata*) often live in schools. The size of fish schools shows strong dependence on the risk of predation. In environments characterized by a high number of predatory fish the size of the fish schools is large, while in environments with few predators the school sizes are significantly smaller (Farr, 1975; Seghers, 1974). As described in section 3.1, the mutual anti-predator benefits of group-living increase with group size.

The analysis of sexual behaviour of guppies shows similar results (Evans and Magurran, 1999). In the presence of many predators male guppies perform relatively few courtship actions and produce a small amount of sperm. In environments with few predators the males are more likely to display courtship behaviour and produce significantly more sperm. This shows that males compete less in high predation risk environments. This phenomenon fits the pattern if we conceptualize competition and cooperation as opponent processes, or as opposite poles of a continuum. It also has something in common with the plant example above, in which both competitive and cooperative interactions are involved.

3.2.5   Mole-rat societies

The African mole-rats (*Bathyergidae*) show a variety of social organizations. Some species of the family live a mainly solitary life style, while others live as eusocial colonies (Spinks et al., 2000). Colonies of the common mole-rat (*Cryptomys hottentotus hottentotus*) are larger in arid areas and smaller in mesic (moderately moist) areas. The movement of individual animals between colonies is also less frequent in arid than in mesic areas. Larger and less variable communities provide the opportunity for the sharing of resources (e.g. food) with more individuals and for the existence of repeated meetings with known individuals, a facilitating factor for the development of cooperative relationships. Arid areas present stronger ecological constraints and greater foraging adversity than mesic areas. This indicates that greater environmental risk results in more cooperative behaviour in these communities.

3.2.6 Human cooperation

Early humans lived in hunter-gatherer communities, in which typically men hunted game and women gathered seeds and other plant parts. Investigation of an existing hunter-gatherer society shows that during the dry season communities are larger and fewer in number in a given area than in the wet season (Hawkes et al., 2001). Thus more adverse conditions trigger the formation of larger groups.

Evidence also shows that men share game after successful hunts (Kaplan and Hill, 1985; Hawkes et al., 2001). Considering the small likelihood of successfully capturing big game, by sharing the meat it is guaranteed that members of the community have the opportunity to eat regularly a small amount of highly nutritious food. In this context the cooperative sharing of meat reduces the uncertainty of gaining highly nutritious food, a risk imposed by the environment on the community.

Anecdotal reports of civil wars, front lines in wars and natural calamities (e.g. earthquakes, flooding, hurricanes) show that cooperation and group cohesiveness among humans increases very much in such situations. For example, in civil wars local populations supportive of the military or paramilitary forces voluntarily collect food and clothing for the fighters. Also a supportive civil population is ready to take the risk of hiding friendly fighters and even to organize their escape. As we write, England is recalling the year-long miner's strike of 20 years ago, a time of hardship for the mining communities, when according to one recollection 'everybody pulled together'. This anecdotal evidence is supported by research both at the macrosocial level of international and interethnic relations and at the microsocial level of small interactive groups (reviewed by Hogg, 1992) and suggests that human cooperation increases under conditions of external threat and intergroup conflict.

Kameda et al. (2002) investigated human cooperative behaviour using lottery games. They found that when gains were more uncertain the willingness for cooperative sharing and the expectation of cooperative sharing was significantly greater than when the gains were less uncertain. A real world example of human cooperation responding positively to environmental uncertainty is the greater endurance of common pool resource groups, such as fisheries and grazing commons, where environmental uncertainty is greater (Ostrom, 1990).

3.2.7 The role of communication

In the above examples the organisms concerned communicate with each other and this communication provides the foundation for the cooperative and altruistic behaviour. For example, in the case of bacteria the individuals communicate by having appropriate proteins incorporated into their outer membrane, and in the case of humans individuals communicate using language and non-verbal communication. Such communications reflect environmental resources and risk factors: for example, the presence of antibiotics triggers protein communications between bacteria; and the opportunity to hunt down big game triggers communication between hunter-gatherer humans.

3.3   Environmental risk and cooperation: a model

We present two versions of a simple model based on the assumption of a particular shape for the relationship between the quality of the environment and the fitness benefit to the individual that results from that quality. Environmental qualities include such things as resources, predators, parasites, competitors and abiotic factors. Assuming also that cooperation, on average, brings greater benefits than non-cooperation, we ask how the marginal benefit of cooperation (i.e. the additional benefit to cooperators over that to non-cooperators) varies with adversity and uncertainty (i.e. the mean and variance of environmental quality). The shape that we assume for the relationship between environmental quality and the benefit to the individual is one of diminishing returns (Figure 3.1) which means that benefit at first increases rapidly with quality but levels off at higher levels of quality. In fact the rate of increase of benefit with quality is always decreasing as quality increases. Since this assumption is basic to all that follows it requires some justification.

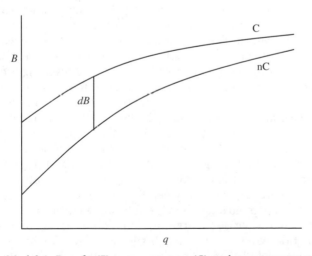

Figure 3.1   Model 1. Benefit (*B*) to cooperators (C) and non-cooperators (nC) as a function of environmental quality (*q*). The two functions converge from the lowest value of *q*.

The assumption is biologically plausible, and is made in many behavioural ecological models (for example, for the way in which benefit to an offspring increases with parental investment in the offspring: Trivers, 1974). Consider first the general case of resource acquisition. The rate of food intake often increases with food density in a diminishing returns fashion since once an animal is satiated, further food intake brings little benefit (or even brings a cost) no matter how much food the environment holds. Taking this further, an animal in a low food density environment has a higher probability of death than one in a food-rich environment and intake of a unit of food (equivalent to a shift to the right along the environmental quality axis) is likely to increase fitness further in the former case; a diminishing returns effect. This is why hungry and thirsty pigeons switch frequently between eating and drinking rather than, say, feeding to satiation before they start drinking (McFarland and Lloyd, 1973); a unit reduction in thirst or hunger increases fitness more when the animal is further from its optimal internal state. A further consideration supporting a diminishing returns relationship for resource acquisition is that the time it takes to handle resources limits the rate at which individuals can exploit an increasing resource density (Stephens and Krebs, 1986).

Consider next the case of abiotic features of the environment – such as temperature, humidity, windspeed, altitude, substrate quality and pH – that influence fitness. For such features there is an optimum value for each species that maximizes an individual's fitness, with fitness declining above and below the optimal value. The environmental quality axis (Figure 3.1) should then be conceptualized as reaching a maximum value at the right that represents the optimal value of, say, temperature for the species. Each point on the axis to the left of this optimal value represents a pair of temperature values – one below the optimum and another above it – that have an equal effect on the fitness of the individual. The axis therefore represents adversity whether due to under- or over-shooting of the optimal environmental value. Imagine now the function relating absolute temperature, say, and resulting fitness; it will take an inverted-U shape, peaking at the optimal temperature. Now, unless the transition through the optimal value is to make a sharp discontinuity, which is biologically very implausible, it follows that the function approaches the optimal value – from both sides – in a diminishing returns fashion. It further follows, therefore, that the quality/fitness function (exemplified by Figure 3.1) is also diminishing returns. (It is possible that fitness functions for resource acquisition and abiotic factors are sometimes sigmoidal. In this case our conclusions are valid over only part of the quality range, since the upper concave part of a sigmoidal function is diminishing returns.)

There is therefore a case for arguing that a diminishing returns quality-benefit function will be common. This leads us to ask whether this relationship alone might be able to explain the positive effects of adversity and uncertainty on cooperation reviewed in the previous section.

As will be clear, our models are conceived in evolutionary terms so that benefits and costs are envisaged as influences on Darwinian fitness. Equivalently, however, the models could describe a human subjective view of quality and benefit (utility) and thus predict cooperation as a function of rational decision making (whether or not one wished to explain rationality in evolutionary terms). Since we assume that cooperation pays more than non-cooperation our results can be applied to any model or empirically known situation where this is the case. The assumption that cooperation pays more than non-cooperation means that in stable populations all individuals are cooperators.

Let:

q = some dimension of environmental quality (e.g. resource, predation risk, temperature)

$B(q)$ = benefit (= fitness increase) to individual as a function of q.

C = cooperate

nC = not cooperate

dB = $B(q, C) - B(q, nC)$ = the increment in fitness due to cooperation as opposed to non-cooperation, as a function of q.

3.3.1 Model 1

Assume that:

(1) $B(q)$ is a diminishing returns function.
(2) $dB = B(q, C) - B(q, nC) > 0$ for all q; i.e. conditions (derivable from various models, for example, or empirically demonstrated) for which cooperation always pays.
(3) $B(q, C)$ and $B(q, nC)$ converge as q increases from its lowest value.

The model is shown graphically in Figure 3.1. The first assumption has already been justified. The second assumption is fundamental to the model. The third assumption follows if non-cooperators can achieve the same asymptotic fitness as the cooperators at some level of q. We return to the second and third assumptions, and relax assumption (3), in Model 2.

First, consider risk as adversity. Figure 3.1 shows directly that as adversity increases (i.e. as environmental quality declines) the marginal benefit of cooperation over non-cooperation (dB) increases. With a greater benefit from cooperative behaviour it follows that where individuals can vary their investment in cooperation (see, for example, Roberts and Sherratt, 1998, for models and data) more cooperation would be expected by individuals in more adverse environments. We ignore any further dynamics between the level of adversity and stability conditions for cooperation.

Second, consider risk as uncertainty, where uncertainty is measured in terms of the variance of q. The model assumptions ((1), (2) and (3) above) imply that if $f(q)$ is the C curve (i.e., $f(q) = B(q, C)$) and $g(q)$ is the nC curve (i.e., $g(q) = B(q, nC)$) then:

(4) $f(q) > g(q)$
(5) $0 < f'(q) < g'(q)$
(6) $0 > f''(q) > g''(q)$

In other words, the two curves should be diminishing return functions such that their difference is acceleratingly decreasing.

We now show that if $p(q)$ is the density function of a probability distribution defined over the q values, then in the high variance case, where the range of existing environmental qualities is greater, $f(q) - g(q) = dB$ has a larger mean value over the interval of interest than the mean value for the low variance case. In other words, the benefit of cooperation increases with variance (uncertainty).

We denote by m the mid-point of the interval; then the two end points can be written as $m - v$ and $m + v$, where $2v$ is the width of the distribution of environmental quality (note that m is the same for any value of v). We wish to show that if $r(v)$ is the mean value of $f(q) - g(q)$ over $[m - v, m + v]$ then the $r(v)$ is an increasing function. This means that if v is larger the mean value is larger. The $r(v)$ being increasing is equivalent to $r'(v) > 0$.

Let $a(q) = f(q) - g(q)$

Then $r(v) = \dfrac{\int_{m-v}^{m+v} a(q) \cdot p(q) dq}{\int_{m-v}^{m+v} p(q) dq}$

Assume that

$AP'(q) = a(q) \cdot p(q), P'(q) = p(q)$

then

$$r'(v) = \frac{\partial}{\partial v} \frac{\int_{m-v}^{m+v} a(q) \cdot p(q) dq}{\int_{m-v}^{m+v} p(q) dq} = \frac{\partial}{\partial v}\left(\frac{AP(m+v) - AP(m-v)}{P(m+v) - P(m-v)} \right) =$$

$$\frac{\frac{\partial}{\partial v}\left(AP(m+v) - AP(m-v)\right) \cdot \left(P(m+v) - P(m-v)\right) - \frac{\partial}{\partial v}\left(P(m+v) - P(m-v)\right) \cdot \left(AP(m+v) - AP(m-v)\right)}{\left(P(m+v) - P(m-v)\right)^2} =$$

$$\frac{a(m+v) \cdot p(m+v) + a(m-v) \cdot p(m-v)}{P(m+v) - P(m-v)} - \frac{\left(p(m+v) + p(m-v)\right) \cdot \left(AP(m+v) - AP(m-v)\right)}{\left(P(m+v) - P(m-v)\right)^2} =$$

$$\frac{a(m+v) \cdot p(m+v) + a(m-v) \cdot p(m-v)}{\int_{m-v}^{m+v} p(q) dq} - \frac{\left(p(m+v) + p(m-v)\right) \cdot \int_{m-v}^{m+v} a(q) \cdot p(q) dq}{\left(\int_{m-v}^{m+v} p(q) dq\right)}$$

so we get

$$r'(v) = \frac{\left(p(m+v)+p(m-v)\right)}{\int\limits_{m-v}^{m+v} p(q)dq} \cdot \left(\frac{a(m+v)\cdot p(m+v)+a(m-v)\cdot p(m-v)}{p(m+v)+p(m-v)} - \frac{\int\limits_{m-v}^{m+v} a(q)\cdot p(q)dq}{\int\limits_{m-v}^{m+v} p(q)dq} \right)$$

If $a''(q) = f''(q) - g''(q) > 0$, i.e., $a(q)$ is convex we get

$\exists \mu \in [m-v, m+v]$ such that

if $AP'(q) = a(q)\cdot p(q)$ and $P'(q) = p(q)$ then, by applying the mean value theorem we get

$$\frac{\int\limits_{m-v}^{m+v} a(q)\cdot p(q)dq}{\int\limits_{m-v}^{m+v} p(q)dq} = \frac{AP(m+v)-AP(m-v)}{P(m+v)-P(m-v)} = \frac{AP'(\mu)}{p'(\mu)} = \frac{a(\mu)\cdot p(\mu)}{p(\mu)} = a(\mu)$$

Since $a(q)$ is convex, $a''(q) > 0 \Rightarrow \lambda \cdot a(m+v) + (1-\lambda)\cdot a(m-v) > a(\mu), \forall \mu \in [m-v, m+v], \lambda \in [0,1]$, and by considering

$$\lambda = \frac{p(m+v)}{p(m+v)+p(m-v)}, 1-\lambda = \frac{p(m-v)}{p(m+v)+p(m-v)} \Rightarrow$$

$$\frac{p(m+v)}{p(m+v)+p(m-v)}a(m+v) + \frac{p(m-v)}{p(m+v)+p(m-v)}a(m-v) > a(\mu), \forall \mu \in [m-v, m+v]$$

$$\Rightarrow \frac{p(m+v)}{p(m+v)+p(m-v)}a(m+v) + \frac{p(m-v)}{p(m+v)+p(m-v)}a(m-v) - \frac{\int\limits_{m-v}^{m+v} a(q)\cdot p(q)dq}{\int\limits_{m-v}^{m+v} p(q)dq} =$$

$$\frac{a(m+v)\cdot p(m+v)+a(m-v)\cdot p(m-v)}{p(m+v)+p(m-v)} - \frac{\int\limits_{m-v}^{m+v} a(q)\cdot p(q)dq}{\int\limits_{m-v}^{m+v} p(q)dq} > 0$$

because

$$\frac{\int\limits_{m-v}^{m+v} a(q)\cdot p(q)dq}{\int\limits_{m-v}^{m+v} p(q)dq} = a(\mu) \text{ for at least one } \mu \in [m-v, m+v]$$

$$\Rightarrow r'(v) = \frac{p(m+v)+p(m-v)}{\int\limits_{m-v}^{m+v} p(q)dq}\left(\frac{a(m+v)\cdot p(m+v)+a(m-v)\cdot p(m-v)}{p(m+v)+p(m-v)} - \frac{\int\limits_{m-v}^{m+v} a(q)\cdot p(q)dq}{\int\limits_{m-v}^{m+v} p(q)dq} \right) > 0$$

since

$$p(q) > 0 \Rightarrow p(m+v)+p(m-v) > 0$$

and

$$\int\limits_{m-v}^{m+v} p(q)dq > 0$$

This shows that indeed, for any probability distribution over the q values, if the difference function between C and nC is convex (assumptions (4)–(6) above) then if v is larger the average value of the difference between C and nC is larger.

As argued for adversity, with a greater benefit from cooperative behaviour it follows that where individuals can vary their investment in cooperation more cooperation would be expected by individuals in more uncertain environments. Again, we ignore any further dynamics between the level of uncertainty and stability conditions for cooperation.

3.3.2 Model 2

Relaxing the third assumption of Model 1, suppose instead that the benefit functions of cooperators and non-cooperators at first *diverge* as q increases, before converging (see Figure 3.2). In the limit assume that assumption two is also relaxed, so that at the lowest environmental quality cooperators and non-cooperators have *equal* and minimal fitness. Then, in the poor quality zone (considered alone) to the left of the point q^*, at which cooperator and non-cooperator benefits maximally diverge (see Figure 3.2), the conclusions of the model for the influence of adversity on dB are reversed. If the population exists across environmental qualities both less than and greater than q^*, cooperation is then most beneficial (and is therefore expected to be most generous) at the intermediate environmental quality q^*, rather than increasing monotonically with adversity.

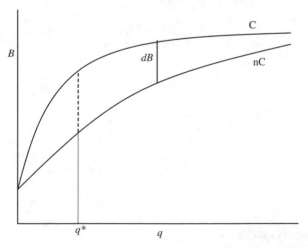

Figure 3.2   Model 2. Benefit (B) to cooperators (C) and non-cooperators (nC) as a function of environmental quality (q). The two functions at first diverge and then converge from the lowest value of q, and C – nC is maximized where q = q*. The two functions may or may not extend to the lowest value of q (where they meet).

The conditions under which the benefit of cooperation (dB) increases with uncertainty are not simple to specify. This is first because the results for Model 1 apply here in reverse for $q < q^*$, and second because the relationship between dB and uncertainty depends on how the population is distributed across environments above and below q^*.

Although in general terms one cannot readily choose between the two models, if our examples in section 3.2 are representative it would seem that Model 1 is the more common representation of reality. Alternatively, Model 2 may represent a fuller account of reality but with most populations existing in relatively good quality environments where $q > q^*$, where results are identical with those of Model 1. The conditions for $q < q^*$ in Model 2 may be quite rare cases of populations *in extremis*, so that circumstances where cooperation is found to be most generous at intermediate levels of adversity are unusual. (They may be unusual simply because populations *in extremis* at $q < q^*$ are more likely to die out.) Whatever is the case, our modelling here would suggest that the common facilitative effect of adversity and uncertainty on cooperation may, at the functional level, be due in part simply to a diminishing returns function of environmental influences on fitness. Selection is then expected to act on proximate mechanisms so that cooperation is enhanced in conditions of greater adversity and uncertainty.

These results complement the predictions of our other models (Andras et al., 2003; Andras, Lazarus and Roberts, in prep.), which are not directly concerned with the shape of the functional relationship between environmental quality and fitness. The first of these shows that the likelihood of cooperation between selfish agents increases with perceived environmental uncertainty (Andras et al., 2003). This model simulated the evolution of societies of simple agents playing a cooperation/cheating game to generate resources spent on living costs. The results show that when the process generating the new resources has a larger variance (i.e. environmental uncertainty is higher) the stable evolved likelihood of cooperation between two agents is also higher.

3.4 Risk, trust and teamwork

Whether cooperation in human societies can flourish successfully without sanctions imposed from outside the group is an old question but there is reason for optimism, from both real life common pool resource groups (Ostrom, 1990) and experimental games (Ostrom et al., 1992). To the extent that the threat of sanctions decreases the perceived uncertainty of the environment – a predictable sanction reducing uncertainty more than the unpredictable possibility of an equivalently costly reprisal – one message of this chapter is that such predictability may also decrease the willingness of individuals to cooperate. Where the spontaneous level of cooperation is low, imposing rules and enforcing cooperative behaviour may increase cooperative acts in the short term. However, unless individuals find personal incentives for cooperation, or make moral choices in this direction, coercion is less likely to encourage the longer-term establishment of cooperative motivation and team thinking.

It is important to understand the basis for the voluntary adherence to behaviour that can lead to the formation of teams. Empirical evidence (Fukuyama, 1996) indicates that trust between humans plays an essential role in the emergence of voluntary cooperation. In the context of our discussion we can view trust as the expectation that rules of behaviour will be followed by individuals within the community. If such expectations are high, and they are reinforced by practice, it is likely that the rules will be closely adhered to, and the formation of cooperative groups, including teams, is likely. When it comes to trusting that others will cooperate, therefore, uncertainty about the *social* environment – about how others will act – *reduces* cooperation. This is because in Prisoner's Dilemma-type situations confidence that others will cooperate is essential for personal and team success, and in public goods situations team success is maximized when all cooperate. Cooperation requires a substrate of trust, of confidence that others will also cooperate. We therefore expect cooperation to be most commonly shown where uncertainty about trust between individuals is *low*, but where the uncertainty and adversity of the environment that impinges on the social group is *high*.

We go further and suggest that trust is logically and functionally prior to cooperation and sets maximum limits to the cooperation that is achievable. Within these limits the level of cooperation is further influenced by the adversity and uncertainty of the environment. The role of communication between individuals is worth stressing here. First, it is necessary for the development of trust and, second, it provides information about the adversity and uncertainty of the environment.

Trust is also relevant to understanding the response to sanctions, considered above. If the adherence to rules is imposed by sanctions their implicit meaning is that such adherence is not expected voluntarily with confidence; trust in the social group is low. This may reduce trust between individuals further and with it the likelihood of cooperation and team formation.

Acknowledgements

We are grateful to Natalie Gold, whose editorial comments significantly improved the chapter, and to Ian Vine for discussion and references. JL remembers the 'Odd One Out' workshop in Oxford in 1996, to which he was invited by Michael Bacharach, as the most stimulating and interdisciplinary meeting he has attended.

Note

Sections 3.2 and 3.4 of the chapter were written largely by Peter Andras. Section 3.1 was written by John Lazarus, who is also responsible for the model in section 3.3 (except for the variance proofs, which are the work of PA).

References

Andras, P., Lazarus, J. and Roberts, G. (In prep.) Environmental adversity and uncertainty favour cooperation. *Mimeo*.

Andras, P., Roberts, G. and Lazarus, J. (2003) Environmental risk, cooperation and communication complexity. In: *Adaptive Agents and Multi-Agent Systems* (edited by Alonso, E., Kudenko, D. and Kazakov, D.), pp. 49–65. Berlin: Springer-Verlag.

Axelrod, R. (1984) *The evolution of cooperation*. New York: Basic Books.

Axelrod, R. and Hamilton, W. (1981) 'The evolution of cooperation'. *Science*, 211, 1390–1396.

Barkow, J. H., Cosmides, L. and Tooby, J. (1992) (eds) *The adapted mind: Evolutionary psychology and the generation of culture*. New York: Oxford University Press.

Boyd, R. and Lorberbaum, J. P. (1987) 'No pure strategy is evolutionarily stable in the repeated Prisoner's Dilemma game', *Nature*, 327, 58–59.

Callaway, R., Brooker, R., Choler, P., Kikvidze, Z., Lortiek, C., Michalet, R., Paolini, L., Pugnaireq, F., Newingham, B., Aschehoug, E., Armasq, C., Kikodze, D. and Cook, B. (2002) 'Positive interactions among alpine plants increase with stress', *Nature*, 417, 844–847.

Caporael, L. R., Dawes, R. M., Orbell, J. M. and van de Kragt, A. J. C. (1989) 'Selfishness examined: Cooperation in the absence of egoistic incentives', *Behavioral and Brain Sciences*, 12, 683–739.

Colman, A. M. (2003) 'Cooperation, psychological game theory, and limitations of rationality in social interaction', *Behavioral and Brain Sciences*, 26, 139–198.

Daly, M. and Wilson, M. (2002) 'Two special issues on Risk', *Evolution and Human Behavior*, 23, 1–2.

Darwin, C. (1872) *The origin of species by means of natural selection, or the preservation of favoured races in the struggle for life* (6th edn). London: John Murray.

de Bono, M., Tobin, D. M., Davis, M. W., Avery, L. and Bargmann, C. I. (2002) 'Social feeding in *Caenorhabditis elegans* is induced by neurons that detect aversive stimuli', *Nature*, 419, 899–903.

Drenkard, E. and Ausubel, F. M. (2002) '*Pseudomonas* biofilm formation and antibiotic resistance are linked to phenotypic variation', *Nature*, 416, 740–743.

Dugatkin, L. A. (1997) *Cooperation among animals: An evolutionary perspective*. Oxford: Oxford University Press.

Evans, J. P. and Magurran, A. E. (1999) 'Geographic variation in sperm production by Trinidadian guppies', *Proceedings of the Royal Society of London B*, 266, 2083–2087.

Farr, J. A. (1975) 'The role of predation in the evolution of social behavior of natural populations of the guppy, *Poecilia reticulata (Pisces: Poeciliidea)*', *Evolution*, 29, 151–158.

Fehr, E. and Fischbacher, U. (2003) 'The nature of human altruism', *Nature*, 425, 785–791.

Fehr, E. and Rockenbach, B. (2003) 'Detrimental effects of sanctions on human altruism', *Nature*, 422, 137–140.

Frank, R. H. (1988) *Passions Within Reason: The Strategic Role of the Emotions*. New York: W. W. Norton.

Frank, R. H., Gilovich, T. and Regan, D. T. (1993) 'The evolution of one-shot co-operation: an experiment', *Ethnology and Sociobiology*, 14, 247–256.

Fukuyama, F. (1996) *Human nature and the reconstruction of social order*. New York: Free Press.

Gigerenzer, G. (2002) *Reckoning with risk: Learning to live with uncertainty*. London: Allen Lane.

Gintis, H., Smith, E. and Bowles, S. (2001) 'Costly signaling and cooperation', *J Theor Biol*, 213, 103–119.

Greenberg, E. P. (2003) 'Tiny teamwork', *Nature*, 424, 134.

Hamilton, W. D. (1964) 'The genetical evolution of social behaviour. I and II', *Journal of Theoretical Biology*, 7, 1–16, 17–52.

Hawkes, K., O'Connell, J. F. and Blurton-Jones, N. G. (2001) 'Hadza meat sharing', *Evolution and Human Behavior*, 22, 113–142.

Hogg, M. A. (1992) *The social psychology of group cohesiveness. From attraction to social identity*. New York: Harvester Wheatsheaf.

Kameda, T., Takezawa, M., Tindale, R. and Smith, C. (2002) 'Social sharing and risk reduction: Exploring a computational algorithm for the psychology of windfall gains', *Evolution and Human Behavior*, 23, 11–33.

Kaplan, H. and Hill, K. (1985) 'Food sharing among Ache foragers – Tests of explanatory hypotheses'. *Current Anthropology*, 26, 223–246.

Lazarus, J. (2003) 'Let's cooperate to understand cooperation', *Behavioral and Brain Sciences*, 26, 169–170.

Maynard Smith, J. (1964) 'Group selection and kin selection', *Nature*, 201, 1145–1147.

Maynard Smith, J. (1976) 'Group selection', *Quarterly Review of Biology*, 51, 277–283.

Maynard Smith, J. (1982) *Evolution and the theory of games*. Cambridge: Cambridge University Press.

McFarland, D. J. and Lloyd, I. (1973) 'Time-shared feeding and drinking', *Quarterly Journal of Experimental Psychology*, 25, 48–61.

Milinksi, M., Semmann, D., Bakker, T. and Krambeck, H.-J. (2001) 'Cooperation through indirect reciprocity: image scoring or standing strategy?', *Proceedings of the Royal Society of London B*, 268, 2495–2501.

Milinski, M., Semmann, D. and Krambeck, H.-J. (2002) 'Reputation helps solve the "tragedy of the commons"' *Nature*, 415, 424–426.

O'Toole, G. A. (2002) 'A resistance switch', *Nature*, 416, 695–696.

Ostrom, E. (1990) *Governing the Commons: The Evolution of Institutions for Collective Action*. Cambridge: Cambridge University Press.

Ostrom, E., Walker, J. and Gardner, R. (1992) 'Covenants with and without a sword: self-governance is possible', *American Political Science Review*, 86, 404–417.

Roberts, G. (1998) 'Competitive altruism: from reciprocity to the handicap principle', *Proceedings of the Royal Society of London B*, 265, 427–431.

Roberts, G. and Sherratt, T. N. (1998) 'Development of cooperative relationships through increasing investment', *Nature*, 394, 175–179.

Seghers, B. H. (1974) 'Schooling behaviour in the guppy (*Poecilia reticulata*): an evolutionary response to predation', *Evolution*, 28, 486–489.

Singh, P. K., Parsek, M. R., Greenberg, E. P. and Welsh, M. J. (2002) 'A component of innate immunity prevents bacterial biofilm development', *Nature*, 417, 552–555.

Sober, E. and Wilson, D. S. (1998) *Unto others: The evolution and psychology of unselfish behaviour*. Cambridge: Harvard University Press.

Sokolowski, M. B. (2002) 'Social eating for stress', *Nature*, 419, 893–894.

Spinks, A. C., Jarvis, J. U. M. and Bennett, N. C. (2000) 'Comparative patterns of philopatry and dispersal in two common mole-rat populations: implications for the evolution of mole-rat sociality', *Journal of Animal Ecology*, 69, 224–234.

Stephens, D. W. and Krebs, J. R. (1986) *Foraging theory*. Princeton, N.J.: Princeton University Press.

Strassmann, J. E., Zhu, Y. and Queller, D. C. (2000) 'Altruism and social cheating in the social amoeba *Dictyostelium discoideum*', *Nature*, 408, 965–967.

Tinbergen, N. (1963) 'On aims and methods of ethology', *Z Tierpsychol*, 20, 410–433.

Trivers, R. L. (1971) 'The evolution of reciprocal altruism', *The Quarterly Review of Biology*, 46, 35–57.

Trivers, R. L. (1974) 'Parent-offspring conflict', *American Zoologist*, 14, 249–264.

Wynne-Edwards, V. C. (1962) *Animal dispersion in relation to social behaviour*. Edinburgh: Oliver and Boyd.

4
The Evolution of Teams
David P. Myatt and Chris Wallace

4.1 Teamwork, coordination and evolution

4.1.1 Public-good provision in teams

Many economic and social activities require a critical number of individuals (referred to here as a 'team') to participate in order to ensure the success of a given project or task. As a result, these kinds of activities frequently experience the well-known problems associated with collective actions.[1] Focus here is directed at two such problems. First, such activities can involve a positive externality: participation in a team leads to a private cost borne by the individual, but the benefits of the team's efforts accrue to all. Second, successful team formation requires coordination: absent the participation of a sufficient number of individuals, the project as a whole would fail.[2]

Sporting activities provide one example of the need for coordination. Many sports are team-based, and without the presence of all participants, the game cannot take place. An example is found in the authors' home town: in May of each year Oxford colleges compete in a rowing tournament known as 'Eights Week'. A team's success in this tournament critically depends upon the ability of its eight members (hence the name) to train on a regular basis. Training sessions are typically conducted in the early morning and require the presence of the entire team – the absence of a member results in cancellation. A rower will find it optimal to wake early and participate if and only if all the other team members do so. Of course, if seven of the rowers are expected to attend the training session, the eighth team member faces a strong incentive to attend – their attendance will enable the training (and potential success) of the entire team rather than merely the element contributed by an individual.

Another example, this time involving a positive externality, is provided by local environmental projects. These projects benefit everyone; however, only those who give up their time to contribute to them bear any of the costs. The Oxford Conservation Volunteers (OCV) has been 'carrying out practical work conserving the wildlife and traditional landscape of the Oxford area since 1977'.[3] Their activities range from hedge-laying to the conservation of wildlife habitats via scrub clearance. The volunteers contribute time and energy (a private cost) to an activity which generates environmental benefits for all (a positive externality).

Both of these examples involve the provision of a public good.[4] According to its classic definition, a pure public good is both non-rival and non-excludable. A good is non-rival if its consumption by one individual does not decrease the amount available for others; for instance, everyone is able to enjoy the pleasures of an improved environment. A good is non-excludable if all individuals are free to consume it once it has been provided; all members of an Oxford college are able to revel in the glory of coming in at the 'Head of the River'.[5]

Here, the focus is on the conditions under which a team might form and successfully provide public goods of this sort. In particular, how do team size, benefit and cost parameters, and the population from which the team is drawn affect the chances of success? In tackling these questions, a game-theoretic approach is taken.[6] However, in so doing, a fundamental problem of game theory arises: the equilibrium-selection problem.

4.1.2 Game theory and the equilibrium-selection problem

According to one possible definition, game theory is the study of strategic decision making. A decision is strategic when the outcome for an individual (a 'player') depends not only upon that player's decision, but also on the decisions made by others. Thus, an optimal move by a thoughtful player will involve some contemplation of the likely moves of others, either simultaneously or in the future. To analyse such problems, a game theorist will map out the critical elements of the game, including the players, the moves that they can make, and the payoff received by each player as a result of the moves made by everyone. With these ingredients in hand, the desire to predict the play of the game will often lead to the consideration of a Nash equilibrium. A Nash equilibrium is a strategy collection (that is, a planned sequence of feasible moves specified for each and every player) such that every player's strategy is an optimal choice of moves, given the prescribed strategies of others.[7] Thus, when it is a convention for a Nash equilibrium to be played, then this convention will often be strategically stable; there is no pressure for any individual player unilaterally to deviate from it.

Unfortunately, the Nash equilibrium concept does not always yield a unique prediction for the play of a game. Even very simple games often have multiple Nash equilibria that are robust to the many 'refinement' procedures by which game theorists attempt to eliminate equilibria via the imposition of more stringent criteria.[8] This means that, from a strategic-stability perspective, there are many modes of behaviour that might survive over time. Game theorists will often refer to this issue as the equilibrium-selection problem: which equilibrium will be played? In everyday terms, this corresponds to a problem of coordination.

The team-based provision of public goods provides the setting for both a simple game and an illustration of the equilibrium-selection problem. The ingredients (players, moves, and payoffs) are all present. The players are the potential contributors to a team-based project. Each player has two alternative moves; to contribute to the project, or to 'free ride' on others. Finally, a player's payoff may consist of a cost and a benefit. The cost is incurred if and only the player contributes. The benefit is enjoyed if and only if a sufficiently large number of players (the critical team size) choose to contribute, ensuring the project's success. This game has two different categories of Nash equilibria.

Firstly, it is a Nash equilibrium for no player to contribute. If no one else is currently contributing to the team, there is no incentive for an individual player to contribute. A new contributor would bear a cost, but gain no benefit; it is pointless for an individual rower to arrive at rowing practice if the remainder of the crew are not expected to do so.

Secondly, a Nash equilibrium arises when the the number of contributors exactly matches the critical number needed for the formation of a successful team. A contributor's attempt to free-ride would result in the team's collapse. Furthermore, players from outside the team have no incentive to join the team, as the private cost they would incur generates no additional benefit. Returning to the example, the eighth member of a rowing team is critical to the success of a practice session, but a ninth rower would find no space in the boat.

The multiplicity of Nash equilibria of this sort has long been recognized as a problem in game theory.[9] It is also a problem for the players engaged in the team-participation game described here. Everyone would wish to see the success of a team (they all reap the benefits, after all) but there is a coordination issue: which group of players will bear the costs of contribution? Recent attempts to provide solutions to this problem include the global-games literature and the evolutionary-dynamics or stochastic-adjustment literature.[10] The latter approach is the one taken here.[11]

4.1.3   The evolution of team contributions

The stochastic-adjustment dynamics literature provides a way to tackle the equilibrium-selection problem.[12] This literature suggests a theoretical analysis of the evolution of play. In a typical model, the participants are repeatedly matched to play a game. Each period, one or more of the players are given the opportunity to revise their current strategy in the light of previous play. For instance, they might begin by observing the current patterns of behaviour adopted by others around them. Following this observation, they might then choose a best response, under the (myopic) assumption that such patterns of behaviour are likely to persist in the near future.[13]

This strategy-revision procedure leads to a dynamic process that is dependent upon its starting point. To see this, consider an individual who has been given the opportunity to revise their current strategy choice – an 'updating' player. With the team-formation game in mind, an updating player will choose to contribute if and only if their contribution would just result in the formation of a successful team. Otherwise, the best response is non-contribution. Each updating player faces a similar choice. The best-response process will lead to one of the Nash equilibria, but which one will depend on where the process began. Once at an equilibrium, no updating player will alter their current strategy and the process becomes 'locked in'. This path dependence provides a critical role for initial historical conditions; mathematically, the associated dynamic process is said to be 'non-ergodic'.

It has been assumed that the payoffs of the game in question are fixed, and that any updating player always chooses a best response to the observed pattern of play. These assumptions ensure that the strategy-revision process can never leave a Nash equilibrium. Such lock-in can be weakened once 'noise' is added to the process.[14] That is, some small probability of the process moving against the best response is introduced. This means that the there is some possibility that the process can escape from a Nash equilibrium. In the short run, a particular equilibrium is likely to persist for some time. In the long run, however, the process may visit a number of different equilibria. Put simply, this means that the initial conditions of history are not critical in the long run; such conditions are 'washed out' by noisy events that occur from time to time. Mathematically, the associated dynamic process is said to be 'ergodic'. This opens up the possibility for a statistical analysis of the strategy-revision process. In the long run, it is possible to calculate the proportion of time that the process spends at or in the vicinity of different Nash equilibria; these time proportions yield what is called an 'ergodic distribution'. In fact, when the noise added to the process is small, the process spends almost all of its time (in the very long run) at only one equilibrium: this is the equilibrium that is 'selected'.

One way of introducing such noise is to allow players to differ.[15] Individuals may well have different costs of contributing to, and different valuations of, the public good that the team might produce. This is modelled in the following way: each period an individual is chosen at random to update their strategy. The payoffs (for either contributing or not) that are specified in the game do not represent the updating player's actual payoffs, but only their means. The actual payoffs are 'perturbed' by the addition of individual-specific payoff heterogeneity. Such 'noise' in the payoffs reflects the fact that individuals are idiosyncratic. Such idiosyncrasies mean that an updating player may sometimes take a decision that runs against the 'flow of play': the eighth member of a rowing crew might wake following a late evening of over-consumption, and find it too costly to get up in the morning, even though their absence will result in the cancellation of the rowing practice.[16]

Under these conditions, it is possible to characterise the long-run behaviour of this strategy-revision process. Furthermore, the noise can be made small by reducing the idiosyncrasy of players' payoffs; this is a situation in which players are almost homogeneous. The formal analysis reveals a mathematical inequality that determines whether, in the long run, teams tend to succeed or fail. Team and population size, and cost and benefit parameters all play a role in determining whether this mathematical inequality will hold; perhaps unsurprisingly, a team is successful when the costs are low, the benefits are high, and when few team members are needed for the public-good's provision. Other effects are more subtle; success is also influenced by the relative variability (that is, idiosyncrasy) of cost and benefit payoffs. For instance, when the net benefit (valuation minus cost) from being a contributing member of a team is particularly variable, then it is quite likely that a contributing member will suddenly decide to leave the team, hence prompting its collapse. Similarly, when the costs of contribution are particularly variable, and especially if there is occasionally a direct private benefit from contributing, then it is more likely that a number of individuals will spontaneously decide to begin contributing, thus initiating a successful team.

4.1.4 A guide to the chapter

Section 4.2 presents the argument formally. Then, in section 4.3, the model is extended to the case where different players may have systematically different costs of contributions. When this is the case, a single 'bad apple' (a player with a higher average cost of contribution) may destabilise an otherwise successful team. This will occur even though that player would rarely be found contributing in a successful team – it is merely their presence in the pool of *potential* contributors that matters.

4.2   A formal model of team formation

In order to both illustrate and verify the intuition offered in section 4.1, a formal model of team formation is developed. A simple teamwork game is described in section 4.2.1, play of which evolves according to the strategy-revision process of section 4.2.2. The main analysis takes place in section 4.2.3. Finally a short discussion of the main results of the section is contained in section 4.2.4.

4.2.1   The game

The central element of the formal model is a simple binary-action game. The n players are indexed by $i \in \{1,2, ..., n\}$, and player i's chosen action is denoted $z_i \in \{0,1\}$. The two possible actions correspond to 'contribute' ($z_i = 1$) and 'don't contribute' ($z_i = 0$). The choice $z_i = 1$ is interpreted as the decision by player i to contribute to the private provision of a public good, whereas $z_i = 0$ is an attempt to free-ride. The actions of all n players may be stacked together to form the $n \times 1$ vector $z \in Z = \{0,1\}^n$; for instance, if the second and third of three players choose to contribute, then $z = [0\ 1\ 1]'$. Thus Z represents the possible set of action combinations. Equivalently, this is the set of pure-strategy profiles in a simultaneous-move game. For a dynamic model, $z_t \in Z$ records the *state of play* at time t. For this reason, Z is the *state space* of the model.

The payoff specification incorporates two features. First, contributions are costly. Second, a benefit is enjoyed by everyone (the team is successful) if and only if a sufficiently large number of players choose to contribute. It follows that it is important to keep track of the number of contributors. To this end, the notation $|z| = \sum_{i=1}^{n} z_i$ is used for this number, where $|z|$ takes values in $\{0, 1, \ldots, n\}$. It is also helpful to partition the state space into subsets of the form $Z_k = \{z \in Z : |z| = k\}$, so that $z \in Z_k$ if and only if k players contribute. Z_k is the kth *layer* of the state space, and contains $\binom{n}{k}$ states; this represents the number of ways in which k contributors may be picked from a pool of n players.

With notation in hand, payoffs may be defined. A contributing player ($z_i = 1$) pays a cost of $c > 0$. If a critical number $m \geq 2$ or more of the players contribute ($|z| \geq m$), then a successful *team* is formed, and all players (both contributors and non-contributors) enjoy a benefit of $v > c > 0$. Writing $I\{\cdot\}$ for the indicator function,[17] player i's payoff is

$$u_i(z) = [v \times I\{|z| \geq m\}] - [c \times z_i].$$

The restriction $m \geq 2$ ensures that genuine teamwork is required for success; this need is central to the many pure-strategy Nash equilibria (that is, states of play in which no player i is able to benefit from a unilateral deviation) of this team-formation game.

One equilibrium is for no player to contribute: $z_i = 0$ for every i, or $|z| = 0$. All players receive a payoff of zero. The only possible unilateral deviation is for a player to begin contributing. Doing so would yield $|z| = 1 < m$ contributions, and hence would not enable the team's success; the deviant would incur a cost with no benefit. This 'team failure' equilibrium corresponds to the 0th layer Z_0 of the state space Z, which has a single member.

The other pure-strategy Nash equilibria consist of the entire mth layer Z_m of the state space Z, where $|z| = m$. These $\binom{n}{m}$ equilibria corresponds to 'team success'. If player i is a contributor ($z_i = 1$) then a deviation would result in the collapse of the team. Similarly, if player i is a non-contributor then a deviation would involve a cost but no extra benefit.

Summarizing, the pure-strategy Nash equilibria consist of the states $Z^* = Z_0 \cup Z_m$. Remaining states are not equilibria. For instance, if $|z| \neq m$ then a contributing player ($z_i = 1$) could deviate and save contribution costs without changing the success of the team.

4.2.2   The dynamic

Attention now turns to the evolution of play. A strategy-revision process is considered in which the decisions of the players are updated one step a time.

At time t the state of play is $z_t \in Z$, and the number of contributors is $|z_t| \in \{0, 1, \ldots, n\}$. Player i's action at time t is denoted z_{it}. At time t, an individual player is chosen randomly (with probability $1/n$) from the population. This player observes the current population state z_t, and is then able to choose a new action. It is assumed that updating players act myopically, by choosing a simple best response to the observed actions of others.

Suppose that player i updates, with an existing contribution state of $z_{it} = 0$. It is a (myopic) best response for this player to begin contributing if and only if $|z_t| = m - 1$, for only then is the player pivotal to a successful team. Suppose instead that player i begins as a contributor, so that $z_{it} = 1$. It is a best response to stop contributing unless $|z_t| = m$. Summarising, the number of contributors evolves as follows

$$|z_{t+1}| = \begin{cases} |z_t| + 1 & |z_t| = m - 1 \text{ and } z_{it} = 0, \\ |z_t| - 1 & |z_t| \neq m \text{ and } z_{it} = 1, \\ |z_t| & \text{otherwise.} \end{cases}$$

Notice that the process is stationary whenever $z_t \in Z_0$, or $z_t \in Z_m$. These absorbing states correspond exactly to the pure-strategy Nash equilibria of the underlying team-formation game. However, starting from any other state, there is positive probability that the process moves. For instance, suppose that $z_t \in Z_k$, where either $|z_t| = k > m$ or $k < m$. If a contributing player is selected to update, then that player will choose to stop contributing, and the process descends from the kth layer to the $(k-1)$th layer. Similarly, if a non-contributor is selected to update from the $(m-1)$th layer, then the process will ascend to Z_m. Put simply, the process will always find its way to a Nash equilibrium, and then stop.

The dynamic, as it stands, is path dependent: the long run state-of-play depends upon initial history. For instance, if the process begins at a Nash equilibrium (either in Z_0 or Z_m) then it will never leave. Ergodicity is, by definition, long-run freedom from the legacy of initial conditions; to obtain such ergodicity, the process must be extended to include 'noise'.

Here, ergodicity is achieved by the addition of a randomly drawn idiosyncratic element in the players' payoffs. In particular, rather than assuming that payoffs are fixed and known, it is assumed that the individual costs and benefits from participating in a team are to some extent different across players. To model this, suppose that a revising player i has a cost parameter $\tilde{c}_i$ and a benefit parameter $\tilde{v}_i$ such that

$$\tilde{c}_i \sim N\ (c,\ \varepsilon\xi^2),\ \text{and}\ (\tilde{v}_i - \tilde{c}_i) \sim N\ (v - c,\ \varepsilon\kappa^2). \tag{1}$$

The parameter ε indexes the overall idiosyncrasy of payoffs, whereas ξ^2 and κ^2 index the relative variability of the contribution cost $\tilde{c}_i$ and the net benefit of being a contributor to a successful team κ^2. Notice that, whenever $\tilde{v}_i$ is constant, then $\xi^2 = \kappa^2$. Furthermore, setting $\varepsilon = 0$ returns the specification to the underlying game described previously.

As long as $\varepsilon > 0$, the dynamic process described above is ergodic. To see this, notice that a revising player i will find it optimal to choose $z_i = 0$ or $z_i = 1$ with positive probability from any state $z \in Z$. This is guaranteed by the full support of the Normal distribution, i.e. a draw from the Normal can take any value between $-\infty$ and $+\infty$. Therefore, for example, there is always positive probability of obtaining a draw that makes it optimal for a player to choose contribute when no one else is, even though a successful team would not be formed as a result (their cost parameter may be drawn negative).[18] Hence the process can move 'up' or 'down' one state (or stay in the same place). Therefore any state can be reached from any other in finite time and with positive probability (states are 'positive recurrent'). Moreover, since there is positive probability of remaining in the same state, every state is 'aperiodic'.[19] A positive recurrent, aperiodic process is ergodic.

Ergodicity guarantees that the long-run behaviour of the stochastic-adjustment dynamic is unambiguous. This long-run behaviour is captured by the ergodic distribution, which describes the probability of different states $z_t \in Z$ for large t; see for example, Grimmett and Stirzaker (2001). Section 4.2.3 calculates the transition probabilities between states for this process and thus the ergodic distribution. Of course, with $\varepsilon > 0$, the distribution will place positive probability on each of the states in Z. However, as $\varepsilon \to 0$, and the 'trembled' game approaches the underlying game of interest, more and more weight in the ergodic distribution will be concentrated on the states corresponding to Nash equilibria; the reduction in payoff idiosyncrasy makes the process more 'sticky'. As a result, a condition arises which allows selection between these multiple equilibria. The condition yields an insight into the sorts of factors that allow a successful team to arise and persist.

4.2.3 Analysis

The first task is to considers transitions: the probability of moving from one state z_t at time t to another state $z_t + 1$ at time $t + 1$ is required.

Suppose that the process is currently at state $z \in Z_k$ (the process is in the 'kth layer') and that $k \leq n - 1$. The process can rise a layer to a state in $Z_k + 1$ only if a non-contributor is selected to revise their strategy *and* that player chooses to contribute as a result. The former occurs with probability $(n - k)/n$ since there are currently $n - k$ non-contributors. The latter occurs with a probability dependent upon whether $k = m - 1$ or not.

First, suppose $k = m - 1$. In this instance, it only takes one more contributor to form a successful team. Therefore, if there were no noise ($\varepsilon = 0$), a revising player i would find it a best response to set $z_i = 1$ (to contribute). However, when $\varepsilon > 0$, this will only happen with high probability. If the revising player chooses to continue with their current strategy ($z_i = 0$), they will receive a zero payoff. If they choose to contribute they will receive $\tilde{v}_i - \tilde{c}_i$, since a successful team forms. Now this payoff is drawn from a Normal distribution as described in Equation (1). Hence they will choose to contribute with probability

$$\Pr[\tilde{v}_i - \tilde{c}_i > 0] = \Phi\left[(v - c)/\kappa\sqrt{\varepsilon}\right],$$

where $\Phi[\cdot]$ is the cumulative density function of the standard Normal distribution. In a similar way, the probability of a non-contributor choosing to contribute when $k \neq m - 1$ can be calculated. In this case, the individual must act 'against the flow of play', choosing an action which would *not* be a best response in the underlying stage game. When $\varepsilon > 0$, however, there is some small probability that such an action would be a best response – given by $1 - \Phi[c/\xi\sqrt{\varepsilon}]$. Hence,

$$\Pr[z_{t+1} \in Z_{k+1} \mid z_t \in Z_k] = \frac{n-k}{n}\begin{cases} 1 - \Phi[c/\xi\sqrt{\varepsilon}] & \text{if } k \neq m-1, \\ \Phi[(v-c)/\kappa\sqrt{\varepsilon}] & \text{if } k = m-1. \end{cases} \quad (2)$$

Similarly, the probability of dropping a layer when $k \geq 1$ can be calculated. In this instance, a *contributor* must be randomly selected (which occurs with probability k/n) and they must choose to stop contributing. This will be a best response with one minus the probabilities shown above. Therefore,

$$\Pr[z_{t+1} \in Z_{k-1} \mid z_t \in Z_k] = \frac{k}{n}\begin{cases} \Phi[c/\xi\sqrt{\varepsilon}] & \text{if } k \neq m, \\ 1 - \Phi[(v-c)/\kappa\sqrt{\varepsilon}] & \text{if } k = m. \end{cases} \quad (3)$$

Of course, a revising player may also decide to keep their action unchanged. In this case, the state remains within the same layer. These probabilities can be calculated in a way analogous to above, but they are not required for the analysis. Note that the players' identities do not enter the transition probabilities – only the aggregate number contributing and not contributing play a role. A more general framework would allow for such asymmetries across players, and is required for the analysis of section 4.3.

For the moment, however, the symmetry allows a simplification of the state space into the layers. This 'reduced' state space may be written

$$Z = \{Z_0, ..., Z_n\}.$$

Figure 4.1 illustrates this reduced-form state space for a simple example with $n = 3$. The arrows represent the possible transitions up and down the layers. The probabilities calculated in Equations (2) and (3) can be associated with each of these arrows. In addition it is always possible to remain in any given state. Figure 4.2 illustrates the possible behaviour of the strategy-revision process over 100 periods. The next step is to use the transition probabilities to deduce the ergodic (long-run) distribution of this stochastic process.

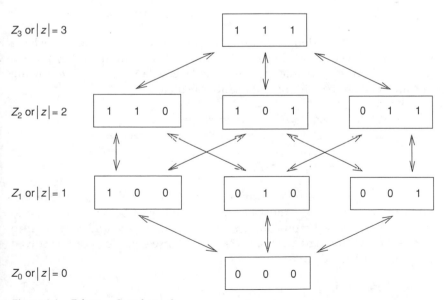

Figure 4.1 Z for $n = 3$ and $m = 2$

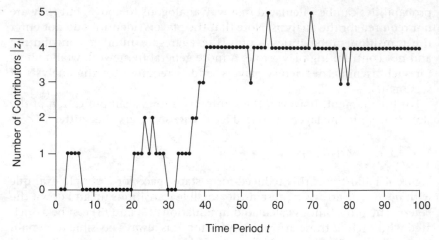

Figure 4.2   Team formation for $n = 5$ and $m = 4$

Having concluded above that the process is indeed ergodic, there will exist a set of probabilities $[\pi^z]_{z \in Z}$ such that $\pi^z = \lim_{t \to \infty} \Pr[z_t = z]$, where $\Sigma_{z \in Z}\, \pi^z = 1$. Put simply, π^z is the probability that state z will occur looking toward a very long horizon. Using the reduced state space, define

$$\pi_k = \sum_{z \in Z_k} \pi^z = \lim_{t \to \infty} \Pr\big[z_t \in Z_k\big].$$

This is the ergodic (long-run) probability of the process being in the layer where k players contribute. Again, $\Sigma_{k=0}^n\, \pi_k = 1$. The reduced Markov process induced by the dynamic moves 'one-layer-at-a-time'. The following 'detailed balance conditions' are readily calculated:

$$\pi_0 = \pi_0\, \Pr[z_{t+1} \in Z_0 \mid z_t \in Z_0] + \pi_1\, \Pr[z_{t+1} \in Z_0 \mid z_t \in Z_1],$$
$$\pi_n = \pi_n\, \Pr[z_{t+1} \in Z_n \mid z_t \in Z_n] + \pi_{n-1}\, \Pr[z_{t+1} \in Z_n \mid z_t \in Z_{n-1}],$$
$$\pi_k = \pi_{k-1}\, \Pr[z_{t+1} \in Z_k \mid z_t \in Z_{k-1}] + \pi_k\, \Pr[z_{t+1} \in Z_k \mid z_t \in Z_k] +$$
$$\pi_{k+1}\, \Pr[z_{t+1} \in Z_k \mid z_t \in Z_{k+1}],$$

where $0 < k < n$. These are intuitive conditions. In the long run, the probability of being in state k must be the probability of being in state k and staying there, plus the probabilities of being elsewhere and moving into state k. Straightforward algebra reveals that these equations can be solved to yield values for π_k. In fact,

$$\pi_k = \frac{q_k}{\Sigma_{j=0}^n\, q_j}, \text{ where } q_k = \prod_{j<k} \Pr\big[z_{t+1} \in Z_{j+1} \mid z_t \in Z_j\big] \times \prod_{j>k} \Pr\big[z_{t+1} \in Z_{j-1} \mid z_t \in Z_j\big].$$

Now consider the relative ergodic probabilities with $j < k$. It is easy to see that

$$\frac{\pi_j}{\pi_k} = \frac{q_j}{q_k} = \prod_{i=j}^{k-1} \frac{\Pr\left[z_{t+1} \in Z_i \mid z_t \in Z_{i+1}\right]}{\Pr\left[z_{t+1} \in Z_{i+1} \mid z_t \in Z_i\right]}. \tag{4}$$

The next step is to replace these probabilities with the ones in Equations (2) and (3), and then allow $\varepsilon \to 0$. The main result of this section follows from this exercise.

Proposition 1. *As $\varepsilon \to 0$ all weight in the ergodic distribution is concentrated on the pure strategy Nash equilibria in $Z_0 \cup Z_m$, and*

$$\frac{(v-c)^2}{\kappa^2} > (m-1)\frac{c^2}{\xi^2} \quad \Rightarrow \quad \lim_{\varepsilon \to 0}\left[\lim_{t \to \infty} \Pr\left[z_t \in Z_m\right]\right] = 1.$$

When the opposite (strict) inequality holds then $\lim_{\varepsilon \to 0} [\lim_{t \to \infty} \Pr[z_t \in Z_0]] = 1$.

Rather than prove this result formally at this stage, an intuition is offered based on Figure 4.1. Appendix A contains the formal proof.

Consider the simple four layer example illustrated in the figure. Selection depends upon the relative difficulty of moving between the different pure equilibria states of the game, at Z_2 and Z_0 in the example with $m = 2$. Suppose the process is currently in a state in Z_2. In order to get to $z \in Z_0$, a revising contributor must choose to stop contributing. This happens with probability

$$1 - \Phi\left[\frac{v-c}{\xi\sqrt{\varepsilon}}\right].$$

For very small (but non-zero) ε this probability will be positive but tiny. The process is now in a state in the layer Z_1. From here it is easy to reach Z_0. All that is required is that a contributor be picked, which occurs with non-negligible probability (a third in this example), and that they then choose to stop contributing. For very small ε, this choice is a best response with a probability close to one.

Thus the 'difficult' part of the journey occurs at the outset when a contributor chooses to stop contributing. The expression above naturally suggests that the term $[(v - c)/\kappa]^2$ acts as an index of this difficulty. As $\varepsilon \to 0$, this is the only part of the process that will matter.

An analogous story can be told starting in the Z_0 Nash equilibrium. Here, a non-contributor must revise their action against the flow of play, and choose to contribute. This will be a best response for them with probability

$$1 - \Phi\left[\frac{c}{\xi\sqrt{\varepsilon}}\right],$$

which again is close to zero when ε is small. Once this has happened the process is at a state in Z_1. With non-negligible probability a non-contributor will be chosen (two thirds in the example) and will find it a best response to contribute with high probability for small ε. Once again, the difficult step is the first, and $[c/\xi]^2$ indexes this difficulty.

A comparison of these two numbers reveals which of the two most difficult steps is *more* difficult than the other, and yields a selection result akin to that in Proposition 1. Of course, when m is larger there are many difficult steps to be taken on the way *up* through the layers, although it does not affect the difficulty of moving *down* (since only the first step has low probability). Thus for general m there are $m-1$ low probability steps to be made when moving from Z_0 to Z_m. Hence the index of difficulty becomes $(m-1)[c/\xi]^2$ and the result of the proposition obtains.

4.2.4 Discussion

Proposition 1 states that whenever

$$\frac{v-c}{\kappa} > \sqrt{m-1} \times \frac{c}{\xi}, \tag{5}$$

all weight in the ergodic distribution is concentrated in Z_m when ε gets vanishingly small. That is, a successful team evolves. If the inequality is reversed, a successful team will not evolve. Rather, the Nash equilibrium in Z_0 is selected where no one contributes. In this section, the selection inequality in Equation (5) is examined.

Notice that n, the population size, does not play a role at all. The other parameters all enter in an intuitive way. The larger $v - c$ (corrected for its variability), the smaller c (again, corrected for variance), and the smaller m, the easier it becomes for a successful team to arise and persist in the long run.

The precise nature of the selection result obtained in the proposition arises when the limit is taken as $\varepsilon \to 0$. Of course, away from the limit, the ergodic distribution can still be calculated numerically for $\varepsilon \gg 0$. When this is done, n *will* play a role in the likely success of a team. Figure 4.3 illustrates this point. The ergodic distribution is shown in the graph for two different values of n.[20]

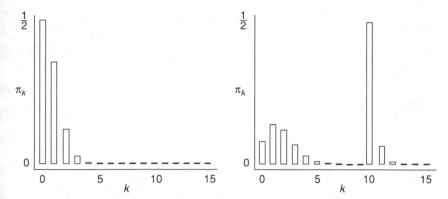

Figure 4.3   Ergodic distributions for $n = 20$ and $m = 50$

In the first graph, where $n = 20$, most weight in the ergodic distribution lies around the $z \in Z_0$ state. That is, nearly all of the time, no successful team is formed. A similar outcome is suggested by Equation (5) – with the parameters used for the figure, the left hand side equals 3 whilst the right hand side is 2. However, although the equation indicates that increasing n should have no impact on selection, once ε is large enough, the limiting result of Proposition 1 ceases to be informative. As can be seen from the second graph in the figure, once $n = 50$, most weight is concentrated around the states $z \in Z_m$, where a successful team is operating.

Why is this? The intuition at the end of section 4.2.3 needs modification. Away from the limit the probabilities of choosing non-contributors as opposed to contributors become important. Consider the states in Z_1. Only one player is currently contributing. The chances of picking this player are much smaller as n gets large, and hence it becomes easier to move away from Z_0 and toward Z_m. A similar change of emphasis occurs at states close to Z_m. Here the team size, m, as well as its relative size to the population at large (m/n) will play a role. As a result, an increase in the population size increases the weight attached to the states in Z_m, making it more likely that a successful team will form. Essentially, there are more non-contributors to pick from and 'many hands make light work'.

The same point can be made in a slightly different way by fixing the population size and increasing ε. Figure 4.4 illustrates. Here, n is fixed at 30 and ε rises from 0.25 to 1. The first ergodic distribution is almost identical to that of the first graph in Figure 4.3. By increasing ε, the population size becomes more important and overturns the selection result that operates in the limit. The intuition is identical. Moving away from the limit, a successful team will operate for more of the time when the population is sufficiently large.

Nor does it take long for this feature to become dominant. Figure 4.5 plots the probability of the process being in any state $z \in Z_k$ where $k \geq m$

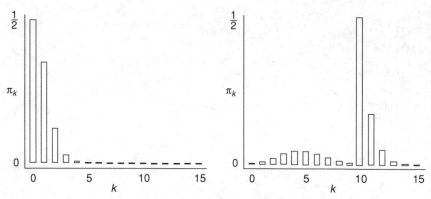

Figure 4.4   Ergodic distributions for $\varepsilon = 20$ and $\varepsilon = 50$

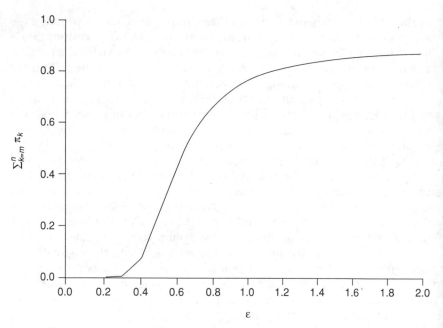

Figure 4.5   Team success and ε

in the long run against ε for $0 \leq \varepsilon \leq 2$ (the other parameters remain as before). Relatively quickly weight moves to the states where a successful team operates.

Of course, these facts do not overturn the statement of Proposition 1, but they do put limiting results of this sort in a proper context. In the next section, a further exercise of this kind helps provide additional insight. Another critical assumption made at the outset was the symmetry between players. Section 4.3 examines the case where there is one 'bad apple' – a single player with a higher cost of contribution.

Although no one would expect such a player to take part in a successful team in the long run, their existence within the population does have important consequences for team formation – both when $\varepsilon = 0$ *and* away from the limit.

4.3 Extensions and simulations

So far, the players in the model have had symmetric payoffs. Interest also lies in the case where individuals differ in this respect. A full model of this kind is beyond the scope of this chapter, and is presented in a companion paper – Myatt and Wallace (2003b). Here a simple example of asymmetric payoffs is considered. One player is assumed to be a 'bad apple', that is, to have a higher average cost of contribution than the others. In the long run this player does not spend much time as part of any successful team (and, as $\varepsilon \to 0$, no time at all), nonetheless, their presence alone can cause a dramatic shift in the fortunes of the population.

The ergodic process is not so readily available in this case. The problem arises because it is no longer possible to simplify the state space into layers. With just one different player, the state space can be simplified to

$$Z = \{Z_0, Z_1^-, Z_1^+, ..., Z_{n-1}^-, Z_{n-1}^+, Z_n\},$$

where Z_k^+ represents all the states such that k players contribute, including the bad apple – and Z_k^- represents the states where k contribute, excluding the bad apple. Thus $Z_k^- \cup Z_k^+ = Z_k$. Formally, if the nth individual is arbitrarily designated the bad apple,

$$Z_k^- = \left\{ z : \sum_{l=1}^{n} z_i = k \quad \text{and} \quad z_n = 0 \right\}, \text{ and}$$

$$Z_k^+ = \left\{ z : \sum_{i=1}^{n} z_i = k \quad \text{and} \quad z_n = 1 \right\}.$$

The difficulty is that this process can no longer be represented by a 'one-step-at-a-time' dynamic. In fact, in this simplified state space, it is possible for the process to transit from a state into itself or to at most three others. Hence it is not possible to apply results from simple birth-death processes, as it was in section 4.2.3.[21]

Transition probabilities can still be found easily. The only additional consideration is the presence of the bad apple. With probability $1/n$, this player is chosen. The probability that they choose to contribute differs from other players, as their cost of contribution is larger. The simplest case is to assume that

$$\tilde{c}_n \sim N\,(C,\ \varepsilon\xi^2), \text{ and } \tilde{v}_n - \tilde{c}_n \sim N(v - C,\ \varepsilon\kappa^2),$$

which is identical to Equation (1) except that the average cost parameter c is replaced by some $C > c$. An identical process to that presented in section 4.2.3 then yields transition probabilities $\Pr[z_{t+1} \in Z_i^+ \mid z_t \in Z_j^-]$, $\Pr[z_{t+1} \in Z_i^- \mid z_t \in Z_j^-]$, $\Pr[z_{t+1} \in Z_i^+ \mid z_t \in Z_j^+]$, and $\Pr[z_{t+1} \in Z_i^- \mid z_t \in Z_j^+]$. For $\varepsilon > 0$, the ergodic distribution is not available in closed form. However, limiting results can be obtained – see Myatt and Wallace (2003b). For the purposes of the current paper, however, the ergodic distribution is of interest away from the limit, as well as when ε is small.

To this end, numerical simulations allow an examination of the ergodic distribution for various parameter values. Figures 4.6, 4.7, and 4.8 show the long run distribution of the process with $c = \xi = \kappa = 1$, $v = 4$, $m = 5$, and $C = 2$, for a variety of values of ε. In each case, the distribution on the left illustrates the ergodic distribution before the addition of a bad apple (and with $n = 6$), whilst the distribution on the right shows the effect of adding a bad apple to the population (and hence $n = 7$).

Figure 4.6 shows the ergodic distributions for $\varepsilon = 1$. Section 4.2.4 argued that increasing the size of the population whilst keeping team size constant would have the effect of increasing the probability that a successful team forms. However, as can be seen from the figure, there is no appreciable increase in the probability of team formation – the two ergodic distributions are almost identical.

Figure 4.7 goes one step further. As ε decreases (to 0.5), the probability of a successful team forming is substantially reduced by the introduction of a bad apple. Even though the population increases from $n = 6$ to $n = 7$, $\Sigma_{k \geq m}\,\pi_k$ is reduced.

The smaller ε becomes, the more pronounced this effect. Figure 4.8 illustrates this for $\varepsilon = 0.25$. Now the introduction of an extra (bad apple) player results in a complete reversal of the team's fortunes. More weight now lies at Z_0 than at Z_m. Without a bad apple, on the other hand, the process spends almost all its time at Z_m.

In all three cases, $Z_m^+ \approx 0$. That is, the bad apple spends little time in successful teams when they form. There are, after all, six other players with lower cost parameters to choose from. Successful teams do not include the bad apple. Nevertheless, it is the bad apple's presence that destroys the successful team. The reason is this: it is very much more likely that a contributing bad apple in a successful team finds it optimal to cease contributing if called upon to update their behaviour. In fact, following the intuition of section 4.2.3, the difficulty of taking such a step is only $[(v - C)/\kappa]^2$ rather than $[(v - c)/\kappa]^2$. Roughly speaking, team formation still

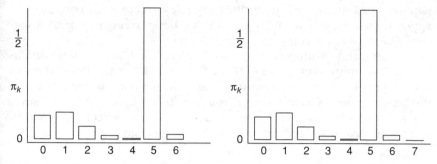

Figure 4.6 Bad apple ergodic distributions for $\varepsilon = 1$

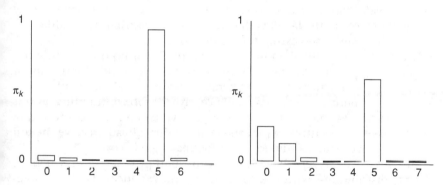

Figure 4.7 Bad apple ergodic distributions for $\varepsilon = 0.5$

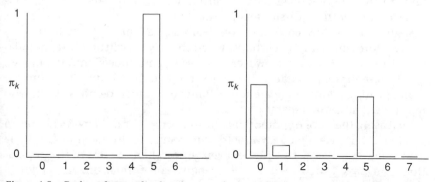

Figure 4.8 Bad apple ergodic distributions for $\varepsilon = 0.25$

requires $m - 1$ steps, each with difficulty $[c/\xi]^2$ (there is no need for bad apples to help form teams). So whilst it has become easier to break a successful team, it has become no easier to form one.

Of course, this intuition (as discussed in section 4.2.4) applies particularly to the limiting case as $\varepsilon \to 0$. Further away from the limit, the bad apple effect becomes less pronounced, and the population size relative to the team size begins to play the critical role. This is apparent from Figures 4.6, 4.7, and 4.8. As ε increases in size, the bad apple effect continues to hamper successful team formation, but to a lesser degree.

4.4 Conclusions

This chapter presents a model of the evolution of team formation. A population of players repeatedly update their decision to either contribute to a potential team or not. If sufficiently many individuals choose to contribute in any given round, a successful team is formed, and *every* player in the population receives the benefits that accrue. Each contributor, regardless of whether the team is successful, must pay a cost.

The game has multiple equilibria. In particular, if no one contributes, then revising players have no incentive to contribute, as they alone cannot form a team and hence derive any benefit. Likewise, if a successful team is formed contributing players have no incentive to stop contributing, as this would result in team collapse and lower payoffs; and non-contributing players have no incentive to join the team, as they already receive the full benefits of successful coordination without paying any cost.

Initially, each player's benefit and contribution cost are drawn from Normal distributions with identical means and variances. Thus, on occasion, players find it optimal to play against the flow of play described in the previous paragraph. As the distributions collapse to their means, and hence noise is driven from the model, a precise condition arises to select between the multiple strict equilibria. Equation (5) gives the condition for the updating process described above to spend nearly all its time in the equilibria associated with successful team formation.

High benefits, low costs and low team size all make team formation easier. More surprisingly, perhaps, when there is very little noise, population size does not matter. However, as noise is reintroduced into the model, an increase in the population size does improve the fortunes of teams. In each updating period there are more non-contributors to choose from who may potentially join a team.

Increasing the pool of potential contributors might not always be such a good idea, however. Once asymmetry is introduced into the model, a single 'bad apple' (a player with a higher average cost than the rest of the population) can have a detrimental effect upon team formation. As section 3 shows, even though the bad apple would not play a part in any successful team, their mere presence in the population can overturn the selection result of the symmetric case. This is most apparent when there is little noise in the process, but can still have an impact away from the limit. At a first glance, increasing the population might seem to improve the chances of successful team formation, but the nature of the individuals being added to the pool plays a critical role.

An interesting extension of the ideas proposed in this paper would allow for general asymmetries across players in the population. This is the direction taken in a companion paper, Myatt and Wallace (2003b). The updating procedure described in section 4.2 can no longer be represented as a simple birth-death process. Limiting results are still available, via the use of Freidlin and Wentzell (1984)-style rooted tree methods, but these go well beyond the analysis required for the ideas presented here.

Appendix   Omitted proofs

Proof of Proposition 1. The 'switching ratios' of Equation (4) can be employed in the first place to eliminate states that will not feature in the limiting distribution. For instance, consider the relative probability of 0 versus 1 contributor. Formally,

$$\frac{\pi_0}{\pi_1} = \frac{\Pr[z_{t+1} \in Z_0 \mid z_t \in Z_1]}{\Pr[z_{t+1} \in Z_1 \mid z_t \in Z_0]} = \frac{(1/n)\Phi[c/\xi\sqrt{\varepsilon}]}{(n/n)(1-\Phi[c/\xi\sqrt{\varepsilon}])} \to \infty, \text{ as } \varepsilon \to 0$$

Similarly, for $k \neq 0$ and $k \neq m$, it is the case that $\lim_{\varepsilon \to 0} \pi_k = 0$. Thus, for vanishingly small ε, the only states that have positive weight in the ergodic distribution are the ones that correspond to pure strategy Nash equilibria, $z \in Z_0 \cup Z_m$.

Equation (4) is again used, this time to compare the pure Nash equilibrium states. π_0/π_m involves the product of m fractions. Substituting with the transition probabilities in Equations (2) and (3) yields the following expression:

$$\frac{m!(1-\Phi[(v-c)/\kappa\sqrt{\varepsilon}])\Phi[c/\xi\sqrt{\varepsilon}]^{m-1}}{(n!/m!)(1-\Phi[c/\xi\sqrt{\varepsilon}])^{m-1}\Phi[(v-c)/\kappa\sqrt{\varepsilon}]} \propto \frac{1-\Phi[(v-c)/\kappa\sqrt{\varepsilon}]}{(1-\Phi[c/\xi\sqrt{\varepsilon}])^{m-1}}.$$

The latter term can be decomposed into ratios of densities and hazard rates for the Normal distribution. The expression becomes

$$\frac{1-\Phi[(v-c)/\kappa\sqrt{\varepsilon}]}{(1-\Phi[c/\xi\sqrt{\varepsilon}])^{m-1}} = \frac{\phi[(v-c)/\kappa\sqrt{\varepsilon}]}{(\phi[c/\xi\sqrt{\varepsilon}])^{m-1}} \times \frac{(\phi[c/\xi\sqrt{\varepsilon}]/(1-\Phi[c/\xi\sqrt{\varepsilon}]))^{m-1}}{\phi[(v-c)/\kappa\sqrt{\varepsilon}]/(1-\Phi[(v-c)/\kappa\sqrt{\varepsilon}])}. \quad (6)$$

Rewriting the first term in the right hand side of Equation (6) explicitly gives

$$
\frac{\phi\big[(v-c)/\kappa\sqrt{\varepsilon}\big]}{\big(\phi\big[c/\xi\sqrt{\varepsilon}\big]\big)^{m-1}} = (2\pi)^{(m-2)/2} \exp\left(-\frac{1}{2\varepsilon}\left[\frac{(v-c)^2}{\kappa^2} - \frac{(m-1)c^2}{\xi^2}\right]\right). \tag{7}
$$

Now consider the denominator of the second term in the right hand side of Equation (6). Notice that $(v-c)/\kappa > 0$, and hence $(v-c)/\kappa\sqrt{\varepsilon} \to +\infty$ as $\varepsilon \to 0$. Since the hazard rate of the Normal distribution is asymptotically linear, it follows that

$$
\lim_{\varepsilon\to 0}\left[\frac{\phi\big[(v-c)/\kappa\sqrt{\varepsilon}\big]}{1-\Phi\big[(v-c)/\kappa\sqrt{\varepsilon}\big]}\right] = \lim_{\varepsilon\to 0}\left[\frac{v-c}{\kappa\sqrt{\varepsilon}}\right].
$$

A similar argument holds for the numerator, so that

$$
\lim_{\varepsilon\to 0}\left[\frac{\phi\big[c/\xi\sqrt{\varepsilon}\big]}{1-\Phi\big[c/\xi\sqrt{\varepsilon}\big]}\right]^{m-1} = \lim_{\varepsilon\to 0}\left[\frac{c}{\xi\sqrt{\varepsilon}}\right]^{m-1}.
$$

Both of these terms are polynomial in ε, whereas the first term of Equation (6) is exponential in ε. The exponential term dominates the polynomial in the limit, and hence determines behaviour as $\varepsilon \to 0$. Examining Equation (7) it is clear that

$$
\frac{(v-c)^2}{\kappa^2} > (m-1)\frac{c^2}{\xi^2} \Rightarrow \lim_{\varepsilon\to 0}\left[\frac{1-\Phi\big[(v-c)/\kappa\sqrt{\varepsilon}\big]}{\big(1-\Phi\big[c/\xi\sqrt{\varepsilon}\big]\big)^{m-1}}\right] = 0,
$$

which yields the desired result.

Acknowledgements

Thanks are due to seminar participants at the Teamwork workshop held at St. Catherine's College, Oxford University, in April 2003.

Notes

1. The classic analysis of collective action problems appears in Olson (1965). The literature which followed is vast and continues to grow in both applied and theoretical directions; see for example, Bardhan, Ghatak, and Karaivanov (2002) and Marx and Matthews (2000) respectively.
2. Both these problems have attracted a great deal of interest, and not only from theorists. For a summary of the experimental approach to these problems, see Ledyard (1995).

3. A description of its activities is available from http://www.ocv.org.uk/.
4. The now-standard economic approach to the problem of public-good provision is presented in the central contributions of Bergstrom, Blume and Varian (1986,1992), and a useful diagrammatic exposition can be found in Ley (1996).
5. In a rowing regatta the overall winner is said to come in at the head of the river.
6. The use of game-theoretic concepts has become standard in the public-goods literature; textbooks commonly employ such language to introduce the problem, for example Cornes and Sandler (1996).
7. This widely used concept is due to Nash (1950), and is central to game theory.
8. Certain Nash equilibria of a game are not robust to the imposition of time consistency. For instance, it can be a Nash equilibrium for one player to threaten an opponent. The opponent believes the threat, and capitulates. In many situations, however, if the opponent were to 'call the bluff' of the first player, then the threat would never be carried out if it is costly to do so. Equilibrium refinements such as 'subgame perfection' of Nash equilibria help to eliminate such non-credible threats.
9. An important early approach is contained in Harsanyi and Selten (1988); their tracing procedure picks out the 'risk dominant' equilibrium in simple games (roughly speaking, the equilibrium from which unilateral deviation is more costly). This need not be a Pareto-superior equilibrium.
10. The former began with the seminal work of Carlsson and van Damme (1993). Briefly, a global game is one in which players do not know all the payoffs of the game, instead receiving noisy signals of their own and their opponents' payoffs. Hence, the true game might be one of several different 'local' kinds; players must consider this 'global' game when making their strategic decisions. For a summary of the literature and its results, see Morris and Shin (2003) or Myatt, Shin and Wallace (2002).
11. Myatt and Wallace (2002) provide an equilibrium-selection argument based on the global-games literature for collective action and public-good provision problems similar to the one discussed here, although the specific application to teams is beyond the scope of that paper.
12. The key contributions in this field are Kandori, Mailath and Rob (1993) and Young (1993). Both provide further arguments for selection of the risk-dominant Nash equilibrium in simple two-player, two-strategy games.
13. This is a standard approach in the stochastic-adjustment dynamics literature. It might be a reasonable assumption if the game is to be played many times between the strategy revisions. However, the results remain unchanged as long as the process moves in the direction of the best response, and any revision procedure that achieves this would be sufficient. Evolutionary models that use this assumption are not generally proposing it as the way in which individual players actually think, but rather as a simple and tractable modelling mechanism which provides an adequate description of observed behaviour. For a more detailed discussion of this methodology, see Myatt and Wallace (2003d).
14. Broadly speaking, Kandori, Mailath and Rob (1993) and Young (1993) do this by allowing individuals to play a strategy which is not a best response with some small probability. This might be interpreted as experimentation on the part of updating players, or simply as mistakes.
15. This is the approach taken in Myatt and Wallace (2003a) and extended to larger games in Myatt and Wallace (2003c). The methods of the latter paper can be brought to bear on the current problem, see Myatt and Wallace (2003b).
16. The authors offer their thanks to Robert McMahon for empirical research on this issue.

17. That is, $I\{\cdot\}$ takes the value 1 if its argument is true, and 0 if its argument is false.
18. This can be interpreted as an individual actually enjoying contributing to a public good even though it is not produced – they receive some utility from the act itself.
19. A state z is aperiodic if the minimum number of periods for which the probability of returning to z given that the process is currently in z is positive is 1.
20. The other parameters have values $v = 3$, $c = \xi = \kappa = 1$, $m = 10$, and $\varepsilon = 0.3$.
21. A 'birth-death' process is simply one in which there is only positive probability of moving up or down a state (or remaining in the same place) in a single time period.

References

Bardhan, P., M. Ghatak and A. Karaivanov (2002) 'Inequality, Market Imperfections, and the Voluntary Provision of Collective Goods' mimeo, University of California at Berkeley.

Bergstrom, T. C., L. Blume and H. R. Varian (1986) 'On the Private Provision of Public Goods', *Journal of Public Economics*, 29(1), 25–49.

—— (1992) 'Uniqueness of Nash equilibrium in Private Provision of Public Goods: An Improved Proof', *Journal of Public Economics*, 49(3), 391–392.

Carlsson, H. and E. Van Damme (1993) 'Global Games and Equilibrium Selection,' *Econometrica*, 61(5), 989–1018.

Cornes, R. and T. Sandler (1996) *The Theory of Externalities, Public Goods and Club Goods*. Cambridge University Press, London, 2nd. edn.

Freidlin, M. I. and A. D. Wentzell (1984) *Random Perturbations of Dynamical Systems*. Springer-Verlag, Berlin/New York.

Grimmett, G. R. and D. R. Stirzaker (2001) *Probability and Random Processes*. Oxford University Press, Oxford, 3rd edn.

Harsanyi, J. C. and R. Selten (1988) *A General Theory of Equilibrium Selection in Games*. MIT Press, Cambridge MA.

Kandori, M., G. J. Mailath and R. Rob (1993) 'Learning, Mutation and Long-Run Equilibria in Games' *Econometrica*, 61(1), 29–56.

Ledyard, J. O. (1995) 'Public Goods: A Survey of Experimental Research' in *The Handbook of Experimental Economics*, ed. by J. H. Kagel and A. E. Roth, chap. 2, pp. 111–194. Princeton University Press, Princeton, NJ.

Ley, E. (1996) 'On the Private Provision of Public Goods: A Diagrammatic Exposition', *Investigaciones Económicas*, 20(1), 105–123.

Marx, L. M. and S. A. Matthews (2000) 'Dynamic Voluntary Contributions to a Public Project', *Review of Economic Studies*, 67(2), 327–358.

Morris, S., and H. S. Shin (2003) 'Global Games: Theory and Application' in *Advances in Economics and Econometrics: Theory and Applications*, ed. by M. Dewatripont, L. P. Hansen and S. J. Turnovsky. Cambridge University Press, London.

Myatt, D. P., H. S. Shin and C. Wallace (2002) 'The Assessment: Games and Coordination', *Oxford Review of Economic Policy*, 18(4), 397–417.

Myatt, D. P. and C. Wallace (2002) 'Equilibrium Selection and Public-Good Provision: The Development of Open-Source Software', *Oxford Review of Economic Policy*, 18(4), 446–461.

—— (2003a) 'Adaptive Play by Idiosyncratic Agents', *Games and Economic Behavior*, in press.

—— (2003b) 'The Evolution of Collective Action', mimeo, Department of Economics, Oxford University.

—— (2003c) 'A Multinomial Probit Model of Stochastic Evolution', *Journal of Economic Theory*, 113(2), 286–301.

—— (2003d) 'Sophisticated Play by Idiosyncratic Agents', *Journal of Evolutionary Economics*, 13(3), 319–345.

Nash, J. F. (1950) 'Equilibrium Points in *N*-Person Games', *Proceedings of the National Academy of Sciences*, 36, 48–49.

Olson, M. (1965) *The Logic of Collective Action: Public Goods and the Theory of Groups.* Harvard University Press, Cambridge, MA.

Young, H. P. (1993) 'The Evolution of Conventions' *Econometrica*, 61(1), 57–84.

5

Cooperation and Communication: Group Identity or Social Norms?

Cristina Bicchieri

A social dilemma is, by definition, a situation in which each group member gets a higher outcome if she pursues her individual interest, but everyone in the group is better off if all group members further the common interest. Overpopulation, pollution, Medicare, public television, and the depletion of scarce and valuable resources such as energy and fish-rich waters are all examples of situations in which the temptation to defect must be tempered by a concern with the public good. There are several reasons why some individuals might not contribute to the provision of public goods or refrain from wasting common resources. Usually these resources are used by or depend upon very large groups of people for their continued maintenance. It is easy, therefore, for an individual to consider her contribution to a public good or her personal consumption of a common resource as insignificant. Furthermore, in social dilemmas there is a huge difference between the costs and benefits accruing to an individual. Gains go to the individual, but the costs are shared by all. Given the structure of social dilemmas, rational, self-interested individuals are predicted to defect always. Yet almost 50 years of experiments on social dilemmas show cooperation rates ranging from 40 per cent to 60 per cent, and everyday experience shows people making voluntary contributions to public goods, giving to charities, volunteering and refraining from wasting resources. One variation in social dilemma experiments, which dramatically increases cooperation rates, is allowing subjects to discuss the dilemma. There are two possible explanations for this 'communication effect'. One is that communication enhances group identity, the other that communication elicits social norms. Though group identity may focus people on group norms, such as in-group loyalty and trust, I argue that the group in this case is only an instrument for the deployment of a norm and not its cause. I shall argue that the reason for cooperative behaviour is the working of norms;[1] if correct, this conclusion has important strategic implications for institutional design and public policies that encourage social cooperation.

5.1 Experiments

To examine how group members make their decisions in social dilemmas, two different research paradigms are used. In a public goods dilemma, such as contributing to the maintenance of a public space or funding a public television, individuals must contribute resources to ensure the provision of the public good. Since one can enjoy public broadcasting without making a financial contribution, groups run the risk that members will not contribute, and that the public good will not be provided at all. In a resource dilemma, such as making use of common grazing land or clean air, groups share a scarce resource from which individual members can harvest. Since individuals' use of the resource, whilst beneficial to them, has negative effects on others, the group runs the risk of excessive harvesting, leading to depletion of the resource.

A typical social dilemma experiment uses the mixed-motive structure of the Prisoner's Dilemma to study choice behaviour. Like Prisoner's Dilemma games, both public goods and resource dilemmas have the property that the individually rational choice is always defection, but if all refuse to cooperate, all are worse off.[2] The usual experimental procedure involves subjects previously unknown to one another, who may receive a monetary payoff or points, and form one or two groupings depending on the experimental design. Subjects are given instructions and are presented with a payoff matrix describing the monetary consequences of their actions. It is individually best for each to keep his money or to appropriate a large amount of a common resource (to defect), but all are better off if everyone makes a cooperative decision to contribute to the public good or take little of the common resource. When two separate groups are formed, subjects are given the choice between allocating money to the in-group or to the out-group; if there is only one group, individuals must choose between giving money to their group or keeping it themselves.[3] Choices are made privately, interactions may be one-shot or repeated, and discussion before playing may or may not be allowed. I shall consider here mainly one-shot interactions, because repeated interactions allow opportunities for reciprocation or reputation formation. In a repeated game, it might work to the advantage of a rational, self-interested player to develop a reputation for being a 'nice guy'. In this case cooperation is not surprising, and it is easily explained by the traditional rational choice model. Only when there is no apparent incentive to cooperate does pro-social behaviour become really interesting.

As an example of what experimental subjects may face, consider the following 'Give Some' game (Dawes, 1980), which is an example of a public goods dilemma. There are five players, and each receives $8 from the experimenter. The choice is between keeping the money or giving it away, in which case every other player gets $3. What a player gets depends on his choice and the choice of the other players.

Table 5.1 shows that it is always better for any individual player to keep the money, at least in terms of monetary payoffs, but the outcome of everyone giving is much better than the outcome of everyone keeping ($8 versus $12).

An example of a resource dilemma is the following 'Take Some' game (Dawes 1980). There are three players and each has to decide whether to pick a red chip, in which case he gets $3 and all three players are fined $1, or pick a blue chip, in which case he gets $1 and there is no fine (Table 5.2). Again, the individual outcome depends upon one's choice, as well as the other players' choices.

In this situation, too, it is better to defect (hold the red chip), but the collective outcome of defection is worse than the cooperative outcome.

What we know from years of social dilemma experiments is that a significant baseline of cooperation is found in all experimental conditions, contrary to the prediction of rational choice theory. Even more interesting, we also know that in one-shot games allowing subjects a short period of communication about the dilemma increases cooperation well above the baseline. Indeed, a meta-analysis of social dilemma experiments conducted from 1958 to 1992 (Sally, 1995) shows that the mean cooperation rate across conditions was 47.4 per cent, that communication increased cooperation by 40 per cent and commitment and promising increased cooperation by 30 per cent. Similar conclusions are drawn by Gerry Mackie (1997), who summarized the results of several social dilemma experiments

Number of givers	Payoff to keep	Payoff to give
5	–	$12
4	$20	$9
3	$17	$6
2	$14	$3
1	$11	$0
0	$8	–

Table 5.1   'Give Some' game

Number picking blue chip	Payoff to red chip	Payoff to blue chip
3	–	$1
2	$2	$0
1	$1	–$1
0	$0	–

Table 5.2   'Take Some' game

devoting particular attention to the role of communication and commitments. His conclusions can be thus summarized:

- discussion about the dilemma (but not 'irrelevant' discussion) increases cooperation rates
- the primary content of discussions about the dilemma is promises and commitments to cooperate
- to be effective, promising must be unanimous
- overhearing spoken commitments from another group does not increase cooperation
- when subjects are instructed that pledges are 'nonbinding', they treat them as such and pledges have no effect on cooperation
- commitments tend to be kept even if the beneficiary is a computer
- commitments made on the initial belief of benefit to the in-group tend to be kept when the locus of benefit unexpectedly switched to the outgroup (carry-over effect)
- discussion improves contribution to a step-level public good even when it is confined to subgroups smaller than the critical number necessary to attain the cooperative payoff
- cooperation declines over repetitions.

A number of suggestions have been advanced to explain the effectiveness of communication in increasing cooperation rates in one-shot games. For example, communication may help subjects to understand the game, facilitate coordinated action, alter expectations of others' behaviour, promote group solidarity, elicit generic norms of cooperation or result in commitments to cooperate (Kerr and Kaufman-Gilliland, 1994). However, since it is now common experimental practice to make sure the subjects understand the game they are going to play, even in the absence of communication, this cannot adequately explain the effects of communication on cooperation rates. Attaining coordination, in turn, is a necessary but not a sufficient condition for cooperation, and it remains to be explained how expectations of others' cooperative behaviour induce subjects to cooperate instead of tempting them to defect. As to the elicitation of 'generic' norms of cooperation, I do not believe such generic norms exist. What we have are specific, contingent norms that apply to well-defined situations. Thus communication may indeed focus subjects on some norms, but they will be specific to the context in which communication takes place. Finally, commitments to cooperate certainly play an important role in increasing cooperation rates, but it remains to be explained why and under which conditions pledges to cooperate in one-shot games in which one's action will remain anonymous do work. Why communication successfully increases cooperation rates is still an open question, but among the former suggestions, only group identity and social norms have not been eliminated by experimentation as possible explanations.

At the heart of the controversy between the group identity and social norms explanations of the effects of communication on cooperation rates lie two different views of the relation between an individual and the groups to which she belongs. In a reductionist perspective, the basic explanatory unit is the individual, and the group is just the aggregate of its members. Group behaviour is thus explained in terms of properties of the individuals that make up the group. Individuals may be motivated by rational considerations, social norms, or be 'driven' to behave in given ways by automatic, unconscious processes. Communication in this view increases cooperation rates by making individuals focus upon particular social norms, such as the norm of promise keeping. A holistic perspective instead views the group as a primitive, distinct explanatory unit. Group membership has important cognitive consequences as to how we perceive ourselves and others, how we process and filter information and how we represent other collectives. Thinking of oneself as a group member causes major shifts in motives and behaviour. A basic tenet of social identity theory is that individuals incorporate groups into their self-concepts, and this internalization precipitates motivational changes, so that often behaviour contrary to self-interest is activated. As far as I know, few have tried to merge the two perspectives.[4] It is entirely possible, however, to view group identity as a trigger for norm-abiding behaviour. When we represent a collection of individuals as a group, we immediately retrieve from memory roles and scripts that 'fit' the particular situation, and have a tendency to follow the appropriate social norms.[5] Notice, however, that though group identity can be a motivating force, it does not seem to be able to elicit cooperative behaviour unless it triggers a pre-existing norm. I shall return to this important point later.

5.2   Group identity

Dawes, Orbell, and van de Kragt are among the leading proponents of the social identity explanation of cooperation in social dilemmas. They reasoned that if individuals incorporate groups into their self-concept, a motivational shift would occur, and group welfare would matter more than individual welfare. Orbell et al. (1988) detail two experiments designed to investigate the role of discussion in increasing cooperation rates via a group identity effect. During each session, multiple groups of 14 subjects were randomly divided into subgroups of seven persons each; afterwards, they went to separate rooms. Each subject was given a promissory note worth $6, which he could keep or give away. If they chose to give the money away, six other subjects would each receive $2. If everyone cooperated, each would get $12. In half of the subgroups, subjects were told that contributions benefited six out-group members, whereas in the remaining half, subjects were told that contributions benefited the other six in-group members. Half of the subgroups could discuss the dilemma for ten minutes before playing. At the end of the discussion period, half of the subgroups who were allowed to discuss were informed that the beneficiaries of their contribution had changed. If subjects were originally told that their contributions would benefit the in-group, they were now told that the out-group would receive the money, and vice versa. All experimental discussions were taped, and I shall later examine them to argue that it is not group identity, but norms of promise-keeping, that explain the high rate of cooperation after a period of discussion.

Subjects contributed much more when both the dilemma was discussed and they initially believed that their contribution would go to the in-group, as Table 5.3 shows.

Since increases in cooperation rates were not uniform across conditions, but appeared only when discussion of the dilemma was allowed, the authors reject the hypothesis that general norms of cooperation motivate contribution. If a general norm of cooperation were at work – they argued – subjects would not have discriminated between groups (as they would not have cared about the recipients of their money). Their conclusion is questionable. If norms are interpreted as generic imperatives, always readily available and invariably followed by those who hold them, then of course Orbell et al. are right. But norms, as I state in Bicchieri (forthcoming), are context-specific, and subjects have to be focused on them. The choice to follow a norm is conditional upon one's beliefs about how many other people are following it and whether one is expected to follow it by a sufficient number of people (in the case of social norms). Discussion may reveal a general willingness to cooperate, and so change one's expectations about others' behaviour, but it may also reveal a potential discontent with non-cooperators, thus engendering normative expectations.[6] The effect of discussion on cooperation rates might precisely be due to the fact that discussing the dilemma often involves an exchange of pledges and promises, and the very act of promising focuses subjects on a norm of promise-keeping, as well as that it fosters expectations that a sufficient number of subjects will fulfill their promises.

Social norms can be thought of as default rules that are activated in the right circumstances.[7] More often than not the activation process is

	Initial belief that money goes to: in-group		Initial belief that money goes to: out-group	
	Belief at time of decision:		*Belief at time of decision:*	
	in-group	*out-group*	*in-group*	*out-group*
No discussion	37.5%	30.4%	44.6%	19.6%
Discussion	78.6%	58.9%	32.1%	30.4%

Table 5.3 Results of Orbell et al. (1988)

unconscious, it does not involve much thinking or even a choice on the part of subjects.[8] We may thus expect that, once a norm has been activated, it will show some inertia, in the sense that unless a major change in circumstances occurs, people will keep following the norm that has been primed. This absence of fine tuning might explain an interesting finding from this experiment: When a group initially believed themselves to be the beneficiaries of their contributions, but were subsequently told prior to their decision that the out-group would benefit instead, 58.9 per cent still cooperated. This carry-over effect of discussion suggests that cooperation results from the activation of a norm of promise-keeping. Such norm would only become salient in the context of in-group giving but, once activated, would show some inertia and still be followed even if the beneficiaries have changed. If instead the commitments and pledges exchanged during the discussion period were just contracts with particular people (the in-group), then knowing that the money will go to the out-group should decrease cooperation rates. Identification with one's own group may encourage cooperative behaviour, but once it becomes apparent that the money would go to the out-group, the motivation to give should disappear.

There is some other indirect evidence supporting a norm-based explanation. The carry-over effect is also present in a very different experiment by Isaac and Walker (1988). In it subjects played a two-period game with ten trials per period. The experiment had three conditions: (1) no discussion in either period; (2) no discussion in period one, but discussion in period two; (3) discussion in period one, but not in period two. The results were as follows: In condition (1), cooperation in period one started at 50 per cent but then declined to 10 per cent. In period two it started at 40 per cent and then declined to zero. In condition (2), cooperation in period one went from an initial 50 per cent to 10 per cent. In period two, it started at 60 per cent and then went to 90 per cent. In condition (3), cooperation remained close to 100 per cent in period one. There was a carry-over effect in the second period (no discussion), since cooperation started at 100 per cent but eventually decreased to 85 per cent. These data seem to indicate that groups quickly agreed on a behavioural norm, which was then adhered to through the trials. In condition (1), for example, subjects observed their partners' behaviour and could then form empirical expectations about their future behaviour. A descriptive norm (defined in Appendix A2) favouring defection quickly emerged and stabilized in both periods. In condition (2), the descriptive norm that emerged in period one was initially 'carried over' into the second period of interaction: Low rates of cooperation carried over into the second period, and cooperation only increased towards the end of the next ten trials. A plausible explanation is that, initially, there might have been some conflict between the previously established descriptive norm and a social norm of cooperation that people focused on through discussion. But inertia, and anchoring to previously established behaviour, were eventually taken over (if slowly) by the agreed upon cooperative behaviour. In condition (3), discussion in period one immediately induced full cooperation. Discussion, I want to suggest, focused subjects on socially desirable behaviour, and induced both empirical and normative expectations of compliance. Interestingly, such expectations stayed high also in the second period, where no discussion occurred, and transgressions were not enough to significantly bring down cooperation levels. These results are in line with my hypothesis about the relative strength and stability of social norms, as opposed to descriptive norms. Whereas a 'good' descriptive norm is vulnerable to small threshold effects, in that few defections lead to the norm's decline (as exemplified in the outcome of condition (1), where cooperation is quickly taken over by defection), a 'bad' descriptive norm is harder to displace. In the first case, it takes a few defectors to tilt the cost/benefit balance of cooperation in favour of costs, whereas in the second case it takes a large number of cooperators to tilt the balance in favour of benefits. When a 'bad' descriptive norm is in place, an effective way to eliminate it is to focus people on beneficial social norms, and this is precisely what the initial discussion period did. As the results of condition (3) exemplify, even in the presence of defections (in period two) normative expectations will stay high. As I will discuss later (and my definition of social norms makes clear), people need not expect universal compliance in order to follow a norm: what matters to them is the belief that enough people comply, where 'enough' may vary from person to person.

The purpose of the second experiment by Orbell et al. (1988) was to clarify the relationship between promise-making and cooperation. This time all groups of 14 subjects participated in an initial discussion of the dilemma. Afterwards they were divided into subgroups of seven as in the first experiment. Half of the subgroups were allowed to discuss the dilemma for another ten minutes. Subjects could make one of three possible choices: They could keep their $5; they could give it to their in-group, in which case the other six members would each receive $2; they could give it to the out-group, in which case all seven out-group members would receive $3 each. Since the initial discussion took place before each group of 14 subjects was split into two subgroups, and the best choice for the whole group of 14 was to give to the out-group, promises to cooperate were exchanged among all the participants, with the understanding that – once they were split into two subgroups – the money would go to the out-group. To investigate the relationship between promise-making and cooperation, the experimenters stratified groups into three categories: (1) groups in which everyone promised to cooperate with the out-group; (2) groups in which some promised to cooperate with the out-group and others didn't; (3) groups in which subjects decided to make their own independent choices. In more than half of the groups there was unanimous promising, and in that case 84 per cent cooperated with the out-group. Without universal promising, cooperation was a meager 58 per cent.

Though this second experiment led Orbell et al. to reject the hypothesis that higher rates of cooperation occurring after discussion are due to generic norms of cooperation, one cannot exclude the possibility that more specific norms are at work. The data indicate that individuals are more likely to cooperate when everyone in the group promises to cooperate, that is, when a consensus on how to behave is reached and an informal social contract is established. But, one might argue, if a specific norm of promise-keeping is responsible for cooperative behaviour, we should observe a linear relationship between the number of subjects who promise and the number of cooperators in each group, and no such relationship is shown by the data. This objection presupposes that the norm of promise-keeping is a personal (and almost unconditional) norm, since in the absence of external sanctions of any kind (choices are one-shot and anonymous) only a personal system of values would have sufficient motivational power to induce subjects to cooperate. Then if discussion is allowed and promises to cooperate are exchanged, those who promised should fulfil their obligations irrespective of how many others in the group promised. If the data show otherwise, cooperation cannot be imputed to the working of personal norms.[9]

The above-mentioned objection presupposes an unduly restrictive view of how norms work. People may not have a personal norm prescribing a given behaviour, yet they may display that behaviour if a social norm encouraging it is made salient (Cialdini et al., 1990).[10] Not unlike Cialdini's littering experiments, unanimous promising points to a consensually held norm. Subjects are faced with both a descriptive norm ('everybody will cooperate') and a social norm ('keeping one's promise to cooperate is the appropriate thing to do'), and will thus be prompted to conform. In fact, my definition of social norms can explain why, in a group where only *some* promise to cooperate, the outcome may turn out to be dismal. A promise to perform a potentially costly action will be kept *if* it is expected that a substantial number of other group members will contribute to the socially desirable outcome. The evidence that some subjects did not promise makes one expect them to defect. Since norm-compliance is conditional upon expectations of others' compliance it may be that, unless a sufficiently high number of people openly commit to cooperate, cooperation will not occur. In this case, even those who promised may decide to defect.

Note that if unanimous promising prompts subjects to cooperate, less than unanimous promising may not necessarily induce complete defection. The data from Orbell et al. suggest that the rate of cooperation is not completely discontinuous, with high cooperation under unanimity and almost no cooperation otherwise. However, apart from the unanimity case, there seems to be no correlation between the number of promisors and subsequent cooperation. As I already mentioned, an individual will follow an existing norm if, among other things, she expects a *sufficient* number of people to follow it *and* she believes a sufficient number of people expect her to follow it. People, however, differ as to their thresholds for conformity. Someone may need 100 per cent promising to be induced to cooperate, whereas another may think that 50 per cent of the group exchanging pledges to cooperate is a sufficient number. Since each group is a composite of heterogeneous individuals, it is not surprising that no correlation is found between numbers of people promising and number of cooperators. Barring the case of unanimity, each group will differ in cooperation rates. This consideration, nonetheless, does not preclude a norm-based explanation of the effect of communication on cooperation rates. Orbell et al., however, maintain that discussion has an effect on cooperative behaviour mainly because it creates group identity. Though the data do not refute their hypothesis, there are several difficulties with it. For one, it is never independently tested and, as we shall see momentarily, the very concept of group identity needs clarification. Furthermore, an analysis of the taped discussions that occurred in Orbell, Dawes and van de Kragt's (1988) first experiment lends support to a norm-based explanation.

5.3   Cheap talk

Though each group had a unique personality and discussion style, there are common themes and concerns that arose in almost all groups, which provide insights into the causes of cooperation.[11] Many groups had leaders who dominated the discussion. They advocated a particular strategy and asked the rest of the group to concur. In the absence of group leaders, subjects found it difficult to reach an agreement, and often opted to end their discussion period early. Recall that in the first experiment discussion took place after the two subgroups were formed, and subjects had to choose whether to keep their money or, depending upon the experimental condition, to give it either to the in-group or the out-group. The content of these discussions is quite different, though, depending on whether the potential beneficiary of the money is the in-group or the out-group.

Groups sometimes wanted to talk with the out-group to check if they planned to cooperate. The implication seemed to be that – if they were to make a commitment – they would be considered more trustworthy. The question of whether to trust the out-group frequently arose, and those groups who initially thought of cooperating with the out-group were worried about being cheated by them. Many groups concluded that most out-group members would defect.[12] This conclusion was reached by projection: If we were in their place – it was argued – we would certainly defect. Group members evidently considered themselves to be a statistically representative sample; knowing their own propensity to defect led them to predict with some confidence the out-group behaviour. The predictability of the out-group's behaviour was grounded upon an expectation that they would behave 'normally', given the circumstances. Why would most groups consider defection on the part of the out-group a normal choice?

It seems that competitiveness, mistrust, discrimination and even aggression towards out-groups are deeply rooted attitudes, ready to emerge even in relatively neutral situations such as those encountered in experiments. In 1948, Sherif's Robber's Cave experiment, in which young boys selected for good psychological adjustment and sociability were separated into two rival groups, showed how quickly hostility and aggression can develop among groups that have no cultural or status differences between them. Tajfel's 'minimal group paradigm' (1973) is even more disturbing, as it shows how the mere grouping of individuals on the basis of arbitrary category differences is sufficient to produce group behaviour. In-group favouritism, group loyalty, and a preference for group members are common effects of arbitrary categorization, as is the tendency to exaggerate the similarities with the in-group and the differences with the out-group. Note that these effects occur in situations in which subjects know almost nothing about other group members, apart from the fact that they all share a common group membership. For example, one may just know that one's group is made of 'overestimators of dots' as opposed to another group of 'underestimators of dots' (after having quickly judged how many dots there are on a wall screen).[13]

Precisely when there is only limited personal information on other subjects, categorization alone can generate impersonal attraction (or preference) for the other group members, as well as a sense of cohesion. This is a particularly interesting observation, since it has been commonly assumed that group cohesiveness is linked to the degree of personal attraction among group members, as well as to how well the group satisfies individual needs. According to Tajfel's theory, group behaviour is ultimately induced by a cognitive effect. The moment we think of ourselves as members of a group, however randomly determined, our perceptions and motives change. We start perceiving ourselves and our fellow group members along impersonal, 'typical' dimensions that characterize the group to which we belong. The generic attraction felt for in-group members is precisely this sense of being similar in those dimensions that make us a group and not an unrelated set of individuals. In well-established ethnic, gender, or professional-based groups, there will be a shared understanding of what the similar traits are. But it is remarkable that even in newly formed and anonymous groups subjects tend to believe that in-group members are more similar to them than out-group members along a series of broad traits, in the absence of any evidence supporting this assumption. If no well-established similarities are accessible, some similarity will nevertheless be presumed. Generic attraction, again, is brought forth by perceived (or presumed) similarity, and both seem to be a consequence of group formation rather than its cause. When more personal information is available, however, for example due to a longer period of interaction, attraction becomes less impersonal and group behaviour is less likely to occur.

Negative and positive stereotyping is the result of our quick, almost unconscious mental habits of categorizing people and groups. A stereotype is nothing but the prototypical description of what members of a given category are (or are believed to be). It is a cluster of physical, mental and psychological characteristics attributed to a 'typical' member of a given group. Stereotyping, like any other categorization process, activates scripts or schemata, and what we call group behaviour is nothing but scripted behaviour. For example, interpreting a situation as 'we' versus 'them', as it frequently occurs even in the minimal group paradigm studied by Tajfel, may activate interactive scripts that contain norms such as 'take care of one's own', which could explain the preferential treatment accorded to in-group members.[14] In one-shot social dilemma experiments, where exposure to one's or another group is minimal, we should observe uncontaminated, basic group behaviour such as loyalty and cooperation with one's group and mistrust and hostility toward the out-group. Indeed, in 'two groups social dilemmas' (Bornstein, 1992) subjects tended to support their own group, to the detriment of the other group and ultimately of themselves.

In the taped discussions of the Orbell et al. experiments, when subjects were discussing with members of their group and in situations in which in-groups benefited from their own decisions, commitments to cooperate with the in-group were frequently made. This choice was often seen as a gamble, and as such involving risk. Discussion probably decreased the perceived risk of a monetary loss, and this did not happen just because one was able to assess the trustworthiness of other members by looking at their facial expressions and body language. An important reason why cooperation was perceived as less risky was the exchange of pledges and commitments that took place during discussion. Such commitments are, in economic parlance, just 'cheap talk'. In a one-shot interaction, given the assurance of anonymity, the temptation to defect is strong. In the absence of a binding mechanism, it may be to one's advantage to make a public pledge to cooperate, but then defect in private. Commitments and promises to the in-group, however, were generally trusted. Is this an effect of categorization alone, or is it mediated by some implicit normative implication produced by categorization? We must not think of an experiment as an isolated, unique situation. Many times, in the course of our lives, we made promises to people we know, to members of one group or another to which we belong. We usually keep our promises, and expect others to keep theirs. The experimental circumstances are similar, in several respects, to many real life situations subjects have experienced.[15] Categorizing a situation as 'we' versus 'them' is bound to activate well-rehearsed scripts about in-group loyalty and trust. If, as I claim elsewhere, norms are embedded into scripts, the categorization process will lead one to think one 'ought to' trust in-group members and, if promises are made, trust that they will be kept.

Precisely because they do not know the other group members well, and have only limited exposure to them, subjects are free to categorize their interaction as typical. In a typical group interaction, one would trust and cooperate with members of one's own group. The default presumption is that they will not cheat on us, that they will be nice and helpful. This may be the reason why betrayal by an acquaintance is much more devastating than betrayal by a stranger. We do not expect the first to occur. Thaler (1992) noted that well-established groups are often less cooperative than newly formed ones. If group identity were the ultimate cause of cooperation, we would expect much higher rates of cooperation in established groups. What may happen instead is that, after an initial period in which a newly formed group adopts cooperative norms by default, 'deviant' behaviour may lead members to reconsider the context of interaction and their understanding of the situation, and possibly reach the conclusion that the dominant descriptive norm is to defect. Similarly, in repeated social dilemma trials with no communication it has been observed that cooperation rates are high in the initial periods, and then steadily decline over trials. This pattern is probably due to the fact that subjects are initially uncertain as to what constitutes appropriate behaviour. Hence they rely on default social norms they deem appropriate to the situation. If, as trials continue, some group members defect, cooperators will revise their expectations and start defecting, too.

Another belief shared by many subjects was that cooperating with the in-group was not that risky.[16] When *all* group members committed to cooperate, some subjects held the belief that at least half of them would keep their word. In this case, a cooperator would not lose her money. Many were even more optimistic, and voiced the belief that more than half of those promising to cooperate would keep their word. Notice that subjects did not naively expect everyone to keep their promise; rather, they realistically expected *most* people to keep their commitments most of the time. Subjects were focused on a shared norm of promise-keeping, and unanimous promising was likely encouraging them to believe that enough other people were keeping their promises, making it worthwhile to follow the norm.[17] Unanimity therefore should not be interpreted as fostering the expectation of universal compliance, nor as an indication that everybody 'buys into the cooperative solution', thereby creating an obligation on the part of the promisor.[18] Note that unanimous promising also signals that there is a consensus on the appropriateness of cooperation, and that the group is highly cohesive in its judgment. This high cohesiveness might in itself be sufficient to create strong conformity pressures.

5.4 Creating identities

When it is suggested that solutions to social dilemmas may be facilitated by exploiting the solidarity and bonding arising from a shared group identity (Brewer, 1979), a big open question remains to be answered. How can we arouse group identification in such a way that group interest is promoted? For the proponents of the social identity explanation, inducing a salient group identity will cause a blurring of the boundaries between personal and group welfare, a change in preferences and perception that is ultimately responsible for the increased rate of cooperation we witness after discussion of the dilemma. It is therefore important to know what makes group identity salient not just in an experimental context, but especially in the large, anonymous groups that are a common setting for social dilemmas.

There are some minimal conditions for a collection of individuals to constitute a psychological group – a state of affairs where they feel to be a group and act as one. A prominent traditional theory defines a psychological group as a collection of individuals characterized by mutual attraction, reflecting the members' interdependence and mutual need-satisfaction. This definition is severely limited, though, since it applies only to small groups, whereas some of our most important group memberships refer to large-scale social affiliations such as nationality, gender, race, religion, and so on. Members of a nation are not usually united around a single common goal, they interact only with small subsets of people and not always amicably, and obey different norms depending upon the organizations and subcultures to which they belong. National membership is not usually chosen, we are born into it, and the moments in which we are most likely to feel psychological membership are not ones in which our individual needs are satisfied. Indeed, our loyalty to our nation may be fiercest in circumstances, such as a war, that require sacrifice and deprivation. Similarly, the fact that some groups of people are treated in a homogeneous way by others due to the colour of their skin, religious background or otherwise, may give them a sense that they belong to a group, even if the grouping is not the result of their choice and membership into the group may involve discrimination and abuse by the rest of society. It is often reported that during the Nazi period, many German Jews felt for the first time an identification with their fellow Jews. They had been completely integrated and considered themselves to be Germans first and foremost, but finding themselves associated with other European Jews in a common fate gave them, for the first time, a sense of their separate identity.

It is the realization that there can be psychological group membership without interdependence, need satisfaction, personal attraction, social structure or common norms and values that led Tajfel, and later Turner and Brewer, to design experiments in the context of the 'minimal group paradigm'. In these experiments, people were divided into distinct groups on the basis of meaningless criteria (such as estimation of the number of dots on a screen), group membership was anonymous and there were no group goals or any apparent link between group membership and self-interest. I discussed some of these experiments elsewhere, observing how individuals systematically discriminate in favour of in-group and against out-group members.[19] The data collected by Tajfel and his colleagues imply that group behaviour and group membership can exist in the absence of any social contact, social structure or interdependence between members. It was concluded that the minimal (sufficient) condition for psychological group formation is the recognition and acceptance of some self-defining social categorization. Social interaction, common fate, proximity, similarity, common goals or shared threats are not necessary for group formation, even if they usually increase the cohesiveness of an existing group. It is an open question whether they can be sufficient conditions for group formation, in the absence of an explicit categorization of people into groups. Presumably the answer will lie in assessing how efficiently and under which conditions such variables function as cues to the formation of social categorizations.

Group behaviour, as opposed to individual behaviour, is characterized by distinctive features such as perceived similarity between group members, cohesiveness, the tendency to cooperate to achieve common goals, shared attitudes and beliefs and conformity to group norms. If social categorization is sufficient for group formation, by which mechanisms does it produce group behaviour? According to Turner's 'self-categorization theory' (1987), group behaviour depends upon the effects of social categorization on the definition and perception of the self. Self-perception, or self-definition, is defined as a system of cognitive self-schemata that filter and process information, and output a representation of the social situation that guides the choice of appropriate behaviour. This system has at least two major components, social and personal identity. Social identity refers to self-descriptions related to group memberships. Personal identity refers to more personal self-descriptions, such as individual character traits, abilities and tastes.

Though personal and social identity are mutually exclusive levels of self-definition, this distinction must be taken as an approximation. There are many interconnections between social and personal identity, and even personal identity has a social component. It is, however, important to recognize that sometimes we perceive ourselves primarily in terms of our relevant group memberships rather than as differentiated, unique individuals. Depending on the situation, personal or group identity will become salient.[20] For example, when one makes interpersonal comparisons between self and other group members, personal identity will become salient, whereas group identity will be salient in situations in which one's group is compared to another group. Within a group, all those factors that lead members to categorize themselves as different and endowed with special characteristics and traits are enhancing personal identity. If a group is solving a common task, but each member will be rewarded according to his contribution, personal abilities are highlighted and individuals will perceive themselves as unique and different from the rest of the group. Conversely, if the reward for a jointly performed task is equally shared by all group members, group identification is going to be enhanced. When the difference between self and fellow group members is accentuated, we are likely to observe selfish motives and self-favouritism against other group members. When instead group identification is enhanced, in-group favouritism against out-group members will be activated, as well as behaviour contrary to self-interest.

According to Turner, social identity is basically a cognitive mechanism whose adaptive function is to make group behaviour possible. Whenever social identification becomes salient, a cognitive mechanism of categorization is activated that produces perceptual and behavioural changes. For example, the category 'Asian student' is associated with a cluster of behaviours, personality traits and values. We often think of Asian students as respectful, diligent, disciplined, and especially good with technical subjects. When thinking of an Asian student solely in terms of her group membership, we attribute her the stereotypical characteristics associated with her group, so she becomes interchangeable with other group members. When we perceive people in terms of stereotypes, we depersonalize them and see them as 'typical' members of their group. The same process is at work when we perceive ourselves as group members. Self-stereotyping is a cognitive shift from perceiving oneself as unique and differentiated to perceiving oneself in terms of the attributes that characterize the group. It is this cognitive shift that mediates group behaviour.

The feature of group behaviour most relevant to social dilemma experiments is the tendency to cooperate with the in-group even when such behaviour is contrary to self-interest. Through common group membership, individuals share the same self-stereotypes, and perceive themselves as 'depersonalized' and similar to other group members in the stereotypical dimensions linked to the relevant social categorization. Insofar as group members perceive their interests and goals as identical – because such interests and goals are stereotypical attributes of the group – self-stereotyping will induce a group member to embrace such interests and goals as his own, and act to further them. The dark side of this process is the shared perception of group members that their interests are in conflict with those of other groups or of unaffiliated individuals. A prediction of social identity theory is thus that the more salient group membership becomes, the greater will be the tendency to display cooperative behaviour toward the in-group and discrimination against out-groups.

How can group identification be aroused in social dilemmas in such a way that cooperation is promoted? In a multi-trial commons dilemma, Kramer and Brewer (1984) showed that subgroup categorization of a six person group decreased cooperation when compared with a condition in which the group was not subdivided.[21] Kramer and Brewer interpreted the result as an instance of in-group favouritism and in-group/out-group competition: the defectors in the subgroup categorization condition wanted to gain as much as possible for their own subgroup in comparison with the other subgroup. However, if we examine the payoff structure it appears that the benefits of defection accrued only to the individual, not the subgroup, whereas the costs of defecting were spread out over the whole group. The choice was thus either to serve one's private interest (to defect) or to serve the interest of the whole six-person group (to cooperate). There was no possibility to differentially benefit one's own subgroup. Also, from the additional results of a questionnaire that was filled after the experiment, it appears that categorization manipulation did not affect subjects' perceptions of the fellow subgroup members and of the members of the other subgroup, contrary to the prediction of social identity theory. However, since subjects received feedback about the other group members' choices after each trial, they may have used this information in their post-trial perception ratings of the other group members, thus mitigating the effects of the induced categorization.

In a subsequent series of experiments, Brewer and Kramer (1986) showed that when the subgroup identity was made salient, and subjects received a feedback suggesting the existence of a descriptive group norm (the group could be made of 'high users', who took large amounts of common resources, or 'low users' who took small amounts), they tended to follow the group norm. When instead a collective identity was made salient, and it was clear that resources were rapidly dwindling, individuals belonging to groups of 'high users' restrained themselves most. It is not clear, however, that this behaviour results from group identification. Subsequent analysis of subjects' expectations of other group members' behaviour revealed no effect of categorization, nor was an in-group bias apparent from the data. The abandonment of the 'high use' subgroup norm in the superordinate identity condition may be due to a perceived conflict between a descriptive subgroup norm and an opposite social norm prescribing restraint. The superordinate identity could have made the social norm salient, and we know from the work of Cialdini et al. (1990) that when there is a conflict between these two kinds of norms, and the social norm is made salient, people tend to follow the latter. The identity manipulation in this case would have mediated the effect of a cooperative social norm (mandating restraint) through the cognitive salience of group membership.

In a typical social dilemma experiment, there is no imposed or suggested categorization on the part of the experimenter. Subjects do not know each other and, in one-shot experiments, do not expect to play or meet again. The minimal group paradigm was successful in producing group behaviour because it created an explicit in-group/out-group categorization that, even in the absence of conflicting interests, induced in-group favouritism. In a typical social dilemma, however, the choice is between favouring oneself and favouring the group. We know that the mere realization that universal cooperation is in the group's interest does not induce cooperative behaviour, but the social identity hypothesis predicts that making group membership salient will induce a cooperative orientation. Common fate, perceived similarities and verbal interactions, among other things, should contribute to the process of perceptual group formation, inducing people to categorize themselves as part of a more inclusive unit. We would expect a period of discussion, especially on a theme close to the subjects' lives, to engender cooperative behaviour, as would the experience of sharing a common fate. There is no apparent reason to expect discussion of the dilemma to be more efficacious than relevant discussion per se, or the experience of a common fate.

5.5 Keeping promises

There is now a handful of experiments aimed at directly testing the group identity hypothesis in social dilemmas. None of them explicitly considers the possibility that social norms are responsible for the increase in cooperation rates observed after a period of discussion of the dilemma, though the data can be interpreted as supporting a norm-based explanation. Since the behavioural effects of group identity might be indistinguishable from the effects of other variables, such as perceived consensus or commitment, these studies introduced an independent measurement of group identity, defined as a sense of belonging or a feeling of membership in a group.

Kerr and Kaufman-Gilliland (1994) used *self-efficacy* as a variable to differentiate between group identity and commitment explanations of the effect of communication on cooperation rates. They proposed a distinction between cooperation-contingent remedies and public-good remedies. The former increase the value one puts on the cooperative choice; they include side-payments, sanctions, and feelings like pride and guilt. The latter increase the value one puts on the group's welfare, and they include altruism and enhanced group identity. They reasoned that if cooperation was motivated by a public good remedy, then as the efficacy of one's contribution declines, it becomes less likely that one cooperates. Since the group identity explanation of the effects of discussion assumes that communication works by increasing the value one puts on group welfare, discussion is a public good remedy. Hence whenever it is evident that one's action is less efficacious, discussion should not be expected to matter much to one's choice. An explanation based on commitments instead assumes that discussion increases the value of the committed choice itself. Hence efficacy of one's action should not matter: committed subjects would cooperate no matter what.

The experiment consisted of groups of five subjects playing an 'investment game'. Each player was given $10 and an allocation of points. In each play, 100 points would be randomly assigned among the five players. Each player only knew her share, but the larger one's share, the more effective one's choice would be in providing for the public good. If choosing to give, a player would donate $10 plus her allocated points. If 51 or more points were contributed to a step-level public good, then each group member would obtain $15. The game was to be played 16 times, and half of the subjects were allowed a period of discussion before making their (anonymous) choices.[22] The discussion effect was replicated, with 74.2 per cent cooperation in groups that discussed, and only 56.8 per cent cooperation in groups in which no discussion was allowed. Cooperation, however, was stable across levels of efficacy, suggesting that the perception of personal significance in providing for the public good was not an important factor in the choice to contribute. As in other experiments, group discussion contained frequent promises to cooperate, and groups varied in the agreements they reached. Some groups achieved unanimous promising, and in those groups cooperation rates were highest and the minimal efficacy level at which subjects were willing to cooperate was lower than in other groups. Some groups agreed to conditionally cooperate depending on each subject's level of efficacy, and other groups decided instead that each individual would make his or her own independent choice.

Different groups thus seemed to develop their own norms, such as 'contribute only if you have a reasonable share' or 'contribute no matter what'. Yet there was no apparent difference in the respective levels of perceived group identity, as measured by Hinkle et al.'s (1989) Group Identity Scale. The conclusion drawn by the experimenters is that group identity is not a good explanation of discussion-induced cooperation. Commitments, and the norm of promise-keeping that supports them, are the most likely candidate. I must hasten to add that, though I sympathize with the conclusions, I find them too swift. The assumption that group identity entails the desire to enhance group welfare overlooks the possibility that many actions we take have also a 'symbolic' value. In some of Tajfel's experiments with allocations, if given the choice subjects tended to maximize the difference between in-group and out-group, and in so doing were ready to sacrifice their own group's welfare. For example, between an equal allocation of $10 to a member of each group and an allocation of $6 to a member of one's own group and $2 to an out-group member, many subjects would choose the second. It is a choice that penalizes both groups, but hurts the out-group more. If actions have a symbolic value for the actor, she might perform them irrespective of their efficacy.

A better way to test the group identity hypothesis is to check whether several presumably equivalent ways to create or enhance group identity produce the same results in terms of cooperation. The group identity explanation predicts that *any* manipulation arousing group identity will be sufficient to induce cooperation. Bouas and Komorita (1996) ran a series of experiments to test whether discussion or common fate would have an effect on cooperation rates. If discussion of the dilemma has an effect on cooperation, but discussion of an irrelevant topic has no effect (Dawes et al., 1977), we cannot rule out the group identity explanation, since an insignificant discussion topic may not be sufficient to elicit group identity. Discussing a relevant issue, such as an increase in students' tuition when the experimental subjects are college students, should instead create a bond among them, as this topic touches their lives and they can sympathize with each other's concerns. Another way to induce group identity is common fate. Common fate may not involve a common objective or shared needs. It may simply mean that certain categories of people are treated in a homogeneous manner by others on the basis of their sex, colour of skin, language, and many other attributes. And it may be as tenuous as participating to a lottery that will determine the monetary worth of the points owned by each subject. Though participating to a common lottery does not strike me as a strong inducement to social identity formation, there is some evidence about its effects on cooperation rates (Kramer and Brewer, 1984; 1986).

The alternative explanation of discussion-induced cooperation that Bouas and Komorita favour is not one based on norms. In their view, discussion has an effect because it creates consensus, and consequently reduces risk and fosters the expectation that other group members will cooperate. Since the only discussion that can create a meaningful consensus is discussion about the dilemma, the perceived consensus explanation predicts that only discussion of the dilemma will increase cooperation rates. To compare the different predictions generated by the social identity and the perceived consensus explanations, it is helpful to draw the following Tables, 5.4 and 5.5.

The experiment consisted of groups of four subjects facing a typical social dilemma and had of four conditions. A control condition in which there was no discussion nor common fate manipulation. A second condition in

	Common fate	*No common fate*
Control condition	–	defect
No discussion	cooperate	defect
Discussion of relevant topic	cooperate	cooperate
Discussion of dilemma cooperate	cooperate	cooperate

Table 5.4 Group identity prediction

which subjects were allowed to discuss a relevant issue and were then exposed to a common fate manipulation. A third condition in which the dilemma was discussed and common fate was present. Finally, a common fate condition in which no discussion was allowed. In the common fate manipulation, subjects' payoffs were determined by the result of a lottery. In this experiment, too, group identity was independently measured through Hinkle et al.'s Group Identity Scale, after the decisions were taken. Consensus perception and expectations of group members' cooperation were also independently measured. The results are reported in Table 5.6.

Whereas 81 per cent of subjects involved in discussion of the dilemma and common fate cooperated, only 17 per cent did so after discussing a relevant issue (an increase in tuition), and common fate manipulation alone did not even raise cooperation rates above baseline. Group identity, however, was higher in both discussion conditions, while common fate had no effect on group identity. What seemed to matter was perceived consensus, which was highest under discussion of the dilemma, but was also quite high in the relevant discussion condition. These results led Bouas and Komorita to reject the group identity explanation.

A few comments on common fate and the effect of perceived consensus are in order. Common fate is introduced here as a chance event (a lottery). As such, it has no effect on cooperation rates. However, Kramer and Brewer (1984) claimed that common fate induces group identity when such identity is superimposed on a pre-existing subgroup identity. In this case, they show that common fate is in fact salient. If there is no prior group identity, perhaps the notion of common fate has to be strengthened to do its job. For example, it would be interesting to see what happens if common fate were to

	Common fate	No common fate
Control condition	–	defect
No discussion	defect	defect
Discussion of relevant topic	defect	defect
Discussion of dilemma cooperate	cooperate	cooperate

Table 5.5   Perceived consensus prediction

	Control	Common fate	Discussion	Discussion of dilemma
Mean cooperation	.13	.13	.17	.81
Group identity[23]	5.1	5.1	6.1	6.3
Consensus perception	2.25	2.40	5.45	6.65
Expected cooperation	1.05	1.20	1.25	2.47

Table 5.6   Results of Bouas and Komorita (1996)

entail interdependence among the parties, as when subjects are involved in a common task, however briefly, before the social dilemma experiment proper. Perceived consensus increased after discussing the dilemma, but it was also high when another relevant topic was discussed. Note that consensus is weaker than universal promising, in that it does not require unanimous agreement and does not elicit normative expectations. Bouas and Komorita argue that perceived consensus is what causes greater expectations of cooperative behaviour, hence it presumably lowers the risk of losing money. However, since discussion of the dilemma often entails promises to cooperate, we cannot rule out as an explanation of risk reduction the expectation that others will keep their commitments because of a shared norm of promise-keeping. If norms were responsible for the increase in cooperation rates we observe after a period of discussion of the dilemma, the prediction of a norm-based explanation would be like the one in Table 5.5. Since this prediction is fulfilled, we cannot exclude that it is norms, and not just perceived consensus, that cause higher cooperation rates. Moreover, perceived consensus in not in conflict with a norm-based explanation. Discussion of the dilemma, with the intervening exchange of promises and pledges, can trigger both a descriptive norm (we are all going to contribute) and a social norm (one should keep one's word). What is perceived is that the group reached a consensus on what the appropriate course of action should be. Reaching a consensus on, say, how unfair an increase in university tuition is does not increase cooperation rates. I want to add that consensus, in my view, may only be useful in focusing people on a descriptive norm, when one exists, or may even create one, but would not be strong enough to focus them on a social norm. Suppose a group of people were to discuss whether cooperation is better than defection in a public goods dilemma, and agree that cooperation is better, or even that cooperation is the most frequent behaviour. However, no pledges or promises are exchanged. In this case, people would be focused on a descriptive norm, but there would be no incentive to follow it, and expecting others to cooperate might tempt an individual to defect.[24] Now, if we allow promising, group members may not only agree on a course of action, but actively promise each other to follow it. The promise indicates a willingness to perform a potentially costly action, a commitment to forgo narrow self-interest in favour of a collective gain. Individuals are now focused on a social norm. But for promise-keeping to be effective, we know that it must be supported by the expectation that enough people are going to keep their promises. Bouas and Komorita do not tell us how many people promised but, since consensus and expectations were pretty high, I suspect promising was widespread. In conclusion, if consensus alone is not sufficient to motivate giving to the group, it must be that the norms activated during discussion are responsible for the perception of reduced risk that accompanies the expectation of cooperative behaviour on the part of other group members.

5.6   Talking to machines

Sometimes support for an hypothesis is found in unexpected places. The norm-based explanation I favour says that norms are like default rules that are triggered in the right circumstances but not otherwise. Since this process is largely unconscious, we do not expect individuals to be very discriminating or strategically oriented in their norm-following behaviour.[25] Whenever a norm is made salient by the situation one is in, the first reaction is to follow the norm, unless something unexpected occurs that forces reconsideration and possibly reinterpretation of the situation. The field of human-computer interaction is particularly interesting in this respect since it studies, among other things, the reactions people have to various kind of computer interfaces and the rules, if any, that people adopt in interacting with computers.

Kiesler, Sproull and Waters (1996) examined human-computer interaction in a social dilemma experiment. Subjects were presented with an 'investment game', which was in fact a common Prisoner's Dilemma in which the choice to cooperate was dubbed 'project green', and the choice to defect was dubbed 'project blue', in order to devoid choices of any evaluative undertone. Subjects played six rounds against one of the following types of partners: a human confederate, a computer who communicated through written text, a computer who communicated with speech, and a computer who communicated with a synthesized face and speech. Subjects knew whether the partner was a human or a computer.

The partner used the same strategy across conditions:

round 1: the partner asks the subject to make a proposal, and then cooperates
round 2: the partner proposes cooperation and then cooperates
round 3: there is no discussion and the partner cooperates
round 4: the partner asks the subject to make a proposal and then defects
round 5: the partner proposes cooperation and then cooperates
round 6: there is no discussion and the partner defects

After each round, the choices of the players were revealed.

The results are surprising, since they show that discussion and commitment have a strong effect on cooperation, regardless of the nature of the discussion partner.[26] In the first round, 80 per cent of the subjects proposed cooperation to the human confederate, and 94 per cent of them kept their commitment. In the same round, 59 per cent of the subjects proposed cooperation to the computer, and 62 per cent of them kept their commitment. Cooperation was consistently high in rounds 1, 2, 4 and 5, that is, when there was discussion with the partner. Even in round 5, after observing a defection in the preceding round, subjects were willing to cooperate with a partner who proposed cooperation. Evidently they trusted their partner's willingness to cooperate despite their previous experience, and this occurred even if the partner was a computer. In this case, discussion had the effect of discounting previous defection. In rounds 3 and 6, there was a sharp drop in cooperation under all conditions; these were the rounds in which there was no communication, hence no commitment to cooperate.

If group identity were elicited through discussion, we would not have observed a drop in cooperation in round 3, since previous discussion and commitments to cooperate should have carried over to this round. At the very least, we should have not observed a drop in cooperation with the human confederate, since identification with a computer may be harder than with another human being. The results offer a strong support for the hypothesis that discussion enhances cooperation rates because of its content: promises to cooperate are made, and subsequently kept. Individuals seem to adopt the same social rules to interact with computers as they do with other human beings, which lends credibility to the view that we are witnessing the operation of default social rules, which are made salient by situational cues pointing to a particular interpretation of the circumstances and hence to appropriate behaviour. If commitments are pledges to behave in accordance with the object of the commitment, regardless to whom the commitment is made, we can easily explain the former results. When a powerful norm of promise-keeping is made salient, most individuals will obey it, whether the promisee is another person or a machine.

5.7 Cognitive misers

To explain what happens in an experimental situation, and to assess the accuracy of the general conclusions we draw about behaviour in social dilemmas, it helps to briefly summarize the cognitive processes that result in a cooperative choice on the part of so many subjects.[27] The methods we use to make inferences are far from ideal. Social inference is heavily schema-driven, we disregard regression effects and base-rate information, and are prone to perceive illusory correlations. We store information in long-term memory and retrieve scripts/schemata to interpret and understand our environment, as well as to make inferences, explain and predict others' behaviour. Such schemata are cognitive structures that represent knowledge about people, events and the self. Most of the time, they work reasonably well, though they bias all aspects of information processing and inference towards conservative, schema-confirming inferential practices. To apply schematic knowledge, one first needs to be able to categorize the person or situation one encounters as fitting a particular schema/script.

When faced with an experimental setup, an individual will first search for cues to categorize, and thus interpret, the present situation as an instance of a well-known schema or script. The fact that the experimental situation is strange and unnatural, since choices are typically anonymous and there may be no prospect of future interaction, is overlooked in favour of an interpretation biased toward what we know well and have frequently experienced. When we retrieve a script (or a schema), it comes with expectations attached. Even if we do not have any information about the people we will be interacting with, our script tells us what to expect. For example, we know that in experiments in which subjects are given the choice to opt out, besides cooperating or defecting, cooperators typically decide to play and defectors instead opt out more frequently.[28] This happens because cooperators expect cooperation from their partners, and defectors instead expect defection. Frequent cooperators activate a cooperative script, which increases their confidence that they will encounter kindred spirits.

When faced with a new collection of individuals, this collection will be mentally compared to past groupings, and this comparison process will provide us with behavioural cues appropriate to the new situation. Categorizing a social situation as fitting a particular schema/script will typically elicit behavioural roles and norms. In similar, previously experienced contexts we had a role and expectations that we import into the new situation. As I already mentioned, interpreting a situation as 'we' versus 'them', as it frequently occurs even in the minimal group paradigm studied by Tajfel, may activate interactive scripts that contain norms such as 'take care of one's own', 'be loyal' and 'trust your group', which would explain the preferential treatment accorded to in-group members. Similarly, when a subject must choose between keeping the money or giving it to the in-group or the out-group, the way she represents the situation will influence her subsequent choice. Indeed, we know that expecting the out-group to benefit from one's contribution consistently dampens the impulse to give, whereas if it is the in-group who benefits from one's act of giving there is much more willingness to part with one's money.

Depending on how a situation is interpreted, different scripts and thus different norms will be activated. Since our interpretation and understanding of a situation will depend both on a frame of reference and on past experience, different people may interpret the same situation differently. I have discussed elsewhere how ambiguity may lead to self-serving biases in judgments of fairness.[29] In the case of social dilemmas in which discussion of the dilemma is allowed, discussion itself may perform a disambiguating role, shaping individuals' perception of the situation they face and allowing a uniform interpretation of the situation to emerge. Discussion of the dilemma may thus perform several functions, all of them important in increasing cooperation rates. When people face a new situation, they often turn to each other for cues as to how to interpret it. In this context, the role of a leader is substantial, since she provides an interpretation of the situation, or suggests a schema, that other group members can recognize as both familiar and relevant. Unanimous agreement on appropriate behaviour is usually reached only with the help of leaders, who are instrumental in lending salience to a particular descriptive norm (i.e. 'what is normally done' in such situations). A 'leader' in this case is simply a person who convincingly argues in favour of interpreting the current situation in a specific way. In the taped discussions we analyzed, leaderless groups were typically groups in which no common agreement emerged, and where subjects' behaviour was similar to the behaviour of control groups, where no discussion was allowed.

Yet discussion also involves promises, and the act of promising has the effect of focusing people on the social norm of promise-keeping by representing the situation as an instance of situations we have experienced in the past, when we made commitments we usually honoured and expected others to do likewise. As I already mentioned, promises will be kept (and thus the norm followed) if subjects believe that a sufficiently high number of other subjects will keep their promises, and also believe that a sufficiently high number of subjects expect them to fulfil their commitment. Unanimous promising generates precisely that expectation, as well as the belief that a sufficient number of subjects expect promises to be kept, and strongly disapprove of betrayals.[30]

Note that discussion of the dilemma, when successful, points to several norms at once: a descriptive cooperative norm that might come to be perceived as prescriptive, or 'the right thing to do', and a social norm of promise-keeping. Disentangling their respective effects on behaviour is very difficult, and we will have to wait for further experiments to provide answers. We already have, however, some scattered evidence hinting at the consequences of making descriptive norms salient in social dilemmas. Schroeder et al. (1983), for example, investigated the effects of observing the behaviour of others in simulated social dilemmas. They found that subjects quickly conformed to the behaviour of the observed players, regardless of whether it was cooperation or defection. Pillutla and Chen (1997) found similar results in a study on the effects of context (economic or noneconomic) and feedback on cooperative behaviour. Information about the other members' behaviour was the sole variable influencing cooperation rates. Similarly, Allison and Kerr (1994) found that individuals behaved consistently with the perceived group norm, which was inferred from information about past group performance. These data are interesting since they contradict some other results that indicate how viewing or listening to other groups' taped pledges to cooperate had no effect on cooperation rates. One wonders whether the positive effect reported in the former studies was due to the fact that subjects observed the behaviour of *their own* group members. If so, individuals were conforming to what they perceived as a descriptive norm, or the 'normal' behaviour of their group. Unanimous promising may play the same role as observing past behaviour, indicating the group's convergence on a behavioural rule. Since conformity to norms is correlated with the perceived cohesiveness of the group, it should come as no surprise that only under unanimous promising we observe almost universal cooperation.

Is an explanation in terms of norms incompatible with the social identity hypothesis? According to social identity theory, self-categorization entails perceiving oneself in terms of the group prototype and behaving in accordance with that. Though norms may regulate group members' behaviour without being considered specific to the group, often groups develop their own special behavioural norms. In that case, group members believe that certain patterns of behaviour are unique to them, and use their distinctive norms to define group membership. Many close-knit groups, such as the Amish or the Hasidic Jews, enforce norms of separation proscribing marriage and intimate relationships with outsiders, as well as specific dress codes and a host of other prescriptive and proscriptive norms that make the group unique and differentiate it from out-groups.

Hogg and Turner (1987) called the process through which individuals come to conform to group norms *referent informational influence*. Group-specific norms have, among other things, the twofold function of minimizing perceived differences among group members and maximizing differences between the group and outsiders. Once formed, such norms are internalized as cognitive representations of appropriate behaviour as a group member. Social identity is built around group characteristics and behavioural standards, hence any perceived lack of conformity to group norms is seen as a threat to the legitimacy of the group. Self-categorization accentuates the similarities between one's behaviour and that prescribed by the group norm, thus causing conformity as well as the disposition to control and punish in-group members that transgress group norms. In this view, group norms are obeyed because one identifies with the group, and conformity is mediated by self-categorization as an in-group member.

Experimental groups, however, have had no time to develop their unique norms, and even if successful discussion points to a descriptive norm (and perhaps a prescriptive norm, too) one can hardly claim that such norms are special to the group, make it unique, or differentiate it from other groups. At most, group identification will elicit generic norms favouring the group. To explain the biased allocation results he obtained after having grouped his subjects into different (but meaningless) categories, Tajfel concluded that in minimal groups there is a generic norm prescribing in-group favouritism (Tajfel, 1970). Similarly, there may be social norms that prescribe cooperation and trust within a group. If so, we should observe higher cooperation rates in all circumstances in which group identity is salient, not just when discussion and unanimous promising occur. A norm-based explanation is independent of group identification, although it recognizes the importance of group identity in making certain group norms salient. Even without identifying with an in-group, however, an individual may get sufficient cues from the environment signalling that a descriptive and/or social norm is in place. Most of the time, one does not need a conscious motivation to follow the norm. The mental process of categorization, searching for a script and finally following what appears to be the appropriate behaviour is entirely automatic. According to this view, discussion of the dilemma, when it ensues in an agreement as to the appropriate behaviour, signals what the descriptive norm is going to be, and offers enough cues to represent the situation as a familiar one in which promises are exchanged and kept, hence activating a social norm of promise-keeping.

Hobbes may have been wrong when saying that 'covenants without swords are nothing but words'. Covenants are made and kept even in the absence of obvious sanctions. The very act of promising, 'cheap talk' of no consequence, might be enough to induce many of us to behave contrary to narrow self-interest. A social norm has been activated and, under the right circumstances, we are prepared to follow it come what may.

Appendix

Conditions for a social norm to exist

Let R be a *behavioural rule* for situations of type S, where S can be represented as a mixed-motive game. We say that R is a social norm in a population P if there exists a sufficiently large subset $P_{cf} \subseteq P$ such that, for each individual $i \in P_{cf}$:

1. *Contingency*: i knows that a rule R exists and applies to situations of type S;
2. *Conditional preference*: i prefers to conform to R in situations of type S on the condition that:

   (a) *Empirical expectations*: i believes that a sufficiently large subset of P conforms to R in situations of type S;
   and either
   (b) *Normative expectations*: i believes that a sufficiently large subset of P expects i to conform to R in situations of type S;
   or
   (b') *Normative expectations with sanctions*: i believes that a sufficiently large subset of P expects i to conform to R in situations of type S, prefers i to conform and may sanction behaviour.

A social norm R is *followed* by population P if there exists a sufficiently large subset $P_f \subseteq P_{cf}$ such that, for each individual $i \in P_f$, conditions 2(a) and either 2(b) or 2(b') are met for i and, as a result, i prefers to conform to R in situations of type S.

Conditions for a descriptive norm to exist

Let R be a *behavioural rule* for situations of type S, where S is a coordination game. We say that R is a descriptive norm in a population P if there exists a sufficiently large subset $P_{cf} \subseteq P$ such that, for each individual $i \in P_{cf}$,

1. *Contingency*: i knows that a rule R exists and applies to situations of type S;
2. *Conditional preference*: i prefers to conform to R in situations of type S on the condition that:
   (a) *Empirical expectations*: i believes that a sufficiently large subset of P conforms to R in situations of type S;

A descriptive norm is *followed* by population P if there exists a sufficiently large subset $P_f \subseteq P_{cf}$ such that for all $i \in P_f$, condition 2(a) is met for i and as a result i prefers to conform to R in situations of type S.

Acknowledgements

Part of this chapter appeared in 'Covenants without sword: Group identity, norms, and communication in social dilemmas' which was published in Rationality and Society, Vol. 14(2), 192–228, Sage Publications, 2002.

Notes

1. My technical definition of social norms is to be found in the Appendix.
2. Another class of social dilemmas is the 'step-level' public goods problem in which, after a threshold number of participants is reached, the public good is provided. These dilemmas involve a coordination element, since less than the total number of participants is needed to provide the public good. Moreover, if one believes that one is the critical person who will 'make or break' the public good, one has an incentive to cooperate. However, in experiments with step-level public goods provision, subjects behave as if they were involved in a pure social dilemma (Dawes et al. 1986).
3. I am referring to the experiments discussed in Orbell et al. (1988).
4. An example of such merging is found in Jetten et al. (1996).
5. For a discussion of scripts, cf. ch. 2 of *The Grammar of Society* (forthcoming). Also, C. Bicchieri (2000). Hertel and Kerr (2001) have provided some evidence for the quick retrieval (via priming) of social norms.
6. For a discussion of the difference between empirical and normative expectations, cf. ch. 1 of *The Grammar of Society*.
7. See, for example, Bicchieri (1997, 2000).
8. Even if I use a belief/desire framework to describe social norms, this does not imply that people must be aware that they hold certain beliefs. In experiments in which beliefs are manipulated, subjects are usually *not* aware of the effect that such manipulation has on their choices.

9. I take personal norms to be unconditional (or nearly so), as opposed to social norms. The main difference between a social and a personal norm is that expectations of others' conformity play a crucial role in the former, much less so in the latter. There is a difference between conforming to a norm because one expects others to conform (and believes others expect one to conform), and conforming because one is convinced of its inherent value. In the first case, the preference for conformity is conditional upon expecting others to conform; in the second case, my preference for conforming is (almost) unconditional. I discuss this point in detail in Chapter 1 of *The Grammar of Society*.

10. See for example chs. 1 and 2 of *The Grammar of Society*.

11. Robyn Dawes was kind enough to make the tapes available to me, so that my student Colleen Baker was able to carefully analyze their content. Colleen recorded, for each group, who spoke first and what he/she said. How the subjects responded and how many responded, whether there was unanimous agreement on the strategy proposed, and how the conclusion about the out-group's expected behaviour was reached.

12. For a discussion of how intergroup schemas that are based on learned expectations about the competitive nature of intergroup relations influence a group's assessment of the out-group behaviour and intentions, see Insko and Schopler (1987, 1992).

13. There are several possible explanations for in-group bias. Tajfel et al. (1971) originally proposed a generic social norm of group behaviour, according to which people should treat in-group members more favourably than out-group members. Later, however, he favoured a different explanation based on social identity (Tajfel 1982). He assumed that, since people are motivated to maintain a positive social identity, they tend to make their social group positively distinct from other groups. Recent experiments conducted by Yamagishi et al. (1998) lend support to a different explanation: In-group favouritism is based upon the expectation that favours made to in-group members are more likely to be reciprocated than favours made to out-group members. Expectations of generalized reciprocity seem to be based upon a 'generic norm' of group behaviour. Such norm is, in turn, sustained by in-group favouritism.

14. Cf. Hertel and Kerr (2001).

15. A similar argument is made by Hertel and Kerr (2001), in their study of how social norms that favour the in-group are primed in the right circumstances.

16. I am referring here to the systematic analysis of the taped discussions done by my student Colleen Baker (cf. Note 11).

17. Indeed, my definition of social norm says that a subject will follow a norm provided she expects a sufficiently high number of people to follow it, and expect her to follow it, in the relevant circumstances. Of course, what 'sufficiently high' means differs for different people.

18. Orbell et al. 1991, p. 121.

19. Cf. Bicchieri (2000), and also ch. 3 of *The Grammar of Society*.

20. Brewer (1991) has developed a theory of 'optimal distinctiveness' to explain under which conditions we make personal (or social) identity relevant.

21. The experimenters manipulated the salience of the collective or subgroup identity. In some conditions subjects were told the experimenters were interested in the choices of psychology students vs. economics students, who were the remotely located members of the collective group. Such instructions aimed to elicit a subgroup identity. In other conditions experimenters told students that they were interested in the decisions of students at their

particular university vs. students at other universities, in order to elicit a collective group identity.

22. The experiment also tested anonymity conditions, showing that anonymity has no effect on the behaviour of subjects. A later study by Kerr, Garst, Lewandowski and Harris (1997) extended the anonymity condition to the experimenters and also found it not to be a significant factor.
23. Social identity and perceived consensus were measured on a nine point scale. Expectation of cooperation refers to the number of others (zero to three) expected to cooperate.
24. Cooperation may be a descriptive norm, or a social norm. It becomes a social norm when there are both empirical and normative expectations that support it. In the case of discussion without commitment, normative expectations would typically be absent.
25. Cf. ch. 2 of *The Grammar of Society*.
26. It is possible that people expect a computer to be programmed to follow simple social norms or rules like keeping one's commitments.
27. I describe such processes in detail in *The Grammar of Society*, ch. 2.
28. Cf. Orbell and Dawes (1993).
29. Cf. ch. 3 of *The Grammar of Society*.
30. Interestingly, subjects in Orbell et al. experiments also exchanged threats, even if it was clear to all that choices would be anonymous and that there would be no chance of recognizing and punishing transgressors.

References

Allison, S. T. and N. L. Kerr (1994) 'Group Correspondence Biases and the Provision of Public Goods', *Journal of Personality and Social Psychology* 21, 563–79.

Bartlett, F. C. (1932) *Remembering: a Study in Experimental and Social Psychology* (Cambridge: Cambridge University Press).

Bicchieri, C. (forthcoming) *The Grammar of Society: The Nature and Dynamics of Social Norms* (New York: Cambridge University Press).

Bicchieri, C. (2000) 'Words and Deeds: a Focus Theory of Norms' In *Rationality, Rules and Structure*, eds. J. Nida-Rumelin and W. Spohn (Dordrecht: Kluwer Academic Publishers).

Bicchieri, C. (1997) 'Learning to Cooperate' In *The Dynamics of Norms*, eds. C. Bicchieri, R. Jeffrey and B. Skyrms (Cambridge: Cambridge University Press).

Bicchieri, C. (1990) 'Norms of Cooperation', *Ethics* 100, 838–861.

Bornstein, G. (1992) 'The Free Rider Problem in Intergroup Conflicts Over Step-level and Continuous Public Goods', *Journal of Personality and Social Psychology* 62, 597–602.

Bouas, K. S. and S. S. Komorita (1996) 'Group Discussion and Cooperation in Social Dilemmas', *Personality and Social Psychology Bulletin* 22, 1144–1150.

Brewer, M. (1991) 'The Social Self: On Being the Same and Different at the Same Time', *Personality and Social Psychology Bulletin* 17, 475–82.

Brewer, M. (1979) 'Ingroup Bias in the Minimal Intergroup Situation: A Cognitive Motivational Analysis', *Psychological Bulletin* 86, 307–324

Brewer, M. B. and R. M. Kramer (1986) 'Choice Behavior in Social Dilemmas: Effects of Social Identity, Group Size, and Decision Framing', *Journal of Personality and Social Psychology* 50, 543–549.

Camerer, C. and R. Thaler (1995) 'Anomalies: Ultimatums, Dictators and Manners', *Journal of Economic Perspectives* 9, 209–219.

Cialdini, R., C. Kallgren and R. Reno (1990) 'A Focus Theory of Normative Conduct: a Theoretical Refinement and Reevaluation of the Role of Norms in Human Behavior', *Advances in Experimental Social Psychology* 24, 201–234.

Dawes, R. (1980) 'Social Dilemmas', *Annual Review of Psychology* 31, 169–293.

Dawes, R., J. McTavish and H. Shaklee (1977) 'Behavior, Communication, and Assumptions About Other People's Behavior in a Commons Dilemma Situation', *Journal of Personality and Social Psychology* 35, 1–11.

Dawes, R., J. Orbell, R. Simmons and A. van de Kragt (1986) 'Organizing Groups for Collective Action', *American Political Science Review* 80, 1171–1185.

Dawes, R., J. Orbell and A. van de Kragt (1988) 'Not Me or Thee But We: The Importance of Group Identity in Eliciting Cooperation in Dilemma Situations', *Acta Psychologica* 68, 83–97.

Dawes, R., A. van de Kragt and J. Orbell (1990) 'Cooperation for the Benefit of Us&Mdash;Not Me, or My Conscience' In *Beyond Self-interest*, ed. J. Mansbridge (Chicago: University of Chicago Press).

Estes, W. K. (1986) 'Memory Storage and Retrieval Processes in Category Learning', *Journal of Experimental Psychology: General* 115, 155–74.

Fiske, S. T. and S. L. Neuberg (1990) 'A Continuum of Impression Formation, from Category-based to Individuating Processes: Influences of Information and Motivation on Attention and Interpretation' In *Advances in Experimental Social Psychology*, vol. 23, ed. L. Berkowitz (New York: Academic Press).

Fiske, S. T. and S. E. Taylor (1991) *Social Cognition* (New York: McGraw-Hill).

Hertel, G. and N. L. Kerr (in press) 'Priming and in-group bias', *Journal of Experimental Social Psychology*.

Hertel, G. and N. Kerr (2001) 'Priming Ingroup Favoritism: The Impact of Normative Scripts in the Minimal Group Paradigm', *Journal of Experimental Social Psychology* 37, 316–324.

Hinkle, S., L. Taylor, D. Fox-Cardamone and K. Crook (1989) 'Intragroup Identification and Intergroup Differentiation: a Multi-Component Approach', *British Journal of Social Psychology* 28, 305–317.

Hogg, M. A. and J. C. Turner (1987) 'Social Identity and Conformity: a Theory of Referent Informational Influence' In *Current Issues in European Social Psychology*, vol. 2, eds. W. Doise and S. Moscovici (Cambridge: Cambridge University Press).

Insko, C. A. and J. Schopler (1987) 'Categorization, Competition, and Collectivity' In *Review of Personality and Social Psychology: Group Processes*, vol. 8, ed. C. Hendrick (Beverly Hills, Ca.: Sage).

Issac, R. and J. Walker (1988) 'Communication and Free-Riding Behavior: The Voluntary Contribution Mechanism', *Economic Inquiry* 26, 585–608.

Jetten, J., R. Spears and A. S. R. Manstead (1996) 'Intergroup Norms and Intergroup Discrimination: Distinctive Self-Categorization and Social Identity Effects', *Journal of Personality and Social Psychology* 71, 1222–1233.

Jones, E. and R. Nisbett (1972) 'The Actor and the Observer: Divergent Perceptions of the Causes of Behavior' In *Attribution: Perceiving the Causes of Behavior*, ed. E. Jones et al. (Morristown, NJ: General Learning Press).

Kahneman, D. and A. Tversky (1973) 'Availability: A Heuristic for Judging Frequency and Probability', *Cognitive Psychology* 5, 207–232.

Kerr, N., J. Garst, D. A. Lewandowski and S. E. Harris (1997) 'The Still, Small Voice: Commitment to Cooperate as an Internalized versus a Social Norm', *Personality and Social Psychology Bulletin* 23, 1300–1311.

Kerr, N. L. and C. Kaufman-Gilliland (1997) '"...and besides, I probably couldn't have made a difference anyway": Rationalizing defection in social dilemmas', *Journal of Experimental Social Psychology*, 33, 211–230.

Kerr, N. L. and C. M. Kaufman-Gilliland (1994) 'Communication, commitment, and cooperation in social dilemmas', *Journal of Personality and Social Psychology*, 66, 513–529.

Kiesler, S., L. Sproull and K. Waters (1996) 'A Prisoner's Dilemma Experiment on Cooperation with People and Human-like Computers', *Journal of Personality and Social Psychology* 70, 47–65.

Kramer, R. M. and M. B. Brewer (1986) 'Social Group Identity and the Emergence of Co-operation in Resource Conservation Dilemmas' In *Psychology of Decisions and Conflict: Experimental Social Dilemmas*, eds. H. A. Wilke et al. (Frankfurt: Verlag Peter Lang).

Kramer, R. M. and M. B. Brewer (1984) 'Effects of Group Identity on Resource Use in a Simulated Commons Dilemma', *Journal of Personality and Social Psychology* 46, 1044–1057.

Mackie, G. (1997) '"Noncredible' Social Contracts Are Credible: Communication and Commitment in Social Dilemma Experiments', *Mimeo*.

Nisbett, R. and T. Wilson (1977) 'Telling More Than We Can Know: Verbal Reports on Mental Processes', *Psychological Review* 84, 231–259.

Orbell, J., A. van de Kragt and R. Dawes (1991) 'Covenants Without the Sword: The Role of Promises in Social Dilemma Circumstances' In *Social Norms and Economic Institutions*, eds. I. K. Koford and D. J. Miller. (Ann Arbor, MI: University of Michigan Press).

Orbell, J., A. van de Kragt and R. Dawes (1988) 'Explaining Discussion-Induced Cooperation', *Journal of Personality and Social Psychology* 54, 811–819.

Orbell, J. and R. Dawes (1993) 'Social Welfare, Cooperators' Advantage, and the Option of Not Playing the Game', *American Sociological Review* 58, 787–800.

Pillutla, M. and X. P. Chen (1997) 'Social Norms and Cooperation: The Effects of Context and Feedback', *Mimeo*.

Rosch, E. (1978) 'Principles of Categorization' In *Cognition and Categorization*, eds. (E. Rosch and B. Lloyd. Hillsdale, NJ: Erlbaum).

Sally, D. (1995) 'Conversation and Cooperation in Social Dilemmas', *Rationality and Society* 7, 58–92.

Schank, R. and R. Abelson (1977) *Scripts, Plans, Goals and Understanding.* Hillsdale, NJ: Erlbaum.

Schopler, J. and C. A. Insko (1992) 'The Discontinuity Effect in Interpersonal and Intergroup Relations: Generality and Mediation' In *European Review of Social Psychology*, vol. 3, eds. W. Stroebe and M. Hewstone, pp. 121–151 (New York: John Wiley).

Schroeder, D. A., T. D. Jensen, A. J. Reed, D. K. Sullivan and M. Schwab (1983) 'The Actions of Others as Determinants of Behavior in Social Trap Situations', *Journal of Experimental Social Psychology* 19, 522–539.

Sherif, M. (1966) *In Common Predicament.* (Boston, MA: Houghton Mifflin).

Tajfel, H. (1982) 'Social Psychology of Intergroup Relations', *Annual Review of Psychology* 33, 1–30.

Tajfel, H. (1973) 'The Roots of Prejudice: Cognitive Aspects' In *Psychology and Race*, ed. P. Watson (Harmondsworth, UK: Penguin).

Tajfel, H. (1970) 'Experiments in Intergroup Discrimination', *Scientific American* 223, 96–102.

Tajfel, H., M. Billig, R. Bundy and C. Flament (1971) 'Social Categorization in Intergroup Behavior', *European Journal of Social Psychology* 1, 149–178.

Tetlock, P. E. and R. Boettger (1989) 'Accountability: a Social Magnifier of the Dilution Effect', *Journal of Personality and Social Psychology* 57, 388–398.

Thaler, R. (1992) *The Winner's Curse: Paradoxes and Anomalies in Economic Life* (New York: Free Press). ⁻

Turner, J. C. et al. (1987) *Rediscovering the Social Group: A Self-Categorization Theory* (Oxford: Blackwell).

Yamagishi, T., N. Jin and T. Kiyonari (1999) 'Bounded Generalized Reciprocity: Ingroup Boasting and Ingroup Favoritism' *Advances in Group Processes* 16, 161–197.

6

The Psychology of Effective Teamworking

Carol S. Borrill and Michael A. West

Teams have become the building blocks of organizations (Lawler, Mohrman and Ledford, 1992). As organizations grow in size and become structurally more complex, groups of people are needed who work together in co-ordinated ways to achieve objectives that contribute to the overall aims, effectiveness and competitiveness of the organization. Team working provides the flexibility needed to respond effectively, appropriately and more quickly than competitors to the constantly changing demands in the organization's environment, and provides a mechanism for bringing together the range of expertise, skills and knowledge required to complete complex work tasks.

The contribution that team working makes to organizational effectiveness has been demonstrated in a range of studies. A review by Weldon and Weingart (1993) revealed that the introduction of groups with shared goals lead to better performance and productivity in a variety of organizational settings. Macy and Izumi (1993) conducted a meta-analysis of 131 field studies of organizational change and found that interventions with the largest effects upon financial measures of organizational performance were team development interventions or the creation of autonomous work groups. Applebaum and Batt (1994) reviewed 12 large-scale surveys and 185 case studies of managerial practices. They concluded that team-based working leads to improvements in organizational performance on measures both of efficiency and quality. Similarly, Levine and D'Andrea-Tyson (1990) concluded that substantive participation leads to sustained increases in productivity and that teams effectively enable such participation. Cotton (1993) confirmed this finding in a study of a variety of forms of employee involvement.

There are two key themes in the research literature on teams; what factors promote effective team processes, and what conditions are needed to maximize team performance. This chapter presents an overview of the research evidence of relevance to these themes. We start by considering the key features of groups or teams at work.

6.1   What is a team?

In this chapter we use the terms 'team' and 'group' interchangeably. The discussion is focused on formal groups; those which have an identity and set of functions derived from, and contributing to achieving the objectives of the organization. There are many different types of teams in organizations. Sundstrom, McIntyre, Halthill and Richards (2000) proposed six team types: *production teams* that represent core employees and produce tangible goods; *service teams* that engage in repeated transactions with customers; *senior managers* who have primary responsibility for directing and coordinating lower level units; *project teams* that execute specialist time-constrained tasks; *action and performing* teams that execute specialized time-constrained performance tasks; and *advisory teams*.

Whatever the type, teams all have common features. First, members of the team have shared objectives in relation to their work, and they must interact with each other in order to achieve these shared objectives. Team members have more or less well-defined and interdependent roles, some of which are differentiated from one another (e.g. a breast cancer care team includes breast care nurses, surgeons, radiologists, oncologists, pathologists and administrative staff), and teams have an organizational identity as a work group with a defined organizational function (e.g. the public relations team for the pharmaceutical division of a major company). Finally, they are not so large that they would be defined more appropriately as an small organization with an internal structure of vertical and horizontal relationships and subgroupings. In practice, this is likely to mean that a work group will be smaller than about 20 members and larger than three people.

Teams are formed to achieve tasks, objectives and goals that are too complex or too large for one person, or number of people working independently, to achieve. What are the main factors influencing the effectiveness of work teams? What processes and mechanisms need to be in place to ensure that the outputs from a team are greater than the outputs achieved by the same individuals working independently?

The input-process-output model has dominated research and theorizing on team effectiveness and is the basis for much of the theory development and research (Campion, Papper and Medsker, 1996; Goodman, Ravlin and Argote, 1986; Guzzo, 1996; Guzzo and Shea, 1992). In the basic form of the model it is proposed that inputs represent the resources available to the team (team size, characteristics of team members, design of team task, organizational context) and these influence processes (the mechanisms that inhibit or enable the ability of the team to work interdependently and combine their knowledge and skills), which determine outputs. There are two main types of outputs, those that relate to the performance or products resulting from team working (team effectiveness, productivity, innovation) and those which relate to the outcomes for team members (well-being, job satisfaction).

Using this basic approach researchers have identified many factors that are important influences on team outputs (Hackman and Morris, 1975; Campion, Papper and Medsker, 1996; Guzzo and Shea, 1992).

In this chapter we consider some of the main factors influencing team outputs, focusing on the contribution that the inputs and processes shown in Figure 6.1, make to team outputs.

6.2 Understanding team effectiveness

6.2.1 Inputs

6.2.1.1 The group's task

A team works towards specific outcomes, designing a mobile phone, performing a surgical operation or producing a television program. Many of the factors or contingencies associated with team effectiveness vary depending on the nature of the team's task. Kent and McGrath (1969) found that group characteristics only explained 3.4 per cent of the variation in teams' performance compared with 87.9 per cent that was explained by task characteristics. Findings such as these highlighted the importance of understanding design and operational factors that would promote team effectiveness in relation to specific types of task. This resulted in the development of a number of schemes for classifying task characteristics with dimensions such as difficulty, solution multiplicity, intrinsic interest, cooperative requirements (Shaw, 1981); unitary versus divisible, conjunctive, disjunctive and additive (Steiner, 1972); conflict

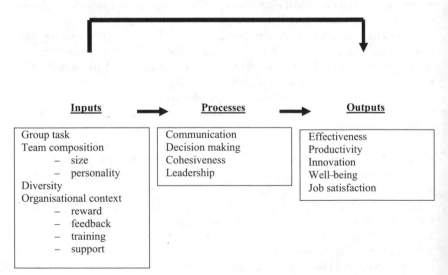

Figure 6.1   An input-process-output model of team performance

versus cooperation, and conceptual versus behavioural (McGrath, 1984). However, such classification systems have proved easier to apply in laboratory settings than with work groups.

Another approach to conceptualizing group tasks is to analyse them in relation to their *hierarchical requirements* (goals and sub goals) and *sequential requirements* (the order in which different parts of a task are carried out), as well as *cyclical process requirements* (generating goals, planning, decision making and executing behaviour) and reviewing performance for each element of the task.

One of the most influential models of task classification, proposed by Hackman and colleagues (Hackman, 1990; Hackman and Lawler, 1971; Hackman and Oldham, 1975) identifies five characteristics of motivating tasks: autonomy (the degree to which the task provides freedom, independence and discretion), task variety (the degree to which the task requires a range of competencies and skills), task significance (the perceived importance of the task), task identity (the degree to which the task requires completion of a whole task and has a visible outcome) and task feedback (the degree to which carrying out the task provides direct and clear information on performance). Variations in these characteristics are related to both job satisfaction (Drory and Shamir, 1988; Hackman and Lawler, 1971) and workgroup effectiveness. These task design characteristics have also predicted facets of team effectiveness for both self-managing and traditional teams (Cordery, 1996).

6.2.1.2 Team composition

The combination of team member attributes (knowledge, skills, abilities, personality), team size, team tenure, team member power and status can have a powerful influence on team processes and team outcomes (Kozlowski and Bell, 2002). As a result there is a considerable amount of research on the nature and attributes of team members.

Team size
Researchers have offered recommendations concerning the best size for teams. Katzenbach and Smith (1993) for example suggest that work teams should contain between 12 and 14 members, while Scharf (1989) suggested that seven was the best size. Evidence from other researchers suggests that size has a curvilinear relationship with effectiveness; too many may reduce performance because it becomes more difficult to integrate and coordinate the activities of team members (Martz, Vogel and Nunamaker, 1992), while others argued that increasing team size improves performance without limits (Campion, Medsker and Higgs, 1993).

Personality
Experience of working in teams suggests that personalities play an important part in the effectiveness of teams working together. The questions

often raised are: What personality types work best together? What mix of personalities is needed for a team to be effective? In what ways must group members be compatible in order to work together effectively?

A number of models of personality in teams have been proposed in the psychological literature. For example, some organizations have sought compatibility in the cognitive styles of team members by using the Myers-Briggs assessment instrument (a questionnaire measure of cognitive style) (Guzzo and Shea, 1992). However, little research has examined relationships between personality compatibility and team performance. An exception is the work of Schutz (1955, 1958, 1967) which seeks to explain how members' personal attributes affect group performance. Some research has shown that compatibility on the dimensions of control predicted time to task completion in groups of managers working in a laboratory setting. However, evidence from other research shows no relationships between compatibility and group performance (for example, Hill, 1982; Moos and Spiesman, 1962; Shaw and Nickols, 1964). Indeed, Hill (1982) found that incompatibility predicted productivity in teams of systems analysts. Researchers using the Big Five personality factors have found that conscientiousness is a strong positive predictor of team effectiveness (Barrick et al., 1998; Neuman, Wagner and Christiansen, 1999). Although this is still the most frequently studied trait, other researchers have shown that extraversion (Barry and Stewart, 1997) and agreeableness (Neuman and Wright, 1999) can also be associated with team effectiveness (Kozlowski and Bell, 2002).

Stevens and Campion (1994) utilize knowledge, skills and abilities (KSAs) in the selection of team members rather than personality, as these are more readily influenced by the organization and not stable traits of the individual. They propose two main requirements each with various KSAs and sub-KSAs. Interpersonal KSAs include conflict resolution, collaborative problem-solving, and communication, while self-management KSAs encompass goal-setting and performance management, and planning and task-coordination.

6.2.1.3 Diversity

Achieving complex tasks requires that team members have a diverse range of knowledge, skills and abilities. The extent to which this diversity within a group impacts on team processes and contributes to or is detrimental to team performance, depends upon a number of factors. Firstly, the effect of diversity depends on the nature of the team task (Jackson, May and Whitney, 1995), having the most positive effect when successful performance of the task requires creativity and innovation. Secondly, the effect of diversity may vary depending on types of team outcomes studied, having a positive effect on team performance but a negative impact on outcomes such as team member turnover (Kozlowski and Bell, 2002) and finally may vary depending on the team member attributes being investigated (Haythorn, 1968; Jackson, 1992, 1996). Team member attributes vary on two main dimensions; attributes that are role-related and task-relevant, (e.g. organizational position and the specialized knowledge of the different team members), and those that are simply inherent in the person and relations-oriented (e.g. age, gender, ethnicity, social status and personality) (Maznevski, 1994). Jackson (1992, 1996), however, identifies another orthogonal dimension along which diversity could be classified: readily-detected or underlying. For example, organizational position is a readily-detected task attribute, while specialized knowledge is an underlying task-related attribute. Readily-detected relations-oriented attributes include age, gender and ethnicity, but social status and personality would be classified as underlying relations-oriented attributes. Here we consider diversity classified along the task-related/relations-oriented dimension.

Task-related diversity
There is remarkable agreement that heterogeneity of skills in teams performing complex tasks is good for effectiveness (e.g. Campion, Papper and Medsker, 1996; Guzzo and Dickson, 1996; Jackson, 1996; Milliken and Martins, 1996; Maznevski, 1994). Heterogeneity of skills and knowledge automatically implies that each team member will bring a different knowledge perspective to the problem, a necessary ingredient for creative solutions (Sternberg and Lubart, 1990; West, 1997). For example, Wiersema and Bantel (1992) reported that strategic management initiatives were more likely in groups that were heterogeneous with respect to educational subject specialization, while Bantel (1993) reported that the management teams of banks which were heterogeneous with respect to education and functional background developed clearer corporate strategies. Several experimental studies, particularly those involving complex tasks or requiring innovation, have shown similar effects (McGrath, 1984).

For tasks requiring creativity and a high quality of decision making, Jackson says that 'the available evidence supports the conclusion that team [task] diversity is associated with better quality team decision-making' (Jackson, 1996, p. 67), citing evidence provided by Filley, House, and Kerr (1976), Hoffman (1959), McGrath (1984), and Shaw (1981).

Although some debate has surrounded the question of whether it is advantageous to have groups that are homogeneous or heterogeneous with respect to the level and type of cognitive ability, most research results support the view that level of ability, not heterogeneity of ability is the critical factor. At least for tasks that are truly interdependent, high ability homogeneous groups outperform, for example, low ability homogeneous groups. This was demonstrated in Tziner and Eden's (1985) study of military groups in which they found that the contribution of one team member of high ability to the performance of the team was greatest when all other crew members were high in ability.

Relations-oriented diversity

Teams that are diverse in relevant task-related attributes are also likely to be diverse in relation to one or more attributes inherent in the individual; personality, status, tenure, gender. How does relations-orientated diversity influence team processes and team outputs?

Differences in relations-oriented characteristics can trigger stereotypes and prejudice (Jackson, 1996) which, via intergroup conflict (Tajfel, 1978; Tajfel and Turner, 1979; Hogg and Abrams, 1988), can affect group processes and outcomes. The research emphasis in this area has changed over the years from a concern with personality differences, that were discussed earlier (e.g. Haythorn, 1968; Hoffman, 1959; Hoffman and Maier, 1961; Tziner and Eden, 1985; Hill, 1982; Moos and Spiesman, 1962; Shaw and Nickols, 1964) to demographic heterogeneity, such as differences in age, tenure and status. Turnover rates are higher in groups that are heterogeneous with respect to age, after controlling for other factors (Jackson et al., 1991; Wagner, Pfeffer and O'Reilly, 1984), and team (or department) tenure (McCain, O'Reilly and Pfeffer, 1983). Status diversity is likely to threaten integration and trust in the group. The threat occasioned by disagreeing with high status members is likely to restrict public speculation by lower status group members. Such status differentials, as much social psychological research has shown, will retard integration because of the barriers to cohesiveness and shared orientation they create. For example, De Dreu (1995) has shown that power and status asymmetries in groups produce hostile interaction patterns in contrast to groups in which there is power balance. Such hostility is clearly likely to inhibit creativity and innovation (West, 2002).

What of ethnic and gender diversity? Two studies that have examined ethnic diversity in groups have suggested that the effects of diversity may change over time. Milliken and Martins (1996) suggested that ethnic diversity in groups can have negative effects on individual and group outcomes, but only early in a group's life. Similarly, in one of the very few longitudinal studies in this area, Watson, Kumar and Michaelsen (1993) reported that groups that were heterogeneous with respect to culture initially performed, on a series of business case exercises, more poorly than culturally homogeneous groups. As group members gained experience with each other over time, however, performance difference between culturally homogeneous and heterogeneous groups largely disappeared.

There is some evidence that heterogeneity in both relations-oriented and task-oriented domains is associated with group innovation, including heterogeneity in personality (Hoffman and Maier, 1961), training background (Pelz, 1956), leadership abilities (Ghiselli and Lodahl, 1958), attitudes

(Hoffman, Harburg and Maier, 1962; Willems and Clark, 1971), gender, (Wood, 1987), occupational background (Bantel and Jackson, 1989) and education (Smith et al., 1994).

The dominant explanation for the positive effects of diversity on team innovation (but not other types of performance) is that the diversity of information, experience and skills brought to the team by members from different professional groups produces more comprehensive and effective decision making. This diversity increases the amount and variety of information that the team can use in collective problem-solving. However, another explanation for the (still debated) effects of task-oriented diversity on team innovation, particularly pertinent in multi-professional teams, is that functional diversity might influence workgroup performance as a result of the higher level of external communication which group members initiate, precisely because of their functional diversity as members of different professional groups (Zenger and Lawrence, 1989). Mohrman, Cohen and Mohrman (1995) have pointed out that there are likely to be innovation benefits of good linkages between groups and teams and across departments within organizations. The cross-disciplinarity, cross-functionality and cross-team perspectives that such interactions can produce are likely to generate the kinds of dividends related to innovation that heterogeneity within teams could offer.

6.2.1.4 Organizational context

Teams are based in organizations and this broader context (the technology, structure, leadership, culture and climate) constrain teams and their responses (Kozlowski and Bell, 2002). One of the major changes in emphasis in research on teams in the last 15 years has been the shift from discussion of intragroup processes to the impact of this organizational context on the team. However, despite the significance attached to the context of team work, there is little empirical, field-based research. This is partly because research with real teams poses greater difficulties in general than work with individuals (e.g. 50 people are needed to cooperate in research with 50 people, but perhaps 300 people are required for work with 50 teams). But it also reflects the difficulty of conducting team research where context is an important variable. Comparing the organizational context of 50 teams requires 50 organizations that have teams carrying out similar tasks.

Various organizational contextual factors have been proposed as important in predicting team effectiveness. Hackman (1990) highlights three factors – reward systems, information and feedback, and training – which, in combination have significant relationships with rated quality of work life and managers' judgments of performance (Cohen, Ledford and Spreitzer, 1994).

Reward systems, such as public recognition, preferred work assignments and money (Sundstrom, De Meuse and Futrell, 1990) have long been known to provide motivation (Vroom, 1964) and affect performance, particularly when the rewards are contingent upon task achievement (Hackman, 1990). Gladstein (1984), in a study of 100 sales teams, found that pay and recognition had an effect, especially upon the leader's behaviour and the way the group structured itself. Hackman (1990) identified two contingencies: whether the rewards are administered to the group as a whole or to individuals, and whether the rewards provide incentives for collaboration or for the delegation of tasks to individuals (the former, in both cases, are associated with positive relationships between rewards and group effectiveness).

The second of Hackman's factors is ready access to data and feedback. Feedback is important for setting realistic goals and fostering high group commitment (Lathom, Erez and Locke, 1988). In addition, accurate feedback from both the task and other group members is associated with job satisfaction (Drory and Shamir, 1988). However, group feedback can be difficult to provide to teams with either long cycles of work or one-off projects (Sundstrom, De Meuse and Futrell, 1990).

Last, Hackman (1990) argued that training and technical assistance should be made readily available for teams to function successfully. Limited empirical evidence suggests training is correlated with both self-reported effectiveness (Gladstein, 1984) and managers' judgments of effectiveness (Campion, Medsker and Higgs, 1993).

A more elaborated consideration of organizational context has been offered by Tannenbaum, Beard and Salas, (1992) who consider eight aspects: rewards systems (individual or team-based); resource scarcity; management control; level of stress in the organization; organizational climate; competition; intergroup relations within the organization; and environmental uncertainty. These factors have high face validity (intuitively they seem to be relevant) in models of work group functioning and effectiveness, but there is still little evidence about their influence on work group effectiveness.

Physical conditions are another situational constraint that can affect the relationship between team processes and effectiveness. For example, a team whose members are dispersed across the countries of the European Union, will find decision making more difficult than a team whose members share the same physical location. Goodman (1986) reports that the relationship between team processes and effectiveness varies depending on whether the physical conditions are good or poor.

6.2.2 Group processes

This section examines the processes within teams that enable them to achieve their goals, examining the main factors that influence these processes and ultimately how effectively teams perform their task.

6.2.2.1 Communication

The study of communication in social groups has a long history in social psychology (see Brown, 1988 for a review), but recent reviews by Guzzo and Dickson (1996) and Guzzo and Shea (1992) revealed the paucity of thorough industrial and organizational research in this area. Blakar (1985) proposes five pre-conditions for effective communication in teams. Team members must have shared social reality – they must have a common 'here and now' within which the exchange of messages can take place, including a shared language base and perception. Team members must be able to 'decentre', to take the perspective of others into account in relation to both their affective and cognitive position (Redmond 1989, 1992). Team members must be motivated to communicate. There must be 'negotiated and endorsed contracts of behaviour' (i.e. agreement among team members about how interactions take place). Finally, the team must attribute communication difficulties appropriately, so if one of the other preconditions is not being met, the team is able to correctly identify the problem and develop a solution.

Research on Team Mental Models provides further insights into factors that can enhance communication in teams. In this approach it is proposed that the extent to which team members have shared cognitive constructs predict team effectiveness. The general thesis is that team effectiveness will improve if team members have an appropriate shared understanding of the task that the team is trying to accomplish, understand the knowledge, skills and preferences of the other members in their team, and have shared knowledge and understanding of the equipment the team has to use (Cannon-Bowers, Salas and Converse, 1993; Klimoski and Mohammed, 1994). There has been limited empirical work exploring this thesis, but preliminary work on team mental models with team working on simulation exercise has provided some support. Mathieu et al. (2000) found that teamwork and taskwork mental models were positively associated with team processes and performance, and that team processes fully mediated the relationship between shared mental models and performance, while Marks, Zaccaro and Mathieu (2000) found that the quality of team mental models positively influenced communication processes and performance.

Research evidence provides no clear understanding of the relationships between team communication dimension, such as frequency of interaction, communication style, communication patterns, and performance. Smith et al. (1994) investigated the relative effects on team performance of demographic factors and team processes, including informal communication, communication frequency. They found that, unusually, communication frequency was significantly, negatively related to performance. Smith et al. (1994) suggested that conflict and disagreement in groups may have resulted in increased communication that was concerned with conflict resolution, rather then with task performance.

More recent experimental research on group communication effectiveness (e.g. Krauss and Fussell, 1990) has been augmented by burgeoning work on computer mediated technology which can aid or hinder work group communication (Finholt, Sproull and Kiesler, 1990; Hollingshead and McGrath, 1995). This technology included voice messaging (e.g. Rice and Shork, 1990), teleconferencing (e.g. Egido, 1990), and group project and decision support systems (Kraemer and Pinsonneault, 1990; Olson and Atkins, 1990; Vogel and Nunamaker, 1990; Guzzo and Dickson, 1996). The results reveal very mixed effects, not surprisingly dependent upon the nature of the task, the group, the context and the technology. Before developing a good understanding of how technology mediates communication in workgroups, however, further theoretical and research progress is needed to understand traditional workgroup communication processes and outcomes.

Keller (1992) studied 93 R&D teams. He found that functional diversity increased external communication and thereby enhanced project performance. However functional diversity also reduced internal communication and cohesiveness. Keller concluded that it is necessary to manage the creative tension between reduced team identification and enhanced organizational integration. Although Keller did not measure whether diversity increased the breadth of team knowledge, his findings illustrate how diversity can impact on both internal and external processes.

Gender diversity can also influence communication in teams. The gender of speakers is an important influence on communication within the group. Not only are men consistently more assertive in public situations and confrontations (Kimble, Marsh and Kiska, 1984; Mathison and Tucker, 1982), but communication expectations differ for men and women. Sex-role stereotypes prescribe passive, submissive and expressive communication for women while men are expected to be active, controlling and less expressive communicators (LaFrance and Mayo, 1978); even in recent years, deviation from these sex-roles has detrimental effects on the perceptions of the speaker (Unsworth, 1995). This punishment for violation of expectations (Jussim, 1986; Jussim, Coleman and Lerch, 1987; Jackson, Sullivan and Hodge, 1993) may influence both the perceptions of women in groups and their willingness to participate in team communication.

6.2.2.2   Decision making

Effective decision making and problem-solving processes are central to effective team performance. A thorough review of the literature on team effectiveness and decision making in organizations (Guzzo and Shea, 1992) and other evidence from both social psychological and organizational research provide support for the general proposition that high quality decision making will be made by groups which are reflexive (are able to use opportunities for learning).

Hackman and Morris (1975) found that in 100 laboratory groups (three persons per group, working on a 15-minute task) only 142 comments were made about the performance strategy of the group (less than two comments per group). However, process discussions following these comments turned out to facilitate the quality of group performance. The judged creativity of group decisions was related to the number of comments made about performance strategy. Previous work also suggests that a conceptually similar factor, task orientation (a focus on quality and continuous improvement) is associated with team innovation and effectiveness (see Ulich and Weber, 1996; West and Anderson, 1996).

A coherent and major body of research developed by Maier and colleagues on decision making in groups suggested that cognitive stimulation in groups may produce novel ideas, a unique combination of sub-ideas, or a complex solution whose total value is 'greater than the sum of its parts'. Group effectiveness might be improved, Maier found, if groups were encouraged to be 'problem minded' rather than 'solution minded' (Maier and Solem, 1962), i.e. were encouraged to question and communicate about its current approach to achieving a task or to consider other aspects of the problem. Maier (1970) also found that group effectiveness was improved when the group analysed problem facets as sub-tasks; members initially worked separately and then combined their individual problem-solving strategies. Similar effects on productivity were found when groups were encouraged to produce two different solutions to a problem, so that the better of the two might be adopted (Maier, 1970). Particularly for complex decision making groups, more planning enhances group performance (Hackman, Brousseau and Weiss, 1976; Smith, Locke and Barry, 1990).

Another line of findings for this comes from research on problem-identification by groups (Moreland and Levine, 1992). Group problem solving, especially early on, is significantly improved when members examine the way in which they have defined the situation and considered whether or not they are solving the 'right' problem (see for example, Bottger and Yetton, 1987; Hirokawa, 1990; Landsberger, 1955; Maier, 1970; Schwenk, 1988). A group that detects problems too slowly or misdiagnoses them will probably fail, whatever solutions it develops for those (Mitroff, Barabba and Kilmann,1977). Indeed, misdiagnosis of problems is a major threat to group effectiveness. Attributing problems to the wrong causes, or not communicating about potential consequences, are common failings which can undermine group effectiveness, especially when group members fail to reflect on the possibility of error (cf. Jervis, 1976; Schwenk, 1988).

A major factor determining group task effectiveness is norms within the group regarding problem-solving. In some groups problems are seen as threats to morale and identification of problems by their members is discouraged (Janis, 1982; Miceli and Near, 1985: Smircich, 1983). Those who become aware of problems in such groups are reluctant to talk about them because they expect to be censored. When problems are brought into the awareness of such groups, the tension produced can prevent appropriate planning and action (cf. Lyles, 1981; Schwenk and Thomas, 1983). Groups that engage in more extensive scanning and discussion of their environments are more effective than those which do not identify problems (Ancona and Caldwell, 1988; Main, 1989; Billings, Milburn and Schaalman, 1980). Moreover, as the environment of groups becomes more uncertain, problem identification becomes more difficult (Hedburg, Nystrom and Starbuck, 1976). Ineffective groups will tend to deny, distort or hide problems and wait and watch to see what occurs with them (Stein, 1996; Moreland and Levine, 1992). In such groups, identifying a problem is more likely to be seen as harmful, by threatening morale or creating conflict over such issues as who caused the problem and who should solve it (cf. Ancona and Caldwell, 1988). Nemeth and Owens (1996) emphasized that in these situations people want to agree: 'They assume that truth lies in numbers and, furthermore, they are motivated to agree with the majority. They fear disapproval and possible rejection which emanates from maintaining a minority view' (p. 128). Indeed Nemeth and Owens (1996) argue this fear of rejection is not illusory. Those who deviate from the majority position are the target of communication aimed at changing their position and, if these attempts are not successful, the person who deviates is rejected (Schachter, 1959).

Tjosvold (1991) described constructive controversy within groups operating in a cooperative context as the open exploration of opposing opinions. He argues for a direct causal relationship with effectiveness and offers empirical support for this proposition (Tjosvold, 1985). Similar notions, though not well developed, have been proposed by Shiflett (1979) in relation to groups. At the organizational level, Argyris (1993) proposed the idea of 'double-loop learning' (identifying a problem and designing a solution that prevents the problem from arising again) in organizations as an indication of members' ability to recognize and modify underlying assumptions about organizational functioning. Dean and Sharfman (1996) studied 52 decisions in 24 companies and demonstrated clearly that the decision process has a sizeable impact on strategic decision making effectiveness.

6.2.2.3 Cohesiveness

Cohesiveness refers to the degree of interpersonal attraction and liking among team members and their liking for the team as a whole. There are sound reasons for arguing that cohesiveness will affect team performance, by influencing team members' helping behaviour and generosity, cooperation and problem-solving orientation during negotiations, and their membership of the team (see Isen and Baron, 1991). This may translate into greater motivation to contribute fully and perform well as a means of gaining approval and recognition (Festinger, Schachter and Back, 1950). However, the reviews of research evidence on the relationship between cohesiveness and team effectiveness are not conclusive. Guzzo and Dickson (1996) comment, 'the topic of cohesiveness is still very much an unsettled concern in the literature.' (p 310), and Guzzo and Shea (1992) observed that the data on the relationship between cohesiveness and performance are 'not unambiguous', concluding that relationship is not simple.

There is some evidence suggesting that members of socially integrated groups experience higher well-being, satisfaction, and exhibit greater efficiency in the coordination of tasks (Shaw, 1981; McGrath, 1984: O'Reilly, Caldwell and Barnett, 1989). Shaw and Shaw (1962) found that highly cohesive groups devoted more time to planning and problem-solving and that group members followed the established plan. Members in low-cohesion groups were hostile and aggressive; they tested each other immediately and did not engage in preliminary planning. Smith et al. (1994) found a substantial positive association between cohesion and the performance of top management teams. One explanation for this link between cohesion and effectiveness is suggested by the work of Ouchi (1980), who showed that highly socialized and cohesive groups have lower communication and coordination costs, are thus more efficient and flexible, and can apply greater attention to problems which require quick action. This explanation is supported by Zaccarro, Gualrtieri and Minionis (1995) who found that highly task-cohesive military teams under high time pressure performed as well on decision making tasks as did either high task-cohesive or low task-cohesive teams under low time urgency. This suggests that task cohesion can improve team decision making under time pressure.

A review (Mullen and Copper, 1994) involved a meta-analytical cross-lagged panel correlation, using 66 tests of the cohesiveness-performance effect. It revealed a consistent and highly significant relationship and that the direction of effect was stronger from performance to cohesion than from cohesion to performance. This is an important finding since it suggests that it is effective performance which influences cohesiveness more than the reverse association.

6.2.2.4 Team leadership

Team performance is determined by a wide range of factors – team composition (size, skills, knowledge, diversity), the team's task, organizational context, team processes, the level effort on the task, appropriateness of the strategies for achieving the task and the resources available to the team (Hackman, 1990; West, 2002). The behaviour of the team leader has the potential to influence all of the factors that contribute to team performance but particularly the team processes we describe above (Tannenbaum, Salas and Cannon-Bowers, 1996). The leader brings task expertise, abilities and attitudes to the team that influence the group design and group norms (Hackman, 1990, 1992, 2002), and, through monitoring, feedback and coaching, develops these processes, which enables the team to achieve its tasks (McIntyre and Salas, 1995). The leader also helps to define work structures and ensures that organizational supports are in place for the team Tesluk and Mathieu, 1999).

Leadership is particularly important for managing the influence of diversity on team processes and performance (discussed above): for ensuring that mechanisms are in place to enable team members to effectively contributes their unique knowledge, skills and experience relevant to the team task, and for ensuring that diverse perspectives are integrated and conflict effectively managed (by, for example, emphasizing shared objectives and vision) (Kim and Yukl, 1995)

Leaders of groups can seek ideas and support their implementation among members; leaders may promote only their own ideas; or leaders may resist change and innovation from any source. The leader, by definition, exerts powerful social influences on the group or team, and this also affects team performance (Beyerlein, Johnson and Beyerlein, 1996; Brewer, Wilson and Beck, 1994; Komaki, Desselles and Bowman, 1989). For example, research in Canadian manufacturing organizations reveals that CEOs' ages, flexibility and perseverance are all positively related to the adoption of technological innovation in their organizations (Kitchell, 1997).

In any discussion of team leadership it is important to acknowledge that leadership processes are not necessarily invested in one person in a team. In most work teams there is a single and clearly defined team leader or manager and his or her style and behaviour have a considerable influence in moderating the relationships between inputs and processes. But leadership processes can be distributed such that more than one or all team members take on leadership roles at various points in the team's activities. Consider for example the breast cancer care team responsible for diagnosis, surgery and post-operative treatment of patients. At various points the oncologist, surgeon and breast care nurse are likely to (and it is appropriate that they should) take leadership roles in the team (Haward et al., 2003).

Team leadership studies (cf. Barry, 1991; Kim, Min and Cha, 1999) have adopted role-based approaches to measure the specific leadership behaviours that team leaders perform in order to facilitate and direct teamwork. The basic premise of these studies is that team leaders must be competent at performing a diverse array of leadership activities. The most comprehensive framework was developed by McCall (1983) and recently reported and tested by Hooijberg and Choi (2000). This framework is based on the 'competing values theory', that leaders must grapple with very different roles, which can be categorized within the quadrant of internal versus external as well interpersonal verses personal. Yukl (2002) refined this taxonomy, drawing upon empirical studies of knowledge work teams, to identify four roles: boundary spanning (management of external relationships including coordinating tasks, negotiating resources and goals with stakeholders as well as scanning for information and ideas); facilitative (encourages an atmosphere conducive to teamwork, ensuring team interactions are equitable and safe; encouraging participation, sharing of ideas and open discussion of different perspectives); innovation stimulating leadership (acts as an innovator, envisions project opportunities and new approaches by questioning team assumptions and challenging the status quo); and directive leadership (drive structured and ordered performance of project work by communicating instructions, setting priorities, deadlines and standards).

Of the four roles described three pertain to leadership activities directed towards stimulating and managing cooperation within the team, whereas the fourth role, leadership boundary spanning, measures the extent to which the leader manages team relationships and coordination with the external environment. Thus while the nature and content of the roles differ, all roles require leader actions to stimulate and direct cooperation between individuals/groups to perform effectively and develop innovations.

No discussion of leadership in social or Industrial/Organizational psychology should neglect the impressive program of work carried out by Norman Maier and his colleagues in the 1960s and 1970s. Maier (1970) conducted a series of experiments with (mostly student) groups exploring the influence of different leadership styles on problem-solving and creativity. The results suggested that the leader should encourage 'problem mindedness' in groups on the basis that exploring the problem fully is the best way of eventually generating a rich vein of solution options. The leader can delay a group's criticism of an idea by asking for alternative contributions and should use his or her power to protect individuals with minority views, so that their opinions can be heard (Maier and Solem, 1962; see also Osborn, 1957). Maier (1970) argued that leaders should delay offering their opinions as long as possible, since propositions from leaders are often given undue weight and tend either to be too hastily accepted or rejected, rather than properly evaluated, a finding since replicated in a variety of applied studies. Maier (1970) concludes that leaders should function as 'the group's central nervous system': receive information, facilitate communication, relay messages and integrate responses – in short, integrate the group. The leader must be receptive to information, but not impose solutions. The leader should be aware of group processes; listen in order to understand rather than to appraise or refute; assume responsibility for accurate communication; be sensitive to unexpressed feelings; protect minority views; keep the discussion moving; and develop skills in summarizing (Maier, 1970).

Leadership processes have a considerable influence in determining whether team inputs, such as team task, team member characteristics, organizational context, are translated into group processes that produce team outputs. Leadership is also critical in reducing the negative impacts of team member diversity discussed above, and ensuring that the positive features of diversity are translated into effective team performance.

6.3   Conclusion

Teams make an important contribution to organizational performance so an understanding of the factors that promote team effectiveness and enable teams to achieve their potential is of interest to both researchers and practitioners. The literature reviewed highlights key factors that promote effective team working. Effective teams have the resources they need to carry out the team's task, this includes having a sufficient number of team members with the appropriate skills to achieve the task. Effective teams are based in an organizational context that is supportive of team working; a context that provides the feedback, rewards, training and support that promotes team working and enables teams to maximize their potential. To ensure that individual team members can contribute their knowledge and skills to achieving the team's tasks, mechanisms and processes must be in place that promote effective communication, decision making strategies and cohesiveness, and that help team members develop a shared understanding. These conditions for effective team working apply to all teams, but promoting effectiveness in teams that have a diverse composition presents additional challenges. As work tasks increase in complexity, the need for heterogeneity of skills within teams increases. It is therefore essential that the barriers to team effectiveness created by relation-orientated diversity are overcome so that the diverse range of knowledge and skills provided by team members can be combined to achieve the task. Team leaders have an important role to play in creating 'integrated' teams, teams that have shared objectives, are motivated to achieve these objectives, have the information and resources they need to achieve the team task, and effective integration processes. Effective leadership makes a critical contribution to maximizing the potential benefits of team working while minimizing the weaknesses, and in heterogeneous team, ensuring that the positive features of diversity in are transformed into effective team performance.

References

Ancona, D. F. and Caldwell, D. F. (1988) 'Bridging the boundary: External activity and performance in organisational teams', *Administrative Science Quarterly*, 37, 634–665.

Applebaum, E. and Batt, R. (1994) *The New American Workplace*. Ithaca, NY: ILR Press.

Argryis, C. (1993) 'On the nature of actionable knowledge', *The Psychologist*, 6, 29–32.

Bantel, K. A. (1993) 'Strategic clarity in banking: Role of top management team demography', *Psychological Reports*, *73*, 1187–1201.

Bantel, K. A. and Jackson, S. E. (1989) 'Top management and innovations in banking: Does the demography of the top team make a difference?, *Strategic Management Journal*, *10*, 107–124.

Barrick, M. R., Stewart, G. L., Neubert, J. M. and Mount, M. K. (1998) 'Relating member ability and personality to work-team processes and team effectiveness', *Journal of Applied Psychology*, 83, 377–391.

Barry, D. (1991) 'Managing the boss-less team: Lessons in distributed leadership', *Organizational Dynamics*, Summer, 31–47.

Barry, B, and Stewart, G. L. (1997) 'Composition, process and performance in self managed groups. The role of personality', *Journal of Applied Psychology*, 82, 62–78.

Beyerlein, M. M., Johnson, D. A. and Beyerlein, S. T. (eds) (1996) *Advances in the interdisciplinary study of work teams (Vol. 2): Knowledge work in teams*. London: JAI Press.

Billings, R. S., Milburn, T. W. and Schaalman, M. L. (1980) 'A model of crisis perception: A theoretical and empirical analysis', *Administrative Science Quarterly*, 25, 300–316.

Blakar, R. M. (1985) 'Towards a theory of communication in terms of preconditions: A conceptual framework and some empirical explorations' In H. Giles and R. N. St Clair (eds), *Recent Advances in Language, Communication and Social Psychology*. London: Lawrence Erlbaum.

Bottger, P. C. and Yetton, P. W. (1987) 'Improving group performance by training in individual problem solving', *Journal of Applied Psychology*, 72, 651–657.

Brewer, N., Wilson, C. and Beck, K. (1994) 'Supervisory behavior and team performance amongst police patrol sergeants', *Journal of Occupational and Organizational Psychology*, 67, 69–78.

Brown, R. J. (1988) *Group Processes: Dynamics Within and Between Groups*. London: Blackwell.

Campion, M. A., Medsker, G. J. and Higgs, A. C. (1993) 'Relations between work group characteristics and effectiveness: Implications for designing effective work groups', *Personnel Psychology*, 46, 823–850.

Campion, M. A., Papper, E. M. and Medsker, G. J. (1996) 'Relations between work team characteristics and effectiveness: A replication and extension', *Personnel Psychology*, 49, 429–689.

Cannon-Bowers, J. A., Salas, E. and Converse, S. A. (1993) 'Shared mental models in expert team decision-making' In N. J. Castellan (ed.) *Individual and group decision making* (pp. 221–246) Hillsdale, NJ: LEA.

Cohen, S. G., Ledford, G. E. and Spreitzer, G. M. (1994) 'A predictive model of self-managing work team effectiveness', *CEO Publications No. T94–28 (271)*, University of Southern California.

Cotton, J. L. (1993) *Employee Involvement*. Newbury Park, CA: Sage.

Cordery, J. L. (1996) 'Autonomous work groups' In M. A. West (ed.), *The Handbook of Work Group Psychology*. Chichester: Wiley.

De Dreu, C. K. W. (1995) 'Coercive power and concession making in bilateral negotiation', *Journal of Conflict Resolution*, 39, 646–670.

Dean, J. W. Jr and Sharfman, M. P. (1996) 'Does decision process matter? A study of strategic decision making effectiveness', *Academy of Management Journal*, 39 (2), 368–396.

Drory, A. and Shamir, B. (1988) 'Effects of organizational and life variables on job satisfaction and burnout', *Group and Organization Studies*, 13 (4), 441–455.

Edigo, C. (1990) 'Teleconferencing as a technology to support cooperative work: Its possibilities and limitations' In J. Galeghar, R. E. Kraut and C. Edigo (eds), *Intellectual Teamwork: Social and Technological Foundations of Cooperative Work*. Hillsdale, NJ: Lawrence Erlbaum.

Festinger, L., Schacher, S. and Back, K. (1950) *Social Pressures in Informal Groups: A Study of Human Factors in Housing*. New York: Harper.

Filley, A. C., House, R. J. and Kerr, S. (1976) *Managerial process and organizational behaviour*. Glenview, IL: Scott Foresman.

Finholt, T., Sproull, L. and Keisler, S. (1990) 'Communication and performance in ad hoc task groups' In J. Galeghar, R. E. Kraut and C. Edigo (eds), *Intellectual Teamwork: Social and Technological Foundations of Cooperative Work*. Hillsdale, NJ: Lawrence Erlbaum.

Ghiselli, E. E. and Lodahl, T. M. (1958) 'Patterns of managerial traits and group effectiveness', *Journal of Abnormal and Social Psychology, 57*, 61–66.

Gladstein, D. (1984) 'Groups in context: A model of task group effectiveness', *Administrative Science Quarterly, 29*, 499–517.

Goodman, P. S. (1986) *Designing Effective Work Groups*. San Francisco: Jossey-Bass.

Goodman, P. S., Ravlin, E. C. and Argote, L. (1986) 'Current thinking about groups: Setting the stage for new ideas' In P. S. Goodman (eds), *Designing Effective Work Groups* (pp. 1–33). San Francisco: Jossey-Bass.

Guzzo, R. A. (1996) Fundamental considerations about work groups. In M. A. West (ed.), *Handbook of Work Group Psychology* (pp. 3–24) Chichester: Wiley.

Guzzo, R. A. and Dickson, M. W. (1996) 'Teams in organisations: Recent research on performance and effectiveness', *Annual Review of Psychology, 46*, 307–338.

Guzzo, R. A. and Shea, G. P. (1992) 'Group performance and intergroup relations in organisations' In M. D. Dunnette and L. M. Hough (eds), *Handbook of Industrial and Organizational Psychology* (vol. 3, pp. 269–313). Palo Alto, CA: Consulting Psychologists Press.

Hackman, J. R. (2002) *Leading teams: Setting the stage for great performances*. Harvard, CN.: Harvard Business School.

Hackman, J. R. (1992) 'Group influences on individual in organisations', In M. D. Dunnette and L. M. Hough (eds) *Handbook of Industrial and Organisational Psychology* (vol. 3). Palo Alto, CA: Consulting Psychologists Press.

Hackman, J. R. (1990) (ed.), *Groups That Work (and Those That Don't): Creating Conditions for Effective Teamwork*. San Francisco: Jossey-Bass.

Hackman, J. R., Brousseau, K. R. and Weiss, J. A. (1976) 'The interaction of task design and group performance strategies in determining group effectiveness', *Organizational Behavior and Human Performance, 16*, 350–365.

Hackman, J. R. and Lawler, E. E. (1971) 'Employee reactions to job characteristics', *Journal of Applied Psychology*, 55 (3), 259–286.

Hackman, J. R. and Morris, C. G. (1975) 'Group task, group interaction process, and group performance effectiveness: A review and proposed integration' In L. Berkowitz (ed.) *Advances in Experimental Social Psychology* (vol. 8). New York: Academic Press.

Hackman, J. R. and Oldham, G. R. (1975) 'Development of the job diagnostic survey', *Journal of Applied Psychology*, 60, 159–170.

Haward, R. Amir, Z., Borrill, C. S., Dawson, J., Scully, J, West, M. A. and Sainsbury, R. (2003) 'Breast cancer teams: The impact of constitution, new cancer workload, and methods of operation on their effectiveness', *British Journal of Cancer*, 89 (1), 15–22.

Haythorn, W. W. (1968) 'The composition of groups: A review of the literature', *Acta Psychologica, 28*, 97–128.

Hedburg, B. L. T., Nystrom, P. C. and Starbuck, W. H. (1976) 'Camping on seesaws: prescriptions for a self-designing organization', *Administrative Science Quarterly*, 21, 41–65.

Hill, G. W. (1982) 'Group versus individual performance: Are n+1 heads better than one?', *Psychological Bulletin*, 91, 517–539.

Hirokawa, R. Y. (1990) 'The role of communication in group decision-making efficacy: A task-contingency perspective', *Small Group Research*, 21, 190–204.

Hoffman, L. R. (1959) 'Applying experimental research on group problem solving to organizations', *Journal of Abnormal and Social Psychology*, 58, 27–32.

Hoffman, L. R., Harburg, E. and Maier, N. R. F. (1962) 'Differences and disagreement as factors in creative group problem solving', *Journal of Abnormal and Social Psychology*, 64, 206–214.

Hoffman, L. R. and Maier, N. R. F. (1961) 'Sex differences, sex composition, and group problem-solving', *Journal of Abnormal and Social Psychology*, 63, 453 456.

Hogg, M. and Abrams, D. (1988) *Social Identifications: A Social Psychology of Intergroup Relations and Group Processes*. London: Routledge.

Hollingshead, A. B. and McGrath, J. E. (1995) 'Computer-assisted groups: A critical review of the empirical research' In R. A. Guzzo and E. Salas (eds), *Team Effectiveness and Decision Making in Organization*. San Francisco: Jossey-Bass.

Hoojberg, R. and Choi, J. (2000) 'Which leadership roles matter to whom? An examination of rater effects on perceptions of effectiveness', *Leadership Quarterly*, 11(3) 341–364.

Isen, A. M. and Baron, R. A. (1991) 'Positive affect as a factor in organizational Behavior' In L. L. Cummings and B. M. Staw (eds), *Research in Organizational Behavior* (vol. 13). Greenwich, CT: JAI Press.

Jackson, L. A., Sullivan, L. A. and Hodge, L. N. (1993) 'Stereotype effects on attributions, predictions and evaluations: No two social judgements are quite alike', *Journal of Personality and Social Psychology*, 65 (1), 69–84.

Jackson, S. E. (1992) 'Consequences of group composition for the interpersonal dynamics of strategic issue processing', *Advances in Strategic Management*, 8, 345–382.

Jackson, S. E. (1996) 'The consequences of diversity in multidisciplinary work teams' In M. A. West (ed.) *Handbook of work group psychology* (pp. 53–75). Chichester, England: Wiley.

Jackson, S. E., Brett, J. F., Sessa, V. I., Cooper, D. M., Julin, J. A. and Peyronnin, K. (1991) 'Some differences make a difference: Individual dissimilarity and group heterogeneity as collates of recruitment, promotions and turnover', *Journal of Applied Psychology*, 76, 675–689.

Jackson, S. E., May, K. E. and Witney, K. (1995) 'Understanding the dynamics of diversity in decision-making teams' In R. A. Guzzo, E. Salas, and Associates (eds) *Team effectiveness and decision making in organizations*. San Francisco: Jossey-Bass.

Janis, I. L. (1982) *Groupthink: A Study of Foreign Policy Decisions and Fiascos*, 2nd edn. Boston: Houghton Mifflin.

Jervis, I. L. (1976) *Perception and Misperception in International Politics*. Princeton, NJ: Princeton University Press.

Jussim, L. (1986) 'Self-fulfilling prophecies: A theoretical and integrative review', *Psychological Review*, 93(1), 429–445.

Jussim, L., Coleman, L. M. and Lerch (1987) 'The nature of stereotypes: A comparison and integration of 3 theories', *Journal of Personality and Social Psychology*, 52 (3), 536–546.

Katzenbach, J. R. and Smith, D. K. (1993) *The wisdom of teams: Creating the high performance organization*. Boston, MA: Harvard Business School Press.

Keller, R. T. (1992) 'Transformational leadership and the performance of research and development research groups', *Journal of Management*, 18 (3), 489–501.

Kent, R. N. and McGrath, J. E. (1969) 'Task and group characteristics as factors influencing group performance', *Journal of Experimental Social Psychology*, 5, 429–440.

Kim, Y., Min, B. and Cha, J. (1999) 'The roles of R & D team leaders in Korea: A contingent approach', *R & D Management*, 29 (2), 153–165.

Kim, H. and Yukl, G. (1995) 'Relationships of managerial effectiveness and advancement to self-reported leadership-reported leadership behaviors from the multiple-linkage model', *Leadership Quarterly*, 6(3), 361–377.

Kimble, C. E., Marsh, N. B. and Kiska, A. C. (1984) 'Sex, age and cultural differences in self-reported assertiveness', *Psychological Reports*, 55, 419–422.

Kitchell, S. (1997) 'CEO characteristics and technological innovativeness: A Canadian perspective', *Canadian Journal of Administrative Sciences*, 14, 111–125.

Klimoski, R. and Mohammed, S. (1994) 'Team mental model: Construct or metaphor?', *Journal of Management*, 20, 403–437.

Komaki, J. L., Desselles, M. L. and Bowman, E. D. (1989) 'Definitely not a breeze: Extending an operant model of effective supervision to teams', *Journal of Applied Psychology*, 74, 522–529.

Kozlowski, S. W. J. and Bell, B. S. (2002) 'Work groups and teams in organizations' In W. C. Borman, D. R. Ligen, and R. J. Klimoski (eds), *Comprehensive handbook of psychology* (vol. 12): *Industrial and organizational psychology* (pp. 333–375). New York: Wiley.

Kraemer, K. L. and Pinsonneault, A. (1990) 'Technology and groups: Assessments of the empirical research' In J. Galeghar, R. E. Kraut and C. Edigo (eds) *Intellectual Teamwork: Social and Technological Foundations of Cooperative Work*. Hillsdale, NJ: Lawrence Erlbaum.

Krauss, R. M. and Fussell, S. R. (1990) 'Mutual Knowledge and communicable effectiveness' In J. Galeghar, R. E. Kraut and C. Edigo (eds) *Intellectual Teamwork: Social and Technological Foundations of Cooperative Work*. Hillsdale, NJ: Lawrence Erlbaum.

LaFrance, M. and Mayo, C. (1978) *Moving Bodies: Nonverbal Communication in Social Relationships*. Monterey, C. A.: Brooks/Cole.

Landsberger, H. A. (1955) 'Interaction process analysis of the mediation of labor management disputes', *Journal of Abnormal and Social Psychology*, 51, 522–528.

Latham, G. P., Erez, M. and Locke, E. A. (1988) 'Resolving scientific disputes by the joint design of crucial experiments by the antagonists: Application to the Erez Latham dispute regarding participation in goal setting', *Journal of Applied Psychology*, 73(4), 753–772.

Lawler, E. E., Mohrman, S. A. and Ledford, G. E. (1992) *Employee involvement and total quality management: Practices and results in Fortune 1000 companies*. San Francisco: Jossey-Bass.

Levine, J. M. and D'Andrea-Tyson, L. (1990) 'Participation, productivity, and the firm's environment' In A. S. Blinder (ed.) *Paying for Productivity* (pp. 183–237). Washington, DC: Brokkings Institution.

Levine, J. M. and Moreland, R. L. (1990) 'Progress in small group research', *Annual Review of Psychology*, 41, 585–634.

Lyles, M. A. (1981) 'Formulating strategic problems: Empirical analysis and problem development', *Strategic Management Journal*, 2, 61–75.

Macy, B. A. and Izumi, H. (1993) 'Organizational change, design and work innovation: A meta-analysis of 131 North American field studies, 1961–1991', *Research in Organizational Change and Design* (vol. 7). Greenwich, CT: JAI Press.

Maier, N. R. F. (1970) *Problem Solving and Creativity in Individuals and Groups*. Monterey, CA: Brooks/Cole.

Maier, N. R. F. and Solem, A. R. (1962) 'Improving solutions by turning choice situations into problems', *Personnel Psychology*, 15, 151–157.

Main, J. (1989) 'At last, software CEOs can use', *Fortune*, 13 March, 77–83.

Marks, M. A., Zaccaro, S. J. and Mathieu, J. E. (2000) 'Performance implications of leader briefings and team interaction training for team adaptation to novel environments', *Journal of Applied Psychology*, 85, 7971–986.

Martz, W. B., Jr., Vogel, R. R. and Nunamaker, J. F., Jr. (1992) 'Electronic meeting systems: Results from the field', *Decision Support Systems*, 8, 141–158.

Mathieu, J. E., Heffner, T. S., Goodwin, G. F., Salas, E. and Connon-Bowers, J. A. (2000) 'The influence of shared mental models on team process and performance', *Journal of Applied Psychology*, 85, 273–283.

Mathison, D. L. and Tucker, R. K. (1982) 'Sex differences in assertive behaviour: A research extension', *Psychological Reports*, 51(3), 943–948.

Maznevski, M. L. (1994) 'Understanding our differences: Performance in decision making groups with diverse members', *Human Relations*, 47(5), 531–552.

McCain, B. R., O'Reilly, C. C. III and Pfeffer, J. (1983) 'The effects of departmental demography on turnover', *Academy of Management Journal*, 26, 626–641.

McCall, M. W. Jr. (1983) 'Developing Leadership' In Galbraith, J. L., Lawler, E. E. III and Associates, *Organizing for the Future: The New Logic for Managing Complex Organizations*. Jossey Bass Series, pp. 256–284.

McGrath, J. E. (1984) *Groups: Interaction and Performance*. Englewood Cliffs, NJ: Prentice-Hall.

McIntyre, R. M. and Salas, E. (1995) 'Measuring and managing for team performance: lessons from complex environments' In R. Guzzo and Salas (eds), *Team effectiveness and decision-making in organizations*. San Francisco, C.A.: Jossey-Bass.

Miceli, M. P. and Near, J. P. (1985) 'Characteristics of organisational climate and perceived wrong-doing associated with whistle-blowing decisions', *Personnel Psychology*, 38, 525–544.

Milliken, F. J. and Martins, L. L. (1996) 'Searching for common threads: Understanding the multiple effects of diversity in organizational groups', *Academy of Management Review*, 21(2), 402–433.

Mitroff, J., Barabba, N. and Kilmann, R. (1977) 'The application of behaviour and philosophical technologies to strategic planning: a case study of a large federal agency', *Management Studies* 24, 44–58.

Mohrman, S. A., Cohen, S. G. and Mohrman, A. M., Sr (1995) *Designing Team-Based Organizations*. San Francisco: Jossey-Bass.

Moos, R. H. and Spiesman, J. C. (1962) 'Group compatibility and productivity', *Journal of Abnormal and Social Psychology* 65, 190–196.

Moreland, R. L. and Levine, J. M. (1992) 'The composition of small groups' In E. J. Lawler, B. Markovsky, C. Ridgeway and H. A. Walker (eds) *Advances in group processes* (Vol. 9, pp. 237–280). Greenwich, CT: JAI Press.

Mullen, B. and Copper, C. (1994) 'The relation between group cohesiveness and performance: An integration', *Psychological Bulletin* 103, 27–43.

Nemeth, C. and Owens, P. (1996) 'Making work groups more effective: The value of minority dissent' In M. A. West (ed.), *Handbook of work group psychology*, (pp. 125–142). Chichester, England: John Wiley.

Neuman, G. A., Wagner, S. H. and Christiansen, N. D. (1999) 'The relationship between work-team personality composition and the job performance of teams', *Group and Organizational Management*, 24, 28–45.

Neuman, G. A. and Wright, J. (1999) 'Team effectiveness: Beyond skills and cognitive Ability', *Journal of Applied Psychology*, 84, 376–389.

O'Reilly, C. A., Caldwell, D. F. and Barnett, W. P. (1989) 'Work group demography, social integration and turnover', *Administrative Science Quarterly*, 34, 21–37.

Olson, G. M. and Atkins, D. E. (1990) 'Supporting collaboration with advanced multi-media electronic mail: The NSF EXPRESS project' In J. Galeghar, R. E. Kraut and C. Edigo (eds), *Intellectual Teamwork: Social and Technological Foundations of Cooperative Work*. Hillsdale, NJ: Lawrence Erlbaum.

Osborn, A. F. (1957) *Applied imagination*. New York: Scribner's.

Ouchi, W. G. (1980) 'Markets, bureaucracies and clans', *Administrative Science Quarterly*, 34, 21–37.

Pelz, D. C. (1956) 'Some social factors related to performance in a research organization', *Administrative Science Quarterly*, 1, 310–325.

Redmond, M. V. (1989) 'The functions of empathy (decentring) in human relations', *Human Relations*, 42, 593–605.

Redmond. M. V. (1992) A multi-dimensional theory and measure of decentring. Unpublished manuscript.

Rice, R. E. and Shork, D. E. (1990) 'Voice messaging, coordination and communication' In J. Galeghar, R. E. Kraut and C. Edigo (eds), *Intellectual Teamwork: Social and Technological Foundations of Cooperative Work*. Hillsdale, NJ: Lawrence Erlbaum.

Schachter, S. (1959) *The Psychology of Affiliation*. Stanford: Stanford University Press.

Scharf, A. (1989) 'How to change seven rowdy people', *Industrial Management*, 31, 20–22.

Schutz, W. C. (1955) 'What makes groups productive?', *Human Relations*, 8, 429–465.

Schutz, W. C. (1958) *FIRO: A three-dimensional theory of interpersonal Behaviour*. New York: Holt Rinehart.

Schutz, W. C. (1967) *JOY: Expanding Human Awareness*. New York: Grove Press.

Schwenk, C. R. (1988) *The Essence of Strategic Decision-making*. Cambridge, NIA: Heath.

Schwenk, C. R. and Thomas, H. (1983) 'Formulating the mess: The role of decision aids in problem formulation', *Omega*, 11, 239–252.

Shaw, M. E. (1981) *Group dynamics: The Psychology of Small Group Behavior*. New York: McGraw-Hill.

Shaw, M. E. and Nickols, S. A. (1964) *Group effectiveness as a function of group member compatibility and cooperation requirements of the task*. (Technical report No. 4, ONR contract NR 170–266, Nonr-580 (111) Gainesville: University of Florida.

Shaw, M. E. and Shaw, L. M. (1962) 'Some effects of sociometric grouping upon learning in a second grade classroom', *Journal of Social Psychology* 57, 453–458.

Shiflett, S. (1979) 'Towards a general model of small group productivity', *Psychological Bulletin* 86, 67–79.

Smircich, L. (1983) 'Organization as shared meaning' In L. R. Pondy, P. Frost, G. Morgan and T. Dandridge (eds), *Organizational Symbolism* (pp. 55–65). Greenwich, CT: JAI Press.

Smith, K. G., Locke, E. A. and Barry, D. (1990) 'Goal setting, planning and organizational performance: An experimental simulation', *Organizational Behavior and Human Decision Processes*, 46, 118–134.

Smith, K. G., Smith, K. A., Olian, J. D., Sims, H. P. Jr, O. Brannon, D. P. and Scully, J. A. (1994) 'Top management team demography and process. The role of social integration and communication', *Administrative Science Quarterly*, 39, 412–438.

Stein, M. (1996) 'Unconscious phenomena in work groups' In M. A. West (ed.), *Handbook of Work Group Psychology* (pp. 143–157). Chichester: Wiley.

Steiner, I. D. (1972) *Group process and productivity*. New York: Academic Press.

Sternberg, R. J. and Lubart, T. I. (1990) *Defying the Crowd. Cultivating Creativity in a Culture of Conformity*. New York: Free Press.

Stevens, M. J. and Campion, M. A. (1994) 'The knowledge, skills and ability requirements for teamwork: Implications for human resource management', *Journal of Management*, 20 (2), 503–530.

Sundstrom, E., De Meuse, K. P. and Futrell, D. (1990) 'Work teams: Applications and effectiveness', *American Psychologist*, 45, 120–133.

Sundstrom, E., McIntyre, M., Halthill, T. and Richards, H. (2000) 'Work groups from Hawthorne studies to work teams of the 1990's and beyond', *Group Dynamics: Theory, Research and Practice*, 4, 44–67.

Tajfel, H. (1978) *Differentiation Between Social Groups: Studies in the Social Psychology of Intergroup Relations* (European Monographs in Social Psychology, No. 14). London: Academic Press.

Tajfel, H. and Turner, J. C. (1979) 'An integrative theory of intergroup conflict' In W. G. Austin and S. Worchel (eds), *Social Psychology of Intergroup Relations*. Monterey, CA: Brooks/Cole.

Tannenbaum, S. I., Beard, R. L. and Salas, E. (1992) 'Team building and its influence on team effectiveness: An examination of conceptual and empirical developments' In K. Kelley (ed.), *Issues, Theory and Research in Industrial/Organizational Psychology* (pp. 117–153). London: North Holland.

Tannebaum, S. I., Salas, E. and Cannon-Bowers, J. A. (1996) 'Promoting team effectiveness' In M. A. West (ed.), *Handbook of Work Group Psychology*. Chichester: Wiley.

Tesluk, P. E. and Mathieu, J. E. (1999) 'Overcoming roadblocks to effectiveness: Incorporating management of performance barriers into the models of work group effectiveness', *Journal of Applied Psychology*, 84, 200–217.

Tjosvold, D. (1985) 'Implications of controversy research for management', *Journal of Management*, 11, 21–37.

Tjosvold, D. (1991) *Team Organisation: An Enduring Competitive Advantage*. Chichester: Wiley.

Tziner, A. E. and Eden, D. (1985) 'Effects of crew composition on crew performance: Does the whole equal the sum of its parts?', *Journal of Applied Psychology*, 70, 85–93.

Ulich, E. and Weber, W. G. (1996) 'Dimensions, criteria and evaluation of work group autonomy' In M. A. West (ed.), *Handbook of Work Group Psychology* (pp. 247–282). Chichester: Wiley.

Unsworth, K. L. (1995) Perceptions of assertion in the workplace: The impact of ethnicity, sex and organizational status. Unpublished manuscript, University of Queensland, Australia.

Vogel, D. R. and Nunamaker, J. F. (1990) 'Design and assessment of a group decision support system' In J. Galeghar, R. E. Kraut and C. Edigo (eds), *Intellectual Teamwork: Social and Technological Foundations of Cooperative Work*. Hillsdale, NJ: Lawrence Erlbaum.

Vroom, V. H. (1964) *Work and Motivation*. New York: Wiley.

Wagner, W. G., Pfeffer, J. and O'Reilly, C. A. (1984) 'Organizational demography and turnover in top management groups', *Administrative Science Quarterly*, 29, 74–92.

Watson, W. E., Kumar, K. and Michaelsen, L. K. (1993) 'Cultural diversity's impact on interaction process and performance: Comparing homogeneous and diverse task groups', *Academy of Management Journal*, 36, 590–602.

Weldon, E. and Weingart, L. R. (1993) 'Group goals and group performance', *British Journal of Social Psychology*, 32, 307–334.

West, M. A. (1997) *Developing Creativity in Organisations*. Chichester: Wiley.

West, M. A. (2002) 'Sparkling fountains or stagnant ponds: An integrative model of creativity and innovation implementation in work groups', *Applied Psychology: An International Review*, 51, 355–424.

West, M. A. and Anderson, N. (1996) 'Innovation in top management teams', *Journal of Applied Psychology*, 81, 680–693.

Wiersema, M. F. and Bantel, K. A. (1992) 'Top management team demography and corporate strategic change', *Academy of Management Journal*, 35, 91–121.

Willems, E. P. and Clark, R. D. III. (1971) 'Shift toward risk and heterogeneity of Groups', *Journal of Experimental and Social Psychology*, 7, 302–312.

Wood, W. (1987) 'Meta-analytic review of sex differences in group performance', *Psychological Bulletin*, 102, 53–71.

Yukl, G. A. (2002) *Leadership in Organizations (5th edn)* New Jersey: Prentice Hall.

Zaccaro, S. J., Gualtieri, J. and Minionis, D. (1995) 'Task cohesion as a facilitator of team decision making under temporal urgency', *Military Psychology*, 7(2), 77–93.

Zenger, T. R. and Lawrence, B. S. (1989) 'Organizational demography: The differential effects of age and tenure distributions on technical communication', *Academy of Management Journal*, 32, 353–376.

7

Teams over Time – a Logical Perspective

Wiebe van der Hoek, Marc Pauly and Michael Wooldridge

Although the notion of 'agency' has always been central to the 50-year old discipline of Artificial Intelligence, the research focus within this field has historically been on isolated, disembodied intelligences. It is only since the early 1980s, and the emergence of the sub-field known as *distributed AI*, that the emphasis within this community began to change, and focus on cooperative problem-solving and teamwork (Bond and Gasser, 1988).

One aspect of this change of focus has been the use of formal methods – including mathematical logic – to formalize and explore the properties of both human and artificial societies. A central concern of these logical approaches to teams is a formalization of team ability, or cooperation. A basic research issue in such work is: How can we create a mathematically precise model of situations where multiple agents interact, and of the powers that different teams have in such a situation? The models used here are essentially game-theoretic in nature, and the logical perspective we apply to these models focuses on logical expressions of the form *[C]p*, which is intended to express the fact that team *C* can achieve or bring about a certain property *p*. We shall use the terms 'team', 'group', and 'coalition' interchangeably, since the logical approach we will present does not distinguish them. In fact, this notion of a team is as simple as one could conceive of: a team is simply a set of individuals. Similarly, teamwork is formalized as the execution of a joint strategy of the members of the team. Using this framework, we can investigate team interaction, and we can compare the efficacy of different teams in order to determine optimal team architecture.

As these remarks suggest, compared to many other approaches to teams and teamwork, our logical approach is very simple, if not naive. The kinds of issues we are interested in here do not even try to address the interesting questions discussed in some of the other contributions of this collection. However, we believe that before addressing more complex questions (such as what makes a group of individuals identify as a team), we should try to develop a mathematically precise structure that can provide a framework within which such questions may be formulated. How far the present logical approach can be developed to address issues relating to teams remains to be seen, as much of the work reported here is of relatively recent origin.

A second argument for the logical approach to teams presented here is the new questions that it raises, even at this admittedly simple level of conceptualization. In section 7.1, we start by considering the basic logic of teams, namely *Coalition Logic* (cf. Pauly, 2002). Already on this level, we can investigate how certain logical properties of team ability are related to the underlying structure of the interaction – for example, whether agents act simultaneously or in turns. Furthermore, how does reasoning about individuals differ from reasoning about teams, e.g. is the latter inherently more complex than the former?

Section 7.2 adds to the basic logical language of team ability new temporal operators, yielding *Alternating-time Temporal Logic* (Alur et al., 1997). Rather than being able to express only what teams can achieve in the short term by coordinating their actions, this extended language allows one to talk about the long-term properties of cooperation. While cooperation may not be profitable in the short term, it may significantly alter the goals that can be achieved at some point in the future, or the desirable properties that can be maintained.

Section 7.3 introduces further expressiveness into the basic logic of teams, by allowing individuals (and hence teams) to have only partial information about the current situation. Members of the team often have very different kinds and levels of knowledge, and their ability to cooperate as a team may be significantly influenced by their knowledge. Defining precisely the knowledge preconditions for team cooperation is one of the main challenges in this area. In terms of the logical language, the resulting *Alternating-time Temporal Epistemic Logic* (van der Hoek and Wooldridge 2003) can express, e.g. that one team can cooperate to get another team to know something at some point in the future. The fact that the precise mathematical formulation of this logic is (at the time of writing) still under discussion demonstrates that the issues involved are by no means trivial.

Note that we have deliberately written this exposition of team logics in a very informal style, choosing to emphasize the intuitions underlying the central concepts, and focusing on some interesting questions arising from the logical perspective. Nonetheless, since a full understanding of the ideas presented here requires more mathematical precision, we hope that the interested reader will feel compelled to study some of the references providing more detail. While much of the work cited resides in the literature of computer science and Artificial Intelligence, we hope that our examples convince the reader that our logical perspective does not apply solely to artificial agents.

7.1 The basic logic of cooperation

On the most basic level, a *team* is a group with a common goal, which can only be achieved by appropriate combinations of individual activities. Similarly, we can view *teamwork* as the cooperation of the team members towards achieving the common goal. These notions have been formalized in *Coalition Logic* (Pauly, 2002), a formal system for reasoning about the ability of coalitions or teams to bring about various goals. The central expression of Coalition Logic is

$[C]p$

which expresses that team C can achieve goal p. Teams here are simply collections of individuals, whereas p is some expression describing the goal state. Besides this modal expression, Coalition Logic also allows for the standard Boolean operations of negation ($\neg$), disjunction ($\vee$), conjunction ($\wedge$) and implication ($\rightarrow$). For example, the expression

$[\{Mike, Wiebe, Marc\}]$ TEAM_PAPER $\wedge \neg[\{Wiebe, Marc\}]$ TEAM_PAPER

states that Mike, Wiebe and Marc can cooperate to achieve a paper on teams, but Wiebe and Marc alone cannot achieve such a paper. In this approach, we also allow for teams consisting of a single individual, e.g.

$\neg[\{Marc\}]$ (HAPPINESS $\vee$ WEALTH)

states that it is not the case that Marc (by himself) can achieve happiness or wealth.

7.1.1 Logical properties of cooperation

Coalition Logic thus allows us to investigate the basic properties of teamwork or cooperation, such as the fact that Marc, Wiebe, and Mike can cooperate to write a paper on teams, and they can also cooperate to not write such a paper. In general, if a team can bring about p, does it follow that it can bring about $\neg p$ as well? Similarly, Mike, Wiebe and Marc can write a paper on teams, they can meet for coffee, and they can also write the paper while meeting for coffee. Again, in general, is it the case that if a team can bring about p and it can bring about q, then it can bring about $p \wedge q$ as well? We will see later that the answer to both questions is negative. Still, we will also be able to formulate some positive properties, some basic laws of teamwork. The central law will specify how the power of a team is related to the abilities of its members.

In order to answer these questions, we need to be more precise about the kinds of situations we are describing with our logical expressions, i.e. we need to define the *semantics* of our language. On the most general level, a situation involving a number of interacting individuals can be modelled as a strategic game (for an introduction to game theory, see e.g. Osborne and Rubinstein, 1994). As an example, suppose Mike and Marc are considering whether or not to go out to dinner together, and if so, to which restaurant. Mike is busy, and hence he will decide on short notice whether the dinner goes through or not. Marc, on the other hand is vegetarian, and since he knows more about the vegetarian options in the different restaurants, the choice of restaurant, *Ego* or *The Other Place (TOP)*, is up to him. The situation is modelled by the game in Figure 7.1.

Each individual has to make a choice from two options, and the resulting states of affairs are given in the matrix. For example, the state s_2 results if Mike decides he is busy while Marc chooses *The Other Place*. We can introduce an expression DINNER which holds at states s_3 and s_4, and an expression DINNER-EGO which holds only at state s_3. Then

$$[\{Mike\}] \text{ DINNER}$$

holds in the sense that Mike has a strategy or action available *(Free)* which guarantees that no matter what Marc does (i.e. independent of whether he chooses *Ego* or *TOP*), DINNER will hold. On the other hand,

$$\neg [\{Mike\}] \text{ DINNER-EGO}$$

holds since neither of Mike's strategies will guarantee a dinner at the *Ego* restaurant (Marc may choose *TOP*). In order to achieve *the* DINNER-EGO goal, both need to cooperate,

$$[\{Marc, Mike\}] \text{ DINNER-EGO}$$

holds, since Mike can choose *Free* and Marc can choose *Ego*. In general, the matrices can be extended to more than two players, but the interpretation we give to team ability remains the same: *[C]p* holds if and only if the members of team *C* can choose their actions in such a way that *no matter*

Mike \ Marc	Ego	TOP
Busy	s_1	s_2
Free	s_3	s_4

Figure 7.1 Strategic game for two players

what the other individuals do (those not in team C), the outcome of the game will satisfy p.

Using this definition of cooperative ability, we can now investigate the logical properties of teamwork. We say that a formula of Coalition Logic is *valid* if it holds in all possible situations (models, strategic games), and we obtain the logical properties of teamwork by investigating the valid formulas of Coalition Logic. First, the earlier dinner example can be utilized to see that

$$[C]p \rightarrow [C]\neg p$$

is not valid, if for p we substitute *¬DINNER-EGO*. For while it is true that *[{Mike}] ¬DINNER-EGO* holds (he can simply decide to be busy), *[{Mike}] DINNER-EGO* does not hold, as we saw earlier. Second, note that *while [{Mike}]DINNER* and *[{Mike}]¬DINNER* both hold, *[{Mike}] (DINNER ∧ ¬DINNER)* does not hold. Hence, $([C]p \wedge [C]q) \rightarrow [C](p \wedge q)$ also is not valid.

There is a list of such axioms for Coalition Logic that has the property of being *logically complete*, in the sense that any valid statement of the logic follows from them. The two central logical properties of this complete axiomatization are *monotonicity* and *superadditivity*. The monotonicity axiom

$$[C]p \rightarrow [C](p \vee q)$$

states that if a team can achieve a goal p, it can also achieve every goal that is weaker than p. The superadditivity axiom, on the other hand, expresses when and how teams can combine their abilities to form bigger super-teams:

$$([C]p \wedge [D]q) \rightarrow [C \cup D](p \wedge q) \ (C \cap D = \varnothing)$$

If team C can cooperate to achieve p and team D can cooperate to achieve q, then they can join into a big team to achieve both p and q together. For this team formation to be possible, however, the two teams must be *disjoint*: they must not have any member in common. We already saw an example of the invalidity of this law when $C = D = \{Mike\}$ in the dinner example. More generally, if C and D share a member, this person has conflicting allegiances. His strategy for achieving p (with team C) may be in conflict with his strategy for achieving q (with team D). If the teams are disjoint, no such conflict can arise.

7.1.2 Dynamic team interaction

So far, we have viewed team interaction as a single, one-shot event. In the restaurant example, both Mike and Marc choose their strategies, an outcome results, and that is the end of the interaction. In many real-life situations, however, individuals interact repeatedly. After having arrived at the restaurant, Mike and Marc might interact with the waiter, who may choose to suggest different dishes on the menu. Hence, at the outcome states s_i of the restaurant game, a new game may be played, whose outcome states again may be associated to a new game, etc. Game theoretically, the resulting dynamic model of team interaction is essentially an *extensive game of almost perfect information* (i.e. allowing for simultaneous moves), and can be pictured as in Figure 7.2.

Hence, in a dynamic interaction model, we have a set of states S such that each state s_i in S is associated with a strategic game, whose outcome states are again states in S. Note that different games may involve different subsets of agents. In the model depicted, the strategic game at state s_0 involves only player 1 who can choose the next state. If he chooses s_1, player 1 and 2 will engage in a strategic game whose outcome is, e.g. s_0 again in case player 1 (row player) chooses r and player 2 (column player) chooses l.

In order to evaluate our logical formulas, we now need to specify a state of the dynamic model. Hence, a coalition C may have a joint strategy to achieve p at state s_1, but not at state s_2. In such a *dynamic* interaction model, Coalition Logic also allows us to express multistage coalitional ability: $[C][D]p$ is true at a state s if coalition C has a joint strategy to achieve some state t at which coalition D has a joint strategy to achieve p.

The picture we have given so far presents the most general case, where we allow arbitrary strategic games to be associated to states. Often, the

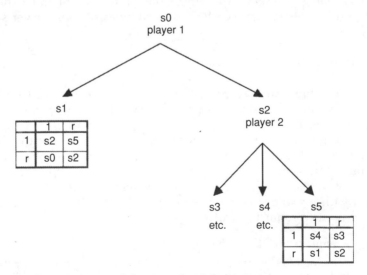

Figure 7.2   Extensive game of almost perfect information

interaction will be much more structured, and the strategic games will then be of a particular type. Hence, we can investigate the typology of interaction by looking at different common subclasses of dynamic models. We will only discuss one particular class of dynamic models, since it allows us to discuss the difference between sequential and concurrent teamwork.

The simplest type of dynamic model allows for interaction only sequentially. In these *turn-based interaction models*, only a single player has a choice to make. Hence, at state s_1, player 2 might be able to determine the next state, and at state s_2, player 1 might be in charge. In the two-player case, this means that the strategic game matrix associated with each state is a single column or row. Game theoretically, these turn-based models are essentially *extensive games of perfect information* – simple game trees such as in Figure 7.3.

In turn-based models, there is no immediate or short-term interaction. Everything that can be achieved by a coalition can already be achieved by one of its members, and hence there is no reason to team up. Formally, this property is expressed by the following axiom, which holds in all turn-based models:

$$[C]p \leftrightarrow ([c_1]p \lor \ldots \lor [c_n]p),$$

where $C=\{c_1,\ldots,c_n\}$. Note that the implication from right to left holds in any dynamic interaction model. The earlier restaurant example shows that the other direction does not hold in general. For while Mike and Marc together have a strategy to dine in *Ego*, neither of them individually has such a strategy. In turn-based models, on the other hand, it is easy to see that this axiom holds. Consider any state s at which individual i can determine the next state. If $[C]p$ holds at s, the members of C have a joint strategy to achieve p at s. Then either i is a member of C and $[i]p$ holds (since i is the only one who influences the outcome), or i is not a member of C, in which

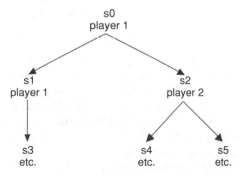

Figure 7.3 Extensive game of perfect information

case *p* must hold at all outcomes independent of *i*'s choice, and hence for every member *c* of *C* we must have *[c]p*.

But note also that while teams appear to add nothing in the short term, this does not necessarily eliminate the need for teamwork. In Liverpool, Mike may have the money to rent a car, but no driver's license, and Wiebe may have a driver's license but no money. Hence, Mike has a strategy for renting a car, and at the resulting state, where Mike has a car, Wiebe has the strategy to get both Mike and himself to London. At each state, one of the two does not need the other's cooperation to get to the next state, but overall, to get from Liverpool (the initial state) to London, Wiebe and Mike still need to cooperate. Formally, *[{Mike}][{Wiebe}]* LONDON holds at the initial state, but there is no single individual *i* for which *[{i}][{i}]* LONDON holds, while *[{Mike,Wiebe}][{Mike,Wiebe}]* LONDON does hold. In other words, while turn-based models eliminate the need for instantaneous or concurrent teamwork, there may still be the need for *sequential* teamwork.

7.1.3   Team design and system verification

The car rental situation also serves as a simple example of how Coalition Logic can be used to investigate optimal team design. As the designer, we may have certain criteria according to which we judge teams to be more or less optimal. As an example, a simple criterion might be that smaller teams are preferable. Given a dynamic interaction model and a goal *p* which we want to achieve, we can test for the smallest coalition *C* for which *[C]p* holds. If *[C]p* does not hold for any coalition *C*, this may be the case because the goal cannot be achieved in one step, as in the car rental example. In that case, we may want to check for the smallest number *k* and the smallest coalition *C* such that $[C]^k p$ holds (i.e. *[C]...[C]* k-times). In our car rental example, the smallest coalition was *{Wiebe,Mike}*, and the smallest *k* was 2. In general, there may be tradeoffs involved, e.g. a bigger coalition may achieve the goal earlier than a smaller coalition. Furthermore, we may also be interested to know that not every member of the team is needed at every step of the plan execution. In the car rental example, Mike was sufficient for the first stage, and Wiebe was sufficient for the second stage.

As we have seen, in Coalition Logic, all these questions can be answered using one and the same mathematical approach, known as *model checking*. We are given a dynamic interaction model and an initial state, and we want to verify whether a formula of Coalition Logic holds at that initial state. To determine an optimal team architecture, multiple formulas may need to be tested or verified. Model checking for Coalition Logic is computationally efficient, in the sense that we have fast and efficient computer programs that can check if a formula holds at some state of an interaction model.

A computationally more complex question is whether, for a given formula, there is an interaction model and a state at which the formula holds. This problem is called the *satisfiability problem* in logic. While model checking can be used to *verify* systems (i.e. check whether they have certain desirable – or undesirable – properties), the *synthesis* of such systems is closely linked to the satisfiability problem. The idea is to start with one or more logical formulas, which specify the desiderata of our system; we can then use the computer to solve the satisfiability problem for this logical specification, and if the answer is 'yes', then a by-product of the satisfiability checking process is a system that satisfies the desirable properties.

As an example, suppose that a student Alice has to decide whether to take a course in logic (*l*) or game theory (*g*). She knows that Wiebe, Mike and Marc all know something about these two areas. Hence, she has decided that the majority opinion among them will determine which course she will take. The formula expressing this specification is the following:

$$F = [\{Mike,Wiebe\}]g \wedge [\{Mike,Wiebe\}]l \wedge$$
$$[\{Mike,Marc\}]g \wedge [\{Mike,Marc\}]l \wedge$$
$$[\{Wiebe,Marc\}]g \wedge [\{Wiebe,Marc\}]l \wedge$$
$$[\varnothing] \neg (g \wedge l)$$

The first part of the formula states that every majority coalition can get Alice to attend either of the two courses. The last conjunct involves the empty coalition, $\varnothing$, and states that Alice cannot choose to attend both courses at once. In general, the expression $[\varnothing]p$ states that p is *guaranteed* to hold at the next step; no individual needs to choose any specific strategy for p to come about.

Clearly, the given specification is satisfiable, and we have already suggested how this can be achieved. We simply need an interaction model with an initial state where Mike, Wiebe and Marc are involved in the following majority voting game (see Figure 7.4).

Mike chooses one of the two tables, the first table for game theory and the second table for logic. Wiebe chooses a row, and Marc a column, **GT** or

Wiebe \ Marc	GT	Logic
GT	*g*	*g*
Logic	*g*	*l*

Wiebe \ Marc	GT	Logic
GT	*g*	*l*
Logic	*l*	*l*

Figure 7.4   Strategic game for three players

Logic. The resulting state satisfies g if a majority of the three individuals has chosen game theory, otherwise l.

To consider a slightly different situation, suppose that Mike, Wiebe and Marc are in three different countries, and hence Alice cannot ask them all to sit around the table for such a vote. Instead, she decides to call the three individually to solicit their opinions. Since she wants to spend as little money as possible, she wonders how many phone calls she will have to make, guaranteeing that any majority can determine the course she will attend. Note that the earlier interaction model is not practicable, since Alice can only call one person individually to get his vote. We thus have to check for satisfiability not in general interaction models, but instead in turn-based models, where at each stage, only one person has a strategic choice to make. Formally, we consider the formula

$$F^k = [\{Mike,Wiebe\}]^k g \wedge [\{Mike,Wiebe\}]^k l \wedge$$
$$[\{Mike,Marc\}]^k g \wedge [\{Mike,Marc\}]^k l \wedge$$
$$[\{Wiebe,Marc\}]^k g \wedge [\{Wiebe,Marc\}]^k l \wedge$$
$$[\varnothing]^1 \neg(g \wedge l) \wedge \ldots \wedge [\varnothing]^k \neg(g \wedge l)$$

This formula expresses that any majority is able to determine the outcome after at most k moves, and that nowhere along the way does Alice take both courses at once. Since $F^1 = F$, we have already seen that F^1 is satisfiable in general interaction models, using the majority voting game we gave. Over turn-based models, it should be clear that F^1 is not satisfiable. Alice needs to make more than one call in order to satisfy her specification. Furthermore, it should not come as a surprise that F^3 is satisfiable. By calling all of Mike, Marc and Wiebe, Alice can choose a course based on majority opinion. The procedure is outlined in Figure 7.5.

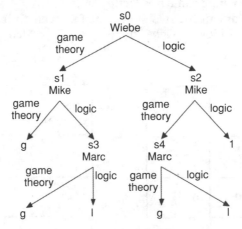

Figure 7.5 Sequential voting procedure involving three votes

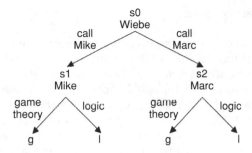

Figure 7.6 Simpler voting procedure involving only two votes

At each position of the game, making the left move corresponds to voting for game theory and making the right move to voting for logic. If Alice is lucky, two telephone calls will suffice. In the worst case, however, the first two people called will have different views and hence Alice needs to call everybody. Consequently, this model only satisfies F^3 and not F^2 at the initial state.

Perhaps surprisingly, it turns out that two telephone calls suffice even in the worst case: F^2 is satisfiable already. The satisfying turn-based model is described by the extensive game of perfect information as shown in Figure 7.6.

According to this model, Alice first calls Wiebe. She explains her situation to him, that she has to choose between two courses, and asks him which of his two colleagues she should call next. This second person chosen (Mike or Marc) will then be able to determine by himself which course Alice will take. This procedure still gives any majority a strategy to determine the course Alice will take. Thus, Alice manages to solve her problem by calling only two of the three people. Hence, this procedure is more efficient (i.e. less costly to Alice) then the naive procedure described earlier of calling people in some order until the majority is clear.

But while this last procedure is more efficient, it puts an additional burden on Mike, Wiebe and Marc. To start with, when called by Alice, Wiebe may not know his colleagues' preferences, so before being able to suggest a colleague to Alice, he may have to call his colleagues to find out their views. If one of his colleagues agrees with him, Wiebe can call Alice back and suggest that colleague, yielding a strategy for these two to achieve the course of their choice. Two things should be noted here: First, while Alice's telephone costs go down, Wiebe's telephone costs may increase. Second, even if Wiebe has found a colleague (say Mike) who agrees with his preference, Mike may, when called by Alice, vote for the other course nonetheless. In other words, Wiebe has no means to enforce an agreement he made with his colleagues.

7.1.4   Individuals vs. teams

Coalition Logic also allows us to investigate some differences between individual reasoning and team reasoning. Using the coalitional modal operator *[C]*, Coalition Logic allows us to write down specifications of group abilities. In order to investigate individual specifications, we consider the *individual fragment* of Coalition Logic. This fragment restricts the modal operator *[C]* to coalitions of size 1. Hence, we can still specify individual abilities using formulas like *[{Wiebe}]p* ∧ *[{Mike}]q*, but formulas like *[{Wiebe,Mike}]q* are not allowed. By comparing Coalition Logic to its individual fragment, we can point out some logical differences between individuals and groups. Two interesting dimensions along which one can compare different logical languages are *expressive power* and *computational complexity*.

The *expressive power* of a language measures the ability of the language to distinguish different situations (i.e. interaction models). The more situations a language can distinguish, the more expressive power it has. For the case at hand, we would like to know whether *full* Coalition Logic is more expressive than its *individual fragment*. For turn-based interaction models, the answer turns out to be negative. Since at every state, there is only a single person who has a choice to make, there is no short-term interaction. Formally, as the axiom for turn-based interaction models suggests, when reasoning about turn-based interaction models, we can replace an expression *[C]p* by *[c_1]p* ∨...∨ *[c_n]p*, where $C = \{c_1,...,c_n\}$. As mentioned, everything the group can bring about can already be achieved by one of its members alone. Note, however, that the resulting formula of the individual fragment may be substantially longer than the original team formula. Thus, even though over turn-based interaction models teams do not add expressive power, they add *succinctness*.

However, for *general* interaction models, *[C]p* cannot be reduced to a formula of the individual fragment. This is because there are situations which are indistinguishable in terms of individual ability but which differ in the abilities of groups. Intuitively, consider a situation where Marc and Wiebe want to move a piano upstairs. In the first situation, the piano is so heavy that neither individually nor together can they manage to get it upstairs. In the second situation, the piano is an electric piano and hence lighter. While they are still unable to get the piano upstairs individually, they can now cooperate to move the piano. Note that these situations are indistinguishable in terms of individual abilities, but they do differ according to team ability. Hence, this is an informal example illustrating that when considering general interaction models, the individual fragment is strictly less expressive than full Coalition Logic. Thus, in general, *team ability is not reducible to individual ability*.

Turning from expressive power to complexity, we can ask whether systems of interacting teams are more complex (in the computational sense

of requiring more computation steps or having larger memory requirements) than systems of interacting individuals. Again, we can distinguish
the task of analysing an interaction model (*model checking*) from synthesiz-
ing an interaction model (*satisfiability checking*). It turns out that verifying a
purely individual specification is not essentially simpler than verifying
general (team) specifications. In both cases, the time it takes to verify
whether a formula holds in some interaction model is bounded by the
length of the formula multiplied by the size of the model. In computational terms, we say thus that the model checking problem is *tractable*,
because the amount of time taken to carry out the model checking computation will be 'manageable'.

For synthesis, we measure the complexity of generating an interaction
model satisfying a given specification, individual or coalitional. Here, the
story gets rather murkier. Within computer science, there is an elaborate
(some would say arcane) theory that attempts to classify computational
problems in terms of their inherent complexity (the number of computation
steps or the amount of memory required to solve them). Unfortunately, for
most of the classes developed within complexity theory, it is as yet
unknown whether they actually are distinct or not. Two central classes are
NP, (formally, 'the class of problems solvable by a nondeterministic Turing
machine in time polynomial in the input size'), and PSPACE, (formally, 'the
class of problems solvable by a deterministic Turing machine in space polynomial in the input size'). The satisfiability problem for the individual fragment of Coalition Logic is known to be in NP, while the satisfiability
problem for Coalition Logic in general is not known to be in NP, but is
known to be in PSPACE. Now, it is known that problems in PSPACE are at
least as difficult as problems in NP, and many computer scientists believe
that problems in PSPACE are strictly more difficult than problems in NP –
but this is at present a belief only, and it remains a major open problem in
theoretical computer science (Papadimitriou, 1994). Hence, the question of
whether there is a complexity difference between coalitional reasoning and
individual reasoning is linked to the most foundational open questions of
theoretical computer science. What all this boils down to is that synthesis
appears to be much harder, in computational terms, than verification; and
synthesis from arbitrary formulae of Coalition Logic appears to be harder
than synthesis from formulas of the individual fragment.

To conclude, recall that we observed that for turn-based interaction
models, coalitional formulas can be replaced by formulas of the individual
fragment. This observation, however, only holds when we restrict ourselves
to the immediate future. Coalition Logic does not contain a formula for
expressing that a team C can guarantee p to hold at some point in the
future (not necessarily in the immediate future). One can show that such
coalitional long-term ability cannot be reduced to individual long-term
abilities, even over turn-based models. Hence, to get more expressive power

out of coalitional specifications, it is natural to add more expressive temporal operators, the subject of the next section.

7.2   Cooperation over time

We now show how the basic structure of Coalition Logic can be usefully extended with expressions for representing the *temporal structure* of events – and we indicate just why such extensions are useful. Formally, the enriched logic is known as *Alternating-time Temporal Logic*, although it is almost universally referred to by its acronym, ATL. To understand how ATL works, it is necessary to have some understanding of temporal logics. Temporal logics basically come with two kinds of semantics: *linear* and *branching-time* structures (Emerson, 1990). Since each branch in the latter structures also represents a linear episode, let us take the time line $\aleph$ as an atomic semantics for our linear time. Temporal formulas are hence interpreted at a time point $n \in \aleph$. The main operators for such a model are O ('next', so $O\varphi$ is true at time n if φ is true at time $(n+1)$), $\Diamond$ ('eventually': $\Diamond \varphi$ being true at n if φ is true in some state $(n+k)$), $\square$ ('always': $\square j$ being true at n if φ is true for all $(n+k)$) and, finally, the binary operator U ('until': $\varphi U \psi$ being true at n if for some k, it is the case that ψ is true at k, and for all m with $n \le m < k$, φ is true at m). ATL combines these temporal operators with cooperation expressions, which have essentially the same meaning as in Coalition Logic – however, one irritation of the literature is that a different notation is used in Coalition Logic and ATL for cooperation expressions: the Coalition Logic expression *[C]* is written in ATL as *<<C>>*. But, whatever the notation, the power should be readily apparent: consider the following ATL formula

$$<< Marc,\ Wiebe,\ Mike >>\ \Diamond\ readerIsBored$$

which says that Mike Marc, and Wiebe can ensure that the reader eventually is bored. A more interesting example, in which the power of the temporal operators is more apparent, is the following.

$$<< Marc,\ Wiebe,\ Mike >> readerIsBored\ U\ readerStopsReading$$

This formula says that the same coalition can ensure that the reader stays bored until he stops reading; after that, the coalition looses control over his level of satisfaction.

Now, the structures in which we interpret formulas in ATL (Alur et al., 1997), are *trees*, and the idea is that the grand coalition G of all agents can cooperate to choose a specific branch in this tree; moreover, all subgroups $C \subseteq G$ can only ensure that some branches will survive, that is, the other branches will not be pursued. As an example, consider the simple system of Figure 7.7 below, inspired by Jamroga and van der Hoek (2004).

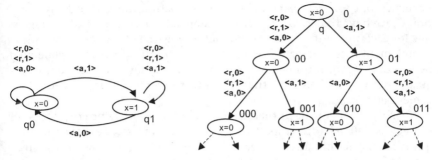

Figure 7.7 Concurrent game structure with all its possible computations

The structure on the left denotes a *concurrent game* structure (with two states $q0$ and $q1$), and the tree on the right denotes all *its possible computations*. The game structure models the simplest kind of two-agent context, one in which we have a server (s) and a client (c). The client can request to set the value of a variable x to 0 or to 1, and the server can either reject (**r**) or accept (**a**) such a request. Thus, the tuple <**r**,0> denotes the strategy profile in which the client c requests the server s to set variable x to 0, whereas s rejects this request (without necessarily knowing what the request was). Such a profile would leave the system in its state, since a rejection from the server implies that the value of x remains unchanged.

Suppose we want to reason about the two basic statements $x = 1$ and $x = 0$, then the following formula is true everywhere in the computational tree: $x = 0 \rightarrow$ <<s>> $O(x = 0)$, expressing that in every state in which x has the value 0, the server has a strategy to enforce that in the next state, x will be 0 again. Formally, this is established as follows. Take any state in which $x = 0$. If the server chooses **r**, there are two possible profiles, i.e., <**r**,0> and <**r**,1>, and no matter what c decides to do, in the next state x will have still have the value 0. Some other properties are the following:

(1) $x = 0 \rightarrow$ <<s>> $O(x = 0)$ (*s can preserve the value of x in one step*)
(2) $x = 0 \rightarrow$ <<s>> $\Box(x = 0)$ (*s can preserve the value of x for ever*)
(3) $x = 0 \rightarrow \neg$ <<s>> $\Diamond(x = 1)$ (*s cannot change the value of x ever in the future on its own*)
(4) $x = 0 \rightarrow \neg$ <<c>> $\Diamond(x = 1)$ (*c cannot change the value of x ever in the future on its own*)
(5) $x = 0 \rightarrow$ <<c,s>> $\Diamond(x = 1)$ (*c and s can cooperate to change the value of x effectively*)
(6)   <<$\varnothing$>>$[\Diamond x = 1 \rightarrow ((<<s>>\Box x = 0) U x = 1)]$ (*see below*)

More formally, let a strategy for player p be a function that assigns to every node a decision, and let a strategy profile for the whole coalition be a set of strategies, one for each player. Then, for any path-formula F and any coalition C, we have that $<<C>>F$ is true in state q if there is a set of strategies, one for each player in C, so that, no matter how the other agents outside C complement these strategies to a strategy profile σ, in the branch generated by this σ, the path-formula F will be true. Thus, what ATL adds to the language that we had before, is that it can reason about what coalitions can achieve *over time*.

We make the following further remarks about ATL. First, since the notion of strategy is defined with respect to the computation tree, our agents have 'perfect recall': for instance, the server in our example could cook up a strategy in which he alternates 'reject' and 'accept' in an eternal repetition, a strategy that would be impossible if he had to base his decision on the states q_0 and q_1 in the concurrent game structure alone. Next, for the grand coalition G and path formula F, the property $<<G>>F$ denotes an extreme case: it denotes that if the grand coalition forms a team, they can guarantee, by each member choosing the appropriate strategy, that F holds. But if every member of G chooses a strategy, we obtain a unique path in the computation tree, so that the meaning of $<<G>>F$ boils down to: for some path, F is true. The other extreme case is yielded by $<<\emptyset>>F$: it says that the empty coalition can choose their strategies, so that, no matter how the other agents complement it to a strategy profile, F will be true. In other words, $<<\emptyset>>F$ holds if F is true on every path.

Finally, we remark that in ATL, we only have formulas of the form $<<C>>F$, where F is a path formula. One might lift this restriction on F, and obtain the language ATL*. An example of an ATL* formula is given as (6) in the list above: the property expresses a kind of 'free will' property for the server: it says that, might x ever become 1 in the future, then it is because s refrains from its power to let it equal 0.

We give some general tautologies of ATL (see van der Hoek and Wooldridge, 2003, for more examples). In the following, G is the grand coalition and C is an arbitrary team from members c of G.

(1)	$<<C>>O\varphi \rightarrow <<C \cup \{c\}>>O\varphi$	*(persistence over supergroups)*
(2)	$<<C>>\Box\ \varphi \rightarrow \neg <<G\backslash C>>\Diamond\neg\varphi$	*(complement)*
(3)	$<<\emptyset>>\Box\ (\varphi \rightarrow \psi) \rightarrow (<<C>>\Diamond\varphi \rightarrow <<C>>\Diamond\psi)$	*(distribution)*

The latter property says, that if on every path, it is always the case that φ implies ψ, then, if C can enforce that sometime in the future φ, it also can enforce ψ. Note that we cannot strengthen this property to $<<C>>\Box\ (\varphi \rightarrow \psi) \rightarrow (<<C>>\Diamond\varphi \rightarrow <<C>>\Diamond\psi)$: if C has a strategy, (say σ_1) to enforce that always φ implies ψ, and C has a strategy (say σ_2) to enforce φ, this does not necessarily mean that C has a strategy to eventually yield ψ. As an example, I may have a strategy that always ensures me nice weather on my holidays if I spend them in Helsinki (the strategy might be that I just do not go to Helsinki), and also do I have a strategy to spend my holidays in Helsinki, yet I lack the strategy to eventually guarantee me nice weather on a holiday to Helsinki.

The model checking problem for ATL is known to be tractable, as with Coalition Logic, see above. Given a concurrent game structure S, a state s in S, and an ATL formula φ, the question whether φ is true in s can be determined in a number of steps linearly depending on the sizes of S and φ. Model checking for ATL has been implemented in MOCHA, a freely available model-checker specifically tailored for ATL (Alur et al., 1998). With respect to satisfiability, however, the problem is *much* worse than the corresponding problem for Coalition Logic. It is EXPTIME-complete, (the 'EXP' here means 'exponential'), which means roughly that adding a single feature (an atomic symbol, say) to the specification φ *doubles* the amount of time required to check whether it is satisfiable. This is regarded as an extremely negative result: it implies there is real doubt as to whether usable programs can ever be developed for checking the satisfiability of ATL formulas, and hence doing synthesis from ATL specifications.

7.3 Cooperation, time and knowledge

Van der Hoek and Wooldridge (2003) proposes to add a notion of knowledge to ATL, the idea being, that ATL is a suitable language for strategic decision making in a team-context, and that the knowledge that team members have when reasoning about each other, is crucial. We restrict ourselves to some examples of what can be expressed in ATEL (Alternating-time Temporal Epistemic Logic) – for a deeper analysis, we refer the reader to van der Hoek and Wooldridge (2003). First of all, to reason about knowledge, we enrich the ATL language with operators K_i (i in G), where $K_i\varphi$ means 'agent i knows φ'. For any team T, $E_T\varphi$ moreover means 'everybody in T knows φ', and, finally, $C_T\varphi$ is short for 'it is common knowledge in the team T that φ', which, in its turn, means that the infinite sequence $E_T\varphi$, $EE_T\varphi$, $EEE_T\varphi$, ... holds.

Now, van der Hoek and Wooldridge (2003) first of all point at the importance of expressing *knowledge preconditions* (the knowledge that is needed by a team in order to achieve certain states of affairs). To say that knowledge in team T about ψ is a precondition for T to bring about φ, can be represented as $<<T>>O\varphi \rightarrow E_T\psi$ but one might also represent it as the path formula $(\neg<<T>>O\varphi)U\ E_T\psi$, expressing for instance that no team can establish the safe to be opened, until it knows the code of the safe. Communication provides a nice area in which agents can *obtain* knowledge, during a run. For instance the property $K_i\varphi \rightarrow <<i,j>>K_j\varphi$ expresses that i can communicate his knowledge to j; by adding more and more assumptions about the communication protocol, one can even assume $K_i\varphi \rightarrow <<i,j>>K_iK_j\varphi$, or, for that matter, $K_i\varphi \rightarrow <<i,j>>C_{\{i,j\}}\varphi$. Sometimes, not only gaining knowledge is important, but also the preservation of ignorance. The following property

$$K_i\varphi \wedge \neg K_j\varphi \wedge \neg K_h\varphi \wedge <<i,j>>O \ (K_i\varphi \wedge K_j\varphi \wedge \neg K_h\varphi)$$

expresses that i and j are able to exchange the information φ, without h being aware, or intercepting it.

The proper ultimate semantics of ATEL is still under debate; we try to hint here at some intricacies. The key idea to interpret K_i is to divide the set of states into a partition for i, each block in such a partition representing a set of states that i cannot distinguish. Given state s, we then say that i knows φ, if φ is true in all states t that i cannot distinguish from s. Let us look at the following simple game, represented in the left structure of Figure 7.8.

Here we have two players: player 1 has the first move (in state a) and he puts a coin under a solid cup, the coin either faces head (**h**) or tail (**t**). While player 2 could only wait (**w**) during this move, in the next step, he is allowed to guess the face of the coin. Let us say that when he guesses right (bringing the game to either hh or tt) he wins, denoted w_2, otherwise player 1 wins (w_1). Does player 2 have a winning strategy in state a? In ATL he would, the strategy being $(a,\mathbf{w})(b,\mathbf{h})(c,\mathbf{t})$, where $(x,\mathbf{y})$ means that in state x player 2 chooses $\mathbf{y}$. This means that in state a we have $<<2>>\Diamond win_2$. Of course, this is not intuitively correct, and to fix this, we require that a strategy for an agent should make the same decisions in states undistinguishable for that agent. Such strategies are called *uniform*. In the example, states b and c are indistinguishable for agent 2, so he should make the same choice in them, and then, $<<2>>\Diamond win_2$ no longer holds in a.

This does not mean that now everything works as expected. Note for instance, that at state b, we still have $<<2>>\Diamond win_2$ and even $K_2<<2>>\Diamond win_2$:

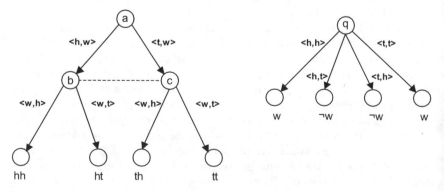

Figure 7.8   Two extensive games of imperfect information

in state b, player 2 knows that he has a winning uniform strategy! From this, we conclude that in a, it holds that $<<\varnothing>>O<<2>>\Diamond win_2$: the grand coalition cannot avoid that, in the next state, player 2 will eventually win! Following work by Moore (1990), Jamroga and van der Hoek (2004) point out that we need to shift from 'having a winning uniform strategy *de dicto*' to 'having a winning uniform strategy *de re*'. In other words, in order to conclude in b, that $<<2>>\Diamond win_2$ we should not just require that 2 knows that there is a strategy that leads to win_2, but there should be a strategy, of which 2 knows that it guarantees win_2! We write $<<i>>_{K(i)}\varphi$ if agent i has a strategy in this sense to guarantee φ. For the example, in order to satisfy $<<2>>_{K(2)}\Diamond win_2$ at state b, it should mean that 2 has a uniform strategy (the only two candidates being $(a,\mathbf{w})(b,\mathbf{h})(c,\mathbf{h})$ and $(a,\mathbf{w})(b,\mathbf{t})(c,\mathbf{t})$), which should in both states indistinguishable for 2 (that is, in b and in c) lead him to win_2 and this is of course not possible.

Using this stronger definition, it is not difficult to define a notion $<<D>>_{E(D)}\varphi$, which means that there is a strategy σ for the coalition D such that it leads to φ, *and everybody in D knows this*. However, for a team of more than one player, this still might not be enough information to act accordingly. Consider the game on the right hand side of Figure 7.8. It is a variant of the matching pennies: both players 1 and 2 are asked to choose form head ($\mathbf{h}$) and tail ($\mathbf{t}$), and if their choices coincide, there is victory (w). There is only one (begin-) state, so everybody has omniscient knowledge about it: it is uniquely distinguishable. Also both one-shot strategies <h,h> and <t,t> lead them to w, and they both know this, so that we have $<<1,2>>_{E(1,2)}Ow$. However, even though there is this team-knowledge about the existence of a successful strategy, the agents still are not guaranteed success, simply because there is too many of such strategies: they won't in general be sure which of the successful strategies will be adopted by the other teammate! Obviously, in order for the team to be successful here, they need a way to communicate their decision, or some strategies should represent a focal point; issues, that are not addressed in current versions of ATEL, however.

7.4 Conclusions and further topics

In this paper, our aim has been to illustrate how researchers in computer science and Artificial Intelligence have gone about developing logics for reasoning about coalitions and teams. These researchers are interested in such ideas because they want to build computers that can work in teams, in much the same way that humans do. In order to do this effectively, it is argued, we must develop computer programs that can reason about teams – their abilities and other properties. Coalition Logic and its relatives provide a powerful tool with which to carry out this kind of reasoning.

The field of logics for reasoning about teams and coalitions is a relatively new one – not just for computer science but also for logic and game theory.

There are many open problems and issues. For example, as the final section illustrated, it is quite natural to wish to extend Coalition Logics not just with an apparatus for reasoning about the temporal ordering of events, but with constructs for referring to the information that agents have about their environment, which may of course include other agents. And, just as we may wish to refer to the information that agents have about their environment, so we may also wish to refer to their *preferences* – and the information they have about the preferences of other agents, which will inform their own strategic reasoning. Although work on such extensions to the basic framework of Coalition Logic is at an early stage, it is worth mentioning some ideas. In *Nash consistent coalition logic* (see Hansen and Pauly, 2002) we replace the basic cooperation expression *[C]* of Coalition Logic with one $[C]_N$, with the interpretation that $[C]_N p$ means that not only do C have a collective strategy to ensure that p, they have such a collective strategy that also has the property of being a Nash equilibrium (i.e. each strategy in this profile is the best response to the strategies of the others). The important point is that no coalition has any incentive to deviate from a Nash equilibrium strategy profile, and so $[C]_N p$ implies the existence of a *stable* strategy profile for p. As yet, the axiomatic and complexity theoretic properties of such logics are not well understood.

References

Alur, R., T. A. Henzinger and O. Kupferman (1997) 'Alternating-time temporal logic', *Proceedings of the 38th IEEE Symposium on Foundations of Computer Science*, 100–109.

Alur, R., T. A. Henzinger, F. Y. C. Mang, S. Qadeer, S. K. Rajamani and S. Tasiran (1998) 'Mocha: Modularity in Model Checking' in *CAV 1998: Tenth International Conference on Computer-aided Verification*, (LNCS Volume 1427), Springer, pp. 521–525.

Binmore, K. (1992) *Fun and Games: A Text on Game Theory* (D. C. Heath and Company: Lexington, MA.).

Bond, A. H. and L. Gasser (eds) (1988) *Readings in Distributed Artificial Intelligence* (Morgan Kaufmann).

Emerson, E. A. (1990) 'Temporal and Modal Logic' in J. van Leeuwen (ed.) *Handbook of Theoretical Computer Science, Volume B: Formal Models and Semantics*, 996–1072.

Hansen, H. and M. Pauly (2002) 'Axiomatising Nash-Consistent Coalition Logic' in S. Flesca, S. Greco, N. Leone and G. Ianni (eds), *Logics in Artificial Intelligence*, LNAI 2424.

Jamroga, W. and W. van der Hoek (2004) 'Agents that Know how to Play'. Accepted for *Informaticae*.

Moore, R. C. (1990) 'A Formal Theory of Knowledge and Action' in J. F. Allen, J. Hendler and A. Tate (eds), *Readings in Planning* (Morgan Kaufmann Publishers) pp. 480–519.

Osborne, M. J. and A. Rubinstein (1994) *A Course in Game Theory* (Cambridge Ma.: MIT Press).

Pauly, M. (2002) 'A Modal Logic for Coalitional Power in Games', *Journal of Logic and Computation* (12)1, 149–166.

Papadimitriou, C. H. (1994) *Computational Complexity* (Addison-Wesley: Reading, Ma.).

van der Hoek, W. and M. J. W. Wooldridge (2003) 'Cooperation, Knowledge, and Time: Alternating-time Temporal Epistemic Logic and its Applications', *Studia Logica* (75)1, 125–157.

8
The Logic of Team Reasoning

Robert Sugden

Almost all decision theory presupposes that agency is invested in *individuals*. Each individual is represented as making decisions in the light of his or her own preferences and beliefs. A person may have preferences about consequences of her actions which affect other people; but these are still *her* preferences. She may have beliefs about what other people will choose; but these are still *her* beliefs. In making decisions, she acts alone.

Opposing this orthodoxy, there is a thin strand of literature which allows *teams* of individuals to count as agents, and which seeks to identify distinctive modes of *team reasoning* that are used by members of teams.[1] In this paper, I offer a new conceptual framework within which theories of team reasoning can be represented. This framework is inspired by David Lewis's game theory. In analyzing the concept of convention, Lewis (1969) develops a distinctive form of game theory, focusing on what individuals have reason to believe.[2] Although Lewis himself is orthodox in treating only individuals as agents, his approach to game theory turns out to be very useful in organizing ideas about team reasoning.

8.1 The Footballers' Problem and the Prisoner's Dilemma: an introduction to team reasoning

My objective is to offer a new analysis of team reasoning. This objective is possible because 'team reasoning' is an imperfectly-defined theoretical concept: different authors use the term (and cognate terms, such as 'collective agency' and 'plural subject') in different ways, and apply it to different but overlapping sets of phenomena. It will be useful to begin with an informal account of what I take to be the core notion of team reasoning.

My starting point is a game which, in various guises, has had a central place in the literature of team agency. A and B are players in the same football team. A has the ball, but an opposing player is converging on him. He can pass the ball to B, who has a chance to shoot. There are two directions in which A can move the ball, *left* and *right*, and correspondingly, two directions in which B can run to intercept the pass. If both choose *left*, there is a ten per cent chance that a goal will be scored. If both choose *right*, the chance is 11 per cent. Otherwise, the chance is zero. There is no time for communication; the two players must act simultaneously. What should they do?

Given the assumption that each player seeks to maximize the probability that a goal is scored, the answer seems obvious: each should choose *right*. But, perhaps surprisingly, this conclusion cannot be derived within conventional game theory. The Footballers' Problem can be represented in that theory as the game shown in Table 8.1. For each player, there are two *strategies* (*left* and *right*); for each *profile* of strategies (that is, each list of strategies, one for each player) there is an array of *payoffs*, representing the desirability to the respective players of whatever outcome results from that profile's being chosen.

The logic of game theory allows us to conclude that it is uniquely rational for A to choose *right* if B is sufficiently likely to choose *right* (more precisely, if the probability that B chooses *right* is greater than 10/21). But, equally, it is uniquely rational for A to choose *left* if B is sufficiently likely to choose *left* (more precisely, if the probability that B chooses *left* is greater than 11/21). In game theory, it is standard to assume that the players have common knowledge of one another's rationality. But in this game, that assumption takes us no further forward. If, say, A tries to predict B's choice by attributing rationality to him, A finds that B's decision problem is symmetrical with his own: what it is rational for B to do depends on what it is rational for B to believe about A's choice. There is an infinite regress.

Notice that the difficulty is not that A and B are self-interested. We have assumed that each individual's preferences fully reflect their common objective as members of the same team (that a goal is scored); but, even so, we cannot show that rationality requires them to make the combination of choices that best promotes that common objective. Thus, the Footballers' Problem is just as much a problem for morally-motivated act-utilitarians as it is for self-seeking individuals.[3] For this reason, it cannot credibly be resolved by means of re-specifying individuals' preferences.[4] The source of the paradox seems to be located in the mode of reasoning by which, in the standard theory, individuals move from preferences to decisions. Intuitively, if we imagine A and B asking, 'What should *we* do?', the answer

		Player B	
		left	*right*
Player A	*left*	10, 10	0, 0
	right	0, 0	11, 11

Table 8.1 The Footballers' Problem as a game

is obvious: *they* should choose the profile (*right, right*). The difficulty is that the syntax of game theory does not allow that question to be asked. Instead, each individual must ask separately, 'What should *I* do?' And then the answer has to be: 'That depends on what the other player can be expected to do'.

Theories of team agency try to reformulate game theory in such a way that 'What should we do?' is a meaningful question. The basic idea is that, when an individual reasons as a member of a team, he considers which *combination* of actions by members of the team would best promote the team's objective, and then performs his part of that combination. The rationality of each individual's action derives from the rationality of the joint action of the team.[5]

A similar analysis can be applied to a much more famous game, the Prisoner's Dilemma. Table 8.2 represents a version of this game. Rather than using the famous story of the prisoners, I will interpret the game in terms of voluntary contributions to a public good: to *cooperate* is to make a contribution and to *defect* is not to make one. To make a contribution is to incur a cost of four units (say, of money) in order to generate six units of total benefit; that benefit is divided equally between the contributor and the other player. Thus, contributions are wealth-creating from a collective viewpoint (each contribution creates two units of net benefit) but not from an individual viewpoint (each contribution leads to a net loss of one unit for the contributor).

If each player is self-interested, each will choose *defect*, irrespective of what she expects the other player to do, and despite the fact that both would be better off if they both chose *cooperate*. But what if they reason as the two members of a team? One possible analysis begins by assuming that the objective of this team is to maximize the sum of C's and D's payoffs. Then the combination of actions which best promotes the team's objective is (*cooperate, cooperate*). Reasoning as a member of the team, each player will choose to do her part in this combination.

8.2 Two problems

It is now time to face one of the central difficulties for any analysis of team reasoning. Roughly speaking, the difficulty is to explain how individuals

		Player D	
		cooperate	*defect*
Player C	*cooperate*	2, 2	–1, 3
	defect	3, –1	0, 0

Table 8.2 The Prisoner's Dilemma

know when to use team reasoning. In fact, there are two distinct problems here. I see one of these problems as internal to the logic of team reasoning, and the other as external to it. It will be easier to explain this distinction after I have discussed the internal problem.

The internal problem is that, from the viewpoint of any individual, the validity or acceptability of team reasoning, narrowly defined,[6] may be conditional on his confidence that other members of the team are reasoning in a similar way. For example, consider player A in the Footballers' Problem. Suppose that A wants a goal to be scored, and that this desire is independent of A's beliefs about B's motivation. Suppose also that A believes that B, for whatever reason, will choose *left*. Then the fact that (*right, right*) is the best profile for the team does not seem to justify A, even if reasoning as a member of the team, in choosing *right*. One way of putting this objection is to say that, given the constraint that B will choose *left*, the best that can be done to achieve the team's objective is for A to choose *left* too. It seems, then, that the logic of team reasoning does not generate an unconditional prescription that each player should play his part in the profile of strategies that is best for the team.

Notice that, in this example, A has a unilateral desire that the team's objective is achieved: his lack of confidence in B does not undermine his commitment to this objective, but only to a particular kind of joint action as the means of achieving it. But what I have called the 'internal problem' can take another form: there can be cases in which lack of confidence in other members of a team undermines commitment to the team's objective itself. Consider player C in the Prisoner's Dilemma, and suppose she believes than D will choose *defect*. Given the constraint that D chooses *defect*, the best profile for the team {C, D} is (*cooperate, defect*): this gives a team payoff of two units, while (*defect, defect*) gives a payoff of zero. In this sense, team reasoning prescribes *cooperate* to each player unconditionally. However, the expectation that D will choose *defect* raises doubts about the appropriateness of team reasoning for C. In part, this is a matter of moral psychology: a person may be willing to play her part in a joint activity which benefits all parties, but not to pay for someone else's free rides. There is also a conceptual issue. It is difficult to make sense of the idea that one person reasons 'as a member of a team' without presupposing that she believes that there *is* a team of which she *is* a member. But, one might think, a two-person team is not something that one person can create unilaterally: for C to conceive of {C, D} as a team, she has to conceive of D conceiving of {C, D} as a team. D's choice of *defect* might be construed as asserting that, for her, {C, D} is not a team at all. Construing D's expected choice in this way, C may conclude that there is no call for team reasoning, since there is no team to activate it.

The common feature of these two examples is the idea that team reasoning may be valid or acceptable for one member of a team only if it is valid or acceptable for the others. We seem to be in danger of being trapped in another infinite regress. One of the main challenges to be met by any analysis of team reasoning is to show how this regress can be escaped. To meet this challenge, we need an internally consistent analysis of a mode of reasoning which tells each member of a team to play his part in the best combination of actions for the team, conditional on the right kind of assurance about the motivation, reasoning or behaviour of other team members. We also need an analysis of how the relevant kind of assurance can be generated. Meeting this challenge is the 'internal' problem.

Notice, however, that a person may still ask: 'Should I endorse this mode of reasoning?' This is the question that I treat as external to the analysis of team reasoning. In taking this position, I am expressing my conception of the scope of decision theory. I do not see it as the task of decision theory to tell us which decisions are 'really' rational for us. For me, decision-theoretic rationality is not an external constraint to which our thoughts must accommodate themselves. The most we can hope for from decision theory, as I understand it, are formal representations of modes of reasoning that people take to be valid, and that they choose to act on.

That is not to say that this is all that is needed in empirical social science. Viewed from the perspective of social science, a decision-theoretic analysis of team reasoning is useful only to the extent that people in fact endorse it and act on it. Thus, a satisfactory empirical theory of team reasoning needs to be able to explain why, under various conditions, people do or do not engage in team reasoning. For those social scientists who believe (as I do) that team reasoning is significant in social life, this is an important explanatory task.[7] But this paper is concerned only with conceptual analysis.

8.3 The logic of reason to believe

Following Lewis (1969) and Cubitt and Sugden (2003), I use a theoretical framework in which the central concept is *reason to believe*. To say that a person *i* has reason to believe a proposition *x* is to say that *x* can be inferred from propositions that *i* accepts as true, using rules of inference that *i* accepts as valid. Notice that a person does not necessarily believe everything that she has reason to believe. To say that *i* actually believes *x* is to assert that she is in a particular psychological state, while to say that she has reason to believe *x* is to assert that *x* is a theorem of a particular form of logic. For example, anyone who accepts the principles of arithmetic has reason to believe the proposition $119 \times 576 = 68,544$, but it is rare for anyone to be in the psychological state of believing that proposition to be true. By conducting game-theoretic analysis in terms of reason to believe, we can use the methods of formal logic to analyse problems faced by real human beings, without committing ourselves to the assumption that those human beings are perfectly rational. Notice also that what a person has reason to believe depends on *her own* standards of reasoning: we (as modellers) may say that i has reason to believe x without committing *ourselves* to any claims about the validity of those reasons.

The proposition 'i has reason to believe x' (where i is a person and x is a proposition) will be written as $R_i(x)$. In interpreting this formula, I assume that there is some reason-to-believe logic, R_i, with its own axioms and inference rules; this logic is *endorsed by i* – that is, i accepts its validity. If R is a reason-to-believe logic, $R(x)$ signifies that x is a theorem of R. (I treat 'x is an axiom of R' as a special case of 'x is a theorem of R'.) For any reason-to-believe logic R, for any propositions x, y, z, I use the notation 'inf(R): x, y → z' to denote that there are inference rules in R which allow z to be inferred from x and y, irrespective of other axioms of R. I assume that every reason-to-believe logic R has the standard rule of *deductive inference*. That is, for all propositions x_1, ..., x_n, z, we have inf(R): x_1, ..., x_n, $\neg(x_1 \wedge ... \wedge x_n \wedge \neg z)$ → z. But a reason-to-believe logic may contain other inference rules, for example, rules of inductive inference or normative principles of practical reason; and different logics may have different combinations of inference rules. Reason-to-believe propositions can be nested; for example, $R_i[R_j(x)]$ denotes 'i has reason to believe that j has reason to believe x'.

In addition to the reason-to-believe logics that are endorsed by individuals, there may be reason-to-believe logics that are *common* to groups of individuals. Roughly, to say that a reason-to-believe logic R^N is common to a group of individuals N is to say that each member of N endorses this logic, and that each individual recognizes that it is so endorsed. Thus, when any member of N reasons in terms of the logic of R^N, she has reason to believe that any inferences she draws are available to other members of N.

Before formalizing the concept of common reason, I need to define a special relationship that may hold between a particular proposition and a particular person. I shall say that a person i *is the subject of* a proposition x_i if x_i makes an assertion about a current or future act of i's will. For the purposes of this paper, there are four relevant ways in which a proposition can have a person as its subject: it may make a prediction about what that person will choose in a future decision problem; or it may make a deontic statement about what she ought to choose; or it may assert that she endorses some inference rule; or it may assert that she has reason to believe some proposition.[8] To get a sense of why being a 'subject' is significant in relation to common reason, consider the following example. Suppose that N is a group of commuters who are in the habit of catching a particular bus each weekday morning. Suppose that one member of this group, person i, has travelled on this bus almost every weekday for the last five years. We might want to say that the proposition 'up to now, i has almost always chosen to travel on this bus' (which we may denote y_i) is an axiom of a common reason-to-believe logic R^N. Now consider the proposition 'next Monday, i will almost certainly choose to travel on this bus' (which we may denote x_i). We might want to assume that other members of N endorse the inductive inference rule 'from y_i, infer x_i'. Thus, each person other than i might have reason to expect i to catch the bus next Monday. Further, we might want to assume that this kind of inductive inference is so natural or customary that everyone can rely on everyone else making it. Thus, for example, i has reason to believe that each of the others has reason to believe that he will catch the bus next Monday. However, in a theory of practical reason, we have to leave each individual free to make his own choices in the light of whatever reasons he endorses. The truth of y_i, and the reliability of the inductive inference from y_i to x_i, do not in themselves provide i with *reason to make x_i true*.[9] In cases such as this, it is useful to have an analysis of common reason which (for distinct i, j) generates $R_j(x_i)$ but *not $R_i(x_i)$*, $R_i[R_j(x_i)]$ but *not $R_j[R_i(x_i)]$*, $R_j[R_i[R_j(x_i)]]$ but *not $R_i[R_j[R_i(x_i)]]$*, and so on.

Now for the definition of common reason-to-believe logic. For any group of individuals N, each of whom has his own reason-to-believe logic R_i, a reason-to-believe logic R^N is *common* to N if it has the following three properties:

> *Awareness of common reason*: for all persons i in N, for all propositions x: $R^N(x) \Rightarrow R_i[R^N(x)]$.
> *Authority of common reason*: for all persons i in N, for all propositions x for which i is not the subject: $\inf(R_i)$: $R^N(x) \to x$.
> *Common attribution of common reason*: for all persons i in N, for all propositions x for which i is not the subject: $\inf(R^N)$: $x \to R_i(x)$.

The *Awareness* condition expresses the intuitive idea that each member of N recognizes the axioms and inference rules of R^N and so, in principle, is capable of reasoning within that logic. Thus, if any proposition x is a theorem of R^N, its being so is a theorem of R_i. The *Authority* condition says that each member of N accepts the validity of all theorems that can be proved in R^N, except in so far as i the subject of those theorems. The *Attribution* condition says that R^N 'recognizes' each individual's awareness of it, and the sense in which each individual treats it as authoritative. The proposition $R^N(x)$ will be read as 'there is common reason to believe x'.

These conditions have a significant implication about the theorems of R^N. Consider any N, any common reason-to-believe logic R^N, any individual i who is a member of N, and any proposition x for which i is not the subject. Suppose that $R^N(x)$ is true. Then, by *Attribution*, we have $R^N[R_i(x)]$. By *Attribution* again, for any individual j in N (where $j \neq i$), we have $R^N[R_j[R_i(x)]]$. And by *Attribution* again, for any individual k in N (where $k \neq j$), we have $R^N[R_k[R_j[R_i(x)]]]$; and so on. From $R^N(x)$, using *Awareness* and *Authority*, we can derive $R_i(x)$. From $R^N[R_i(x)]$, using *Awareness* and *Authority*, we can derive $R_j[R_i(x)]$. From $R^N[R_j[R_i(x)]]$, using *Awareness* and *Authority*, we can derive $R_k[R_j[R_i(x)]]$. And so on. In other words, all finite propositions of the form 'k has reason to believe that j has reason to believe that i has reason to believe x' (where i, j, k are members of N, and $i \neq j$ and $j \neq k$) can be derived from $R^N(x)$.

This result is closely related to a theorem proved by Lewis (1969), which plays a central role in his analysis of common knowledge.[10] It shows how arbitrarily high orders of reason-to-believe can be generated from simple principles of common reason, given the existence of states of affairs that, in a certain sense, are 'self-revealing'. For example, let N be a group of passengers waiting for a particular flight at an airport departure gate. Let A be the state of affairs that an announcement is made over the public address system, stating that the flight will be delayed. Leaving aside complications about deafness, language comprehension and so on, we might say that A has self-revealing properties such that, if in fact A holds, then $R^N(A$ holds) holds too. Suppose we assume also that R^N has an inductive inference rule which allows 'the flight will probably be delayed' to be inferred from 'A holds'. (In Lewis's language, A *indicates* to all members of N that the flight will probably be delayed.) Then, if we (as modellers or observers) know that the announcement has been made, we can infer such propositions as the following: for distinct passengers i and j, i has reason to believe that j has reason to believe that i has reason to believe that the flight will probably be delayed.

8.4   Team maximizing

Consider a strategic interaction among some set of individuals M; the number of individuals in M in m. For each individual i in M, there is a set S_i of alternative *strategies*, from which she must choose one and only one. For each *profile* of strategies $s = (s_1, \ldots, s_m)$ such that each s_i is an element of S_i, there is an *outcome* – that is, the state of affairs that will come about if those strategies are chosen. In the language of game theory, this provides a description of a *game form*. For example, in the Footballers' Problem, $M = \{A, B\}$, and the game form is represented by the matrix shown in Table 8.3.

		Player B	
		left	*right*
Player A	*left*	10 per cent chance that goal is scored	no chance that goal is scored
	right	no chance that goal is scored	11 per cent chance that goal is scored

Table 8.3   The Footballers' Problem as a game form

I use the notation 'choice(i, s_i)' to denote the proposition 'individual i chooses strategy s_i'. I use 'ought(i, s_i)' to denote 'individual i ought to choose strategy s_i'. The latter form of proposition will be used in representing practical reason. For example, the proposition R_i[ought(i, s_i)] denotes that individual i has reason to believe that she ought to choose s_i, or in short, that i has *reason to choose* s_i. In these formulations, 'reason to ...' is to be understood relative to principles of practical reason that are endorsed by i. Just as reason to believe is not the same as actual belief, so reason to choose is not the same thing as actual choice. I shall say that an individual *acts on reasons* if, for her, reasons to choose *do* translate into choices. That is, i acts on reasons if, for all s_i: R_i[ought(i, s_i)] $\Rightarrow$ choice(i, s_i).[11]

In conventional game theory, the information in the game form would be supplemented by the specification of a utility function u_i for each individual i, assigning a utility value to each possible outcome. The analysis of the game thus defined would then proceed under the assumption that each individual seeks to maximize her own (expected) utility. For my purposes, however, a more general approach is more helpful.

For the purposes of the analysis, I take the game form as given. I define a *value function* for the game form as *any* function which assigns a real number to each possible outcome. At this stage, I am merely presenting a definition: I am not assuming anything about how particular kinds of value function might motivate particular players of the game. Viewed in this perspective, the individual utility functions assumed by conventional game theory are merely particular instances of value functions.

For any value function v, and for any set of individuals $N \subseteq M$, the following general concept of optimality can be defined. A *joint strategy* for N, denoted s^N, is a list of strategies, one strategy s_i for each individual i in N. Given information about the actions of any individuals outside N, we can ask which joint strategy or strategies, if chosen by the members of N, would maximize the expected value of v. If this question has a unique answer, the joint strategy it picks out is *uniquely v-maximizing for N*. The *optimality* proposition 's^N is uniquely v-maximizing for N' will be written as 'opt (v, N, s^N)'. For example, consider the Footballers' Problem, and let v be the value function in which, for each possible value of n, the value assigned to the outcome 'n per cent chance that a goal is scored' is n. Then the joint strategy (*right, right*) is uniquely v-maximizing for {A, B}, or in my notation, opt[v, {A, B}, (*right, right*)].

Notice that individual rationality, as represented in conventional game theory, can be interpreted as a special case of the concept of optimality I have just defined. If i is some member of M and if u_i is i's utility function, we can ask which strategy for the one-member set of individuals {i} maximizes the expected value of u_i, given information about the actions of individuals outside {i}. If this question has a unique answer, the strategy that is picked out for i is, by my definition, uniquely u_i-maximizing for {i}. For example, in the Footballers' Problem, if A's utility function u_A evaluates outcomes in terms of the probability that a goal is scored, the following proposition is true: choice(B, *left*) $\Rightarrow$ opt[u_A, {A}, (*left*)].

I now have the ingredients to define a mode of team reasoning. For any set of individuals $N \subseteq M$, for any individual i who is a member of N, for any value function v, i *endorses team maximizing with respect to N and v* if and only if the following condition holds for all joint strategies s^N (with s_i denoting i's component of s^N):

inf(R_i): R^N[opt(v, N, s^N)], R^N[each member of N endorses team maximizing with respect to N and v], R^N[each member of N acts on reasons] $\rightarrow$ ought(i, s_i).

Thus, i's endorsement of team maximizing is represented an inference rule of i's reason-to-believe logic.

Notice that this definition is recursive: the inference rule which constitutes i's endorsement of team maximizing refers to a proposition about the endorsement of team maximizing. However, this recursion is not circular. Because of the role played by the concept 'is the subject of' in the definition of common reason, i's having reason to believe that there is common reason to believe that each member of N endorses team maximizing does *not* entail that i has reason to believe that *he* endorses team maximizing himself. On this analysis, 'team maximizing with respect to N and v' is a rule of practical reason that can be (but need not be) endorsed unilaterally by each person i who is a member of N. However, i's endorsement of the rule has no implications for what he has reason to choose unless he has reason to believe that *everyone else* endorses it and acts on it, that *everyone else* has reason to believe that *everyone else* endorses it and acts on it, and so on.

This kind of recursive structure is common in contracts. Think of a contract of exchange between persons A and B, by which A promises to deliver goods to B and B promises to make a payment to A. One mechanism for finalizing such a contract is for the terms of the agreement to be put in writing, and then for each person to sign the document. Suppose A signs first. What does this signature commit her to? By signing, she does not make an unconditional promise to deliver goods to B, which is binding on her even if B then fails to sign. But nor does she promise to deliver the goods conditional on receiving B's payment. (That would require B to perform his part of the contract before A was obliged to perform hers.) Her commitment is conditional on B's signature, just as B's commitment is conditional on hers. As another example of the same phenomenon, international treaties often stipulate that they become binding only if a certain number of nations ratify them. In ratifying such a treaty, a nation makes a unilateral act of commitment which will activate obligations if and only if other nations make similar commitments. More generally: in a contract with this kind of recursive structure, each party undertakes to abide by the terms of the contract, conditional on having the appropriate kind of assurance that other parties have undertaken to do the same. As these examples illustrate, the recursive structure of my analysis of team maximizing is not an infinite regress.

By virtue of this recursive structure, an individual who endorses team maximizing is committed to playing his part in would-be joint actions only in situations in which he has reason to believe that the other parties to those actions will play their parts too. Thus, in the Footballers' Problem, A can endorse team maximizing without being committed to choosing *right* when he has reason to believe that B will choose *left*. In the Prisoner's Dilemma, C can endorse team maximizing without being committed to choosing *cooperate* when she has reason to believe that D will choose *defect*.

Notice that no restriction is placed on the composition of the group *N*, or on the nature of the value function *v*. Thus, *N* does not necessarily contain all those individuals who might naturally be thought of as having a responsibility for, or an interest in, the maximization of *v*. For example, consider a football team in which one member cannot be relied on to act in the best interests of the team as a whole. (Perhaps this player seeks to score goals *himself*, rather than committing himself to the joint aim that *the team* scores goals.) If the other ten players in the team recognize this particular player's weakness, it is still possible for them to engage in team maximizing as a set of ten players, pursuing the collective objective of the whole team, but treating the actions of the eleventh player as external to their collective reasoning.[12]

8.5 Team satisficing

Team maximizing is a mode of reasoning which can allow groups of individuals to coordinate their actions while acting simultaneously and without communication. It is most applicable in situations in which a well-defined group of individuals recognizes a well-defined collective objective. Since team games usually have clearly-specified rules about what counts as a team and about what counts as winning and losing, team maximizing is particularly well adapted to the coordination problems that such games generate. For similar reasons, it can work well in the model games that are analyzed in game theory and investigated in experiments. However, for many of the strategic interactions of ordinary life, team maximizing seems to demand too much of common reason.

For example, consider the practices by which road-users coordinate their behaviour. For concreteness, take the practice among American drivers of taking turns to pass through 'four-way stop' intersections (at which everyone is required to stop, but rights of way are not defined).[13]

The strategic interaction that takes place at such intersections combines elements of the Footballers' Problem and the Prisoner's Dilemma.[14] Analogously with the Footballers' Problem, two drivers who approach an intersection on collision courses have a common interest in their both following the same right-of-way rule; and some rules are more efficient than others in inducing a smooth flow of traffic. (Depending on the traffic density, the rule of taking turns may be less efficient than a rule that allows, say, two vehicles entering the intersection from the same road to move through together, and allocates turns between *pairs* of vehicles. Traffic signals work in this way, allocating turns between relatively long sequences of vehicles.) But, analogously with the Prisoner's Dilemma, there are cases in which an individual driver can gain at the expense of others by deviating from a right-of-way rule that is followed by everyone else. (Suppose everyone else takes turns. If the vehicle in front of you is taking its turn, it may be safe to follow close behind it. You will occupy the contested area of road before the driver whose turn it is has the chance to do so.)

Intuitively, the practice of turn-taking might seem to reveal a kind of team reasoning: when a driver waits for her turn, one might suggest, she construes herself as playing her part in a joint action of turn-taking which furthers the common objective of a smooth flow of traffic. But it would be much less plausible to claim that each driver independently identifies turn-taking as the *uniquely optimal* solution to a traffic management problem. In fact, as I have said, it is not at all clear that this *is* the optimal solution. We do not expect drivers to try to work out independently which traffic management rules would be optimal, and then to follow the rules they so construct for themselves. Rather, we expect them to fall in line with common practices *which already exist* and which, if generally followed, work *adequately* in achieving common objectives.

To deal with such cases, I define another form of team reasoning (drawing on Herbert Simon's notion of 'satisficing' as an alternative to maximizing). For any set of individuals $N \subseteq M$, for any value function v, a joint strategy s^N is *v-satisficing for N* if, were it chosen by the members of N, the objective expressed by v would be achieved to an adequate degree. The proposition 's^N is *v-satisficing for N*' is denoted by sat(v, N, s^N). Clearly, this is a vaguer concept than maximization; its interpretation depends on common understandings of 'adequacy'. For any individual i who is a member of N, *i endorses team satisficing with respect to N and v* if and only if the following condition holds for all joint strategies s^N (with s_i denoting i's component of s^N):

inf(R_i): R^N[sat(v, N, s^N)], R^N[each member of N endorses team satisficing with respect to N and v], R^N[each member of N acts on reasons], R^N[for each j in N: choice(j, s_j)] → ought(i, s_i).

If *i* endorses team satisficing, he stands ready to participate in joint actions which make an adequate contribution to the team's objective; but in order for this commitment to be activated, *i* must have reason to believe that there is common reason to believe that each member of the team will in fact participate in some *specific* joint action which contributes to that objective.

8.6 Assurance

On my analysis, team reasoning does not generate reasons for choice unless each member of a team has reason to believe that there is common reason to believe that each member of the team endorses and acts on team reasoning. This is a condition of *assurance*. How can such assurance be generated? I have already shown how, in general, common reason to believe in a proposition can be generated by self-revealing states of affairs. But we need to ask what kinds of states of affairs might generate common reason to believe that each member of a group of people endorses and acts on team reasoning.

One possible starting point would be to claim that the relevant principles of team reasoning are entailed by a valid theory of rationality (using 'rationality' in a broad sense, to include moral principles that are held to be discoverable by, and binding on, rational agents). On this account, to engage in team reasoning is simply to be rational. For example, Donald Regan (1980, p. 124) summarizes his principle of *cooperative utilitarianism* by asserting that 'what each agent ought to do is to co-operate, with whoever else is co-operating, in the production of the best consequences possible given the behaviour of non-co-operators'. This is a principle of team reasoning in which the value function to be maximized is a measure of the goodness of consequences, all things considered. Regan's concept of goodness is agent-neutral: it is not goodness *for* any particular individual or group. His prescription is that all rational agents ought to form themselves into a single team with the objective of maximizing goodness. Susan Hurley (1989, pp. 136–159) takes a somewhat similar line. Her prescription to us (as rational and moral agents) is that, having first specified agent-neutral goals, we should 'survey the units of agency that are possible in the circumstances at hand and ask *what the unit of agency, among those possible, should be*'; then we should 'ask ourselves *how we can contribute to the realization of the best unit possible in the circumstances*' (p. 145). I take her to mean that if the achievement of the best possible outcome requires a set of individuals to act as a team, then each of those individuals is obligated to act as a member of that team, provided there is assurance that the others will do so too. On Regan's and Hurley's accounts, then, assurance could be generated by a self-revealing state of affairs which indicates that each member of the team is rational. This approach assimilates the assurance required for team reasoning to the familiar game-theoretic assumption of 'common knowledge of rationality' – while, of course, appealing to a more morally-charged understanding of 'rationality' than is conventional in game theory. However, given my conception of the scope of decision theory (as explained in section 8.2), this approach is not open to me. I have not claimed that my analysis of team reasoning is 'really' valid. All I have claimed is that it is an internally coherent mode of reasoning which people might *take to be* valid. So I cannot assume that some class of people, independently identifiable by their being rational, take it to be valid. In more concrete terms, I do not want to claim that, merely by virtue of being in the situation described by the game form of the Footballers' Problem, player A is *rationally required* to play his part in scoring a goal. Nor do I want to claim that, in the Prisoner's Dilemma, player C is *rationally required* to contribute to the public good. If A conceives of his problem, or if C conceives of hers, as posing the question 'What should I do?', I see no way in which decision theory can tell them that they are mistaken.

A second way of thinking about how the endorsement of team reasoning becomes a matter of common reason is to focus on *agreement*. If we take one form of agency as morally fundamental, and treat its legitimacy as axiomatic, we can consider how, from within that form of agency, a transition to another form might legitimately be made. The most familiar version of this mode of argument treats individual agency as fundamental, and treats a transition to group agency as legitimate if and only if every member of the group consents to the transition.[15] This idea of legitimate transition is central to social contract theory, particularly the more radical form proposed by Jean-Jacques Rousseau.[16] It also underlies most understandings of what is involved in marriage: before their marriage, the two partners are independent agents, but, in marrying, each agrees that he or she will (at least in certain respects) from then on act as member of a two-person partnership. If team agency is instituted by agreement, we might expect assurance to be generated by public acts of joint commitment, as in the paradigm cases of constitutional conventions and marriage ceremonies. In understanding more informal kinds of team agency, we might look for forms of tacit agreement, and for ways in which individuals can express publicly their commitment to collective agency. This seems to be the approach favoured by Margaret Gilbert (1989, 1999). One consequence of this approach is that assurance and obligation are closely connected. If making a commitment implies some obligation to act in accordance with the commitment, the mechanisms which generate the assurance of team reasoning also generate obligations to engage in, and act on, team reasoning.

Clearly, there are many cases in which teams are instituted by agreement. However, I think it is unhelpful to propose an analysis of teams (or, to use Gilbert's term, 'plural subjects') in which some form of open expression of joint commitment is *essential* to their formation. An insistence on this kind of analysis can lead to strained interpretations of what constitutes a 'tacit agreement' or 'expression of commitment', and to correspondingly severe judgments about the obligations that individuals have acquired.[17] I want to emphasize the possibility of a third form of assurance, which relies on experience.

Take the case of the drivers who take turns at intersections. Suppose that this practice is well-established in some American city. Suppose I am a visitor from Britain, where four-way stop intersections are unknown. Through repeated experience of driving in the city, I gradually come to understand the practice. At first, this understanding might be purely behavioural: I learn that which driver moves forward can be predicted by a turn-taking rule. I might still be puzzled about *why* individual drivers follow this rule in those cases in which it appears to be in their interests to act otherwise. But then, perhaps by recognizing analogies with other cooperative practices, I may begin to understand that these drivers are (if only in a rough and ready way) acting on a principle of team satisficing. It is not necessary for the argument that I (as the British visitor) take such a behaviourist approach to understanding the local conventions. I might ask American friends to explain what the right-of-way rule is, and why people follow it. Or I might try to interpret the words or gestures of drivers when they appear to be telling me that I have breached a local rule. The point is that, by whatever means, I can learn that the other drivers are team satisficers without endorsing their mode of reasoning.

If I am to satisfy myself that these drivers are acting on the prescriptions of team reasoning, I need to understand what gives each of them the assurance that other drivers are doing the same. But that is not a problem. I can recognize that each of them is able to observe the behaviour of the others, talk to other people, and so on; each can make inferences, just as I have done, about other people's motivations. The source of the assurance lies in the public nature of the practice itself.

Crucially, each driver's confidence in other drivers extends to confidence in me: each of them, when beginning an interaction with me, has reason to believe that I am using team reasoning – even if, in fact, I am not. This is because, to each of them, I am just one of an anonymous population of drivers, and because team reasoning is the norm in that population. So, without endorsing team reasoning myself, I can learn that the others use team reasoning, that they believe that I use it, that they believe that I believe that they use it, and so on.

Notice that this form of assurance, unlike those based on rationality and on agreement, is not conceptually linked to an obligation to endorse team reasoning. I can understand that the other drivers' turn-taking is generated by a certain mode of reasoning, and I can understand that they believe that I use this mode of reasoning, without concluding that it is prescribed to me by some conception of rationality or morality that is binding on me. Nor do I need to construe the practice as an agreement to which I have tacitly consented. Having understood how other people reason, it remains an open question for me whether I should reason in the same way. But then, if I try to imagine how the practice looks from other people's points of view, I can recognize that what are open questions for me are also open questions for them. They too are not required by rationality or morality to follow the practice; they too are not bound by any explicit or implicit promises. That they have endorsed a mode of team reasoning is simply a fact about them, the evidence for which is revealed in their behaviour. As an individual driver, then, I do not need an explanation of *why* the others endorse this mode of reasoning; I have all the assurance I need to act on the prescriptions of team reasoning. But I still have to decide whether team reasoning is a mode of reasoning that I want to endorse.

8.7 Conclusion

Some readers may think that, by emphasizing the role of experience in generating assurance, I am devaluing team reasoning as a theoretical concept. The idea of team reasoning was first proposed in response to a puzzle posed by the Footballers' Problem, interpreted as a one-shot game (that is, as a game played once and once only). That puzzle is that conventional game theory cannot tell us that *right* is the uniquely rational choice while, intuitively speaking, it seems obviously rational for each player to choose this strategy. Team reasoning has often been seen as a way of delivering the desired result.[18]

On my analysis, however, team reasoning cannot deliver an unconditional recommendation in favour of *right* to either player in a one-shot Footballers' Problem. It can deliver an unconditional recommendation in favour of the joint strategy (*right*, *right*) to the two players collectively, as a team. And, if one of the players endorses team reasoning, it can recommend *right* to that player, provided there is common reason to believe that both players endorse and act on team reasoning. That assurance might be induced by the players' common experience that, in some analogous class of recurrent interactions, people like them do in fact engage in team reasoning. But, in the absence of common experience of team reasoning, and in the absence of any prior agreement to engage in it, assurance may not be possible.

I acknowledge that my approach will not appeal to those decision theorists who hope to find universal theories of rationality in which what it is rational for a person to do in a well-specified decision problem is independent of the contingencies of experience. Nevertheless, I believe that my analysis represents, in an idealized form, an internally consistent and psychologically intelligible mode of reasoning that human beings are sometimes inclined to use. Perhaps that is all that conceptual analysis can deliver in decision theory.

Acknowledgements

This essay will be published in *Philosophical Explorations*, volume 6 (2003), pp. 165–181. I am grateful to the editors of that journal for permission to reprint the essay. It originated in a lecture that I gave at a Colloquium on Collective Intentions at Erasmus University Rotterdam. I thank participants, and particularly Govert den Hartogh, for comments. The analysis presented in this paper is an offshoot of a larger project, which uses David Lewis's work as the starting point for a reconstruction of the foundations of game theory. That project is joint work with Robin Cubitt. The specific idea of using this approach to analyse team reasoning grew out of a discussion with Michael Bratman. My work was supported by the Leverhulme Trust.

Notes

1. As far as I know, this literature begins with the work of Hodgson (1967) and Regan (1980), both of whom discuss what I will call the Footballers' Problem. In decision theory, these ideas have been developed by Hurley (1989, p. 136–170), Sugden (1991, 1993, 1995, 2000) and Bacharach (1993, 1999). Closely related, but less directly concerned with decision theory, are the literatures of collective attitudes (e.g. Gilbert, 1989; Tuomela, 1995) and collective intentions (e.g. Searle, 1990; Bratman, 1993).
2. Cubitt and Sugden (2003) reconstruct and extend Lewis's theory, and point out the ways in which it differs from conventional game theory.
3. The problem was first presented as a problem for act-utilitarianism, which rule-utilitarianism can overcome (Hodgson, 1967; Regan, 1980).
4. Game theorists often claim that apparently counter-intuitive implications of conventional game theory result from the mis-specification of players' preferences (e.g. Binmore, 1994, pp. 97–117).
5. In this respect, the rationality of acting as a member of a team is analogous with that of acting according to a *plan* or long-term *intention*. For example, I may choose to eat fruit rather than cake today as part of a plan to lose weight. I do not evaluate today's action in isolation, taking my future behaviour as given; rather, I evaluate plans as wholes and then, having chosen a particular plan, perform the individual actions that comprise the plan. It is because of this analogy that the literature of team thinking overlaps with the literature of intention.
6. By 'team reasoning, *narrowly defined*' I mean a mode of reasoning, followed by one individual, which prescribes that he should perform his part of whichever profile is best for the team. This mode of reasoning may be embedded in a larger logic which specifies the conditions under which team reasoning, narrowly defined, should be used. In this paper, I will formulate such a logic, which I will call a logic of 'team reasoning'.
7. For some preliminary attempts to tackle it, see Bacharach (1999) and Sugden (2002). This enquiry is one of the main themes of the book that Michael Bacharach was working on when he died, and which I hope to edit for posthumous publication.

8. Notice that, in asserting that i has reason to believe some proposition, one is indirectly making an assertion about the axioms and/or inference rules that i endorses.
9. Given further assumptions, they may *contribute to* such a reason – for example, if i has some reason to want to conform to other people's expectations about what he will do.
10. For more on this, see Cubitt and Sugden (2003).
11. Since the proposition 'i acts on reasons' makes a statement about i's choices, it has i as its subject.
12. Such possibilities are allowed for in Regan's (1980) concept of *cooperative utilitarianism*, which I discuss below. Bacharach (1999) develops the related idea of *circumspect team reasoning*. Bacharach allows there to be some probability that any given member of a team will be *unreliable*, that is, will fail to act on the reasons that apply to that team. These probabilities are assumed to be common knowledge among all players. Circumspect team reasoning requires each individual (when acting reliably) to find the set of actions for the set of reliable players which maximizes the value of the team's objective function, given the expected behaviour of the unreliable players, and then to perform her part of this joint action.
13. I have been told that, officially, the right of way is given by the rule of 'priority to the right'. My American informants differ on how far this rule is followed in practice. From my experience, I infer that taking turns (the first turn going to the first arrival) is the norm.
14. I offer an analysis of this class of games in Sugden (1986, pp. 34–54).
15. Symmetrically, there can be transitions in the opposite direction: a group that is constituted as a collective agent, acting in pursuit of a collective objective, may choose that, in certain respects, its members act as individual agents. For example, a nation which has previously organized its economic life on democratic socialist principles may choose to dismantle its central planning institutions and delegate economic decision making to individuals. It could be judged to be in the best interests of the nation as a collective that individuals act on their private interests in the economic sphere.
16. Rousseau's (1762/1988) picture of the social contract as involving a 'most remarkable change in man' seems to imply a transition from individual to collective agency. Hollis (1998) discusses Rousseau's account of the social contract in the light of recent theories of team thinking.
17. On Gilbert's account, a teenager can acquire obligations to her family merely by openly going along with statements which refer to the family as 'we', and political obligations can arise from expressions of commitment that are elicited under coercion (1989, pp. 171–172; 1999, p. 254)
18. In doing so, it has seemed to open the way for rational-choice explanations of how people use 'focal points' to solve one-shot coordination problems – a phenomenon first noticed by Schelling (1960). Such explanations work by transforming coordination problems into variants of the Footballers' Problem in which the focal point of the coordination problem maps on to (*right*, *right*). See Gauthier (1975), Sugden (1991, 1995), Bacharach (1993) and Janssen (2002).

References

Bacharach, Michael (1993) 'Variable universe games' in Ken Binmore, Alan Kirman and P. Tani (eds), *Frontiers of Game Theory* (pp. 255–275) (Cambridge, Mass.: MIT Press).

Bacharach, Michael (1999) 'Interactive team reasoning: a contribution to the theory of cooperation', *Research in Economics* (53), 117–147.

Binmore, Ken (1994) *Playing Fair* (Cambridge, Mass.: MIT Press).

Bratman, Michael E. (1993) 'Shared intention', *Ethics* (104), 97–113.

Cubitt, Robin and Robert Sugden (2003) 'Common knowledge, salience and convention: a reconstruction of David Lewis's game theory', *Economics and Philosophy* (19), 175–210.

Gauthier, David (1975) 'Coordination', *Dialogue* (14), 195–221.

Gilbert, Margaret (1989) *On Social Facts* (London: Routledge).

Gilbert, Margaret (1999) 'Reconsidering the 'actual contract' theory of political obligation' *Ethics* (109), 236–260.

Hodgson, D. H. (1967) *Consequences of Utilitarianism* (Oxford: Clarendon Press).

Hollis, Martin (1998) *Trust within Reason* (Cambridge: Cambridge University Press).

Hurley, Susan L. (1989) *Natural Reasons* (Oxford: Oxford University Press).

Janssen, Maarten (2002) 'Rationalizing focal points', *Theory and Decision* (50), 119–148.

Lewis, David (1969) *Convention: A Philosophical Study* (Cambridge, Mass.: Harvard University Press).

Regan, Donald (1980) *Utilitarianism and Cooperation* (Oxford: Clarendon Press).

Rousseau, Jean-Jacques (1762/1988) 'On social contract' in Alan Ritter and Julia Conaway Bondanella (eds) *Rousseau's Political Writings* (New York: Norton).

Schelling, Thomas (1960) *The Strategy of Conflict* (Cambridge, Massachusetts: Harvard University Press).

Searle, John R. (1990) 'Collective intentions and actions', in Philip R. Cohen, Jerry Morgan and Martha E. Pollack (eds) *Intentions in Communication* (pp. 410–415) (Cambridge, Mass.: MIT Press).

Sugden, Robert (1986) *The Economics of Rights, Co-operation and Welfare* (Oxford: Basil Blackwell).

Sugden, Robert (1991) 'Rational choice: a survey of contributions from economics and philosophy', *Economic Journal* (101), 751–785.

Sugden, Robert (1993) 'Thinking as a team: toward an explanation of nonselfish behavior', *Social Philosophy and Policy* (10), 69–89.

Sugden, Robert (1995) 'A theory of focal points', *Economic Journal* (105), 1269–1302.

Sugden, Robert (2000) 'Team preferences', *Economics and Philosophy* (16), 175–204.

Sugden, Robert (2002) 'Beyond sympathy and empathy: Adam Smith's concept of fellow-feeling', *Economics and Philosophy* (18), 63–87.

Tuomela, Raimo (1995) *The Importance of Us* (Stanford, California: Stanford University Press).

9
Rational Agency, Cooperation and Mind-reading

Susan Hurley

In this paper I argue for three claims concerning rationality and units of activity. As I use the term 'unit of activity', activity within a unit of activity has consequences that are calculated against a background of what happens and is done beyond that unit; such consequences can be evaluated instrumentally, in light of the goals of the whole unit or of parts of it. I argue, first, that rational agency does not require individual units of activity; participation in collective units of activity in problems of cooperation (such as Prisoner's Dilemma) and of coordination (such as Hi-Lo) can be rational, as well as natural and beneficial. Second, collective units of activity can arise by means of global or local processes. Third, at least some such processes require more than merely tracking the behaviour of others; they require the understanding of others as rational agents, or 'mind-reading'.[1] Mind-reading may function in part to enable solutions to problems of coordination and cooperation. Note that my topic 13 collective *activity*, not collective *intentions* or *goals*; that is, collective means, not collective ends.

9.1 Rationality does not require individualism

Orthodox rational choice theory suffers from a variety of limitations, charted in a recent article by Andrew Colman (2003). A significant source of these limitations is the assumption of individualism made by orthodox rational choice theory: that rational agency necessarily presupposes individual units of activity in the service of goals. But the limits of individualism are not the limits of rationality (Hurley, 2003c).

Prisoner's Dilemma and Hi-Lo games exemplify the limits of individual rationality (Hurley, 1989). In Prisoner's Dilemmas, individuals have different goals, and individual rationality guarantees that the players obtain an outcome worse for them all than another available outcome, which would result from cooperation. This type of game is so familiar that I will not take space to describe it here. Hi-Lo games are coordination games in which individuals have the same goals, yet individual rationality fails to guarantee the players the best available outcome (see Regan, 1980; Hurley, 1989; Colman, 2003). This type of game may be less familiar, so I will describe it briefly.

A simple Hi-Lo game is shown in Figure 9.1. The problem in a nutshell is that, while both would be better off if both do Act B, neither individually has any reason to do Act B unless she has a reason to expect the other to do Act B, since each is better off if both do Act A than if they fail to do the same act (for discussion, see Colman, 2003, 144–145; Regan, 1980; Hurley, 1989). Both the shaded boxes represent equilibria from an individualistic perspective: each has done the act with the best consequences, given what the other has done. It may seem that if each assigns 50 per cent subjective probability to the other doing Act A and to the other doing Act B, the problem can be solved, since a 50–50 mixture of best and worst outcomes is better than a 50–50 mixture of second best and worst outcomes. However, even if this ploy works in simple cases, there will be other cases of Hi-Lo in which it does not work.[2]

The source of these problems of cooperation and coordination is not the nature of individuals' goals, or the instrumental character of rationality. Rather, it is individualism about rationality, which holds the unit of activity exogenously fixed at the individual.

When I speak of a unit of activity, I mean that activity within certain boundaries (which may be defined in spatial or other terms) has consequences, calculated against a background of what happens and is done outside those boundaries; the consequences of this activity can be evaluated instrumentally, in light of the goals of the unit or of parts of it. I will

Simple Hi-Lo		Player 1	
		Act A	Act B
Player 2	Act A	2nd best outcome for both	Worst outcome for both
	Act B	Worst outcome for both	Best outcome for both

Figure 9.1 A simple Hi-Lo game

develop the conception of units of activity by making a series of specific points. My conclusion will be that, once scrutinized, the assumption of a fixed individual unit of activity cannot be justified, on instrumental, theoretical, psychological, or explanatory grounds.

First, instrumental evaluation does not require that the unit whose activity is evaluated have particular boundaries, fixed at the individual unit or otherwise. Instrumental rationality is a general conception of rationality that recommends action that is an effective means to achieving goals. It does not dictate that the units of activity that furthers given goals *must* be formed, constituted or bounded in a particular fixed way. On the contrary, innovative units of activity may be effective means of achieving goals. It would be contrary to instrumental rationality to neglect such opportunities.

Second, various units of activity are possible, and may have overlapping boundaries. Larger units of activity can subsume smaller units; instrumental evaluation can be applied to the different units, with different results. I-now could do this or that, with these or those consequences. But I-over-the-next-year may have larger options and control quite different consequences. So again may you-and-I. (See Parfit, 1984.) We can think of individuals over time as composed of individuals-at-times (or in other ways, as in multiple personality syndrome, or bipolar illness); similarly, we can think of collective agents as composed of persons. In both cases, irrationality (or rationality) at the higher level may co-exist, or even be explained in terms of, rationality (or irrationality) at the lower level. For example, we understand from social dilemmas and social choice theory how a group considered as a unit can behave irrationally even though the agents that compose it are individually rational (see Arrow, 1963; Sen, 1970, 1982; and the large literature on social choice theory). To take a simple example, majority rule applied to transitive individual preference orderings can produce an intransitive social preference ordering. Intrapersonal analogues of social dilemmas may explain some forms of individual irrationality (see Hurley 1989 for a reading of bipolar illness in terms of an intrapersonal prisoners' dilemma). Conversely, agents can behave irrationally as individuals, yet their actions fit together so that the group they compose behaves rationally. For example, some ways (but not others) of organizing interactions within a group eliminate confirmation bias[3] in the group, despite its presence in the individuals that compose the group (see Hutchins, 1995, 235ff).

Third, there is no theoretical need to identify the unit of activity with the source of evaluations of outcomes. Thus, collective activity does not require collective goals or preferences. While formulations of team reasoning may assume team preferences (see Colman, 2003, section 8.1), what is distinctive about collective activity comes into sharper relief when it is made clear that the source of evaluations need not match the unit of activity (this is emphasized in Hurley, 1989). That is, collective action does not require that individual preferences be shared or even aggregated into some collective preference.[4]

Fourth, different units of activity can have different causal powers, even when units overlap. Individualism about rationality requires the individual unit of activity to do the individual act available that will have the best expected consequences, given what other individuals are expected to do. Given what others are expected to do, an individual agent has certain possible outcomes within her causal power. The best of these may not be very good, and what others are expected to do may be indeterminate. But a group of individuals acting as a collective unit can have different possible outcomes within its causal power, given what agents outside the group are expected to do. A collective unit may thus be able to bring about an outcome that is better than any outcome the individual unit can bring about – better for that individual, inter alia.

Fifth, acting as part of a group rather than as an individual can be rational. Since different units of activity can have different causal powers, the issue is not just what a particular unit of activity should do, given what others are expected to do, but also *which unit* should operate. The theory of rationality has yet to endogenize the latter question; Michael Bacharach calls this 'an important lacuna' (1999, 144, but cf. Regan, 1980). As an individual I can recognize that a wholly distinct agent can bring about results that I prefer to any I could bring about, and that my own acts would interfere with this process. This point does not lapse when the boundaries of units overlap. Thus, as an individual I can recognize that a collective unit of which I am merely a part can bring about results that I prefer to any I could bring about by acting as an individual unit, and that my acting as an individual would interfere with this process. I can instead act in a way that partly constitutes the valuable collective action, and in so doing, act rationally.

Of course, it is not controversial that it can best serve my goals to tie myself to the mast of unit extended through time or across a group or both.[5] What is incompatible with individualism is the view that rationality could directly so bind me, rather than just prompt me to use rope.

Sixth, the assumption of a fixed individual unit is also hard to justify on psychological grounds. Acting as part of a group rather than as an individual is often psychologically possible and natural. Nature does not dictate that the individual unit of activity must always operate. Persons are capable of participating in different units, and regularly do. Hence they face the normative question which unit of activity they *should* participate in. This is an aspect of the capacity for character formation and self-determination characteristic of persons.

Finally, the possibility of flexible units and collective activity has explanatory power. It's widely recognized that cooperating in the Prisoner's Dilemma can be interpreted as the result of discredited evidential reasoning: 'Since the other prisoner and I are in exactly the same situation, whatever we do, we will do the same thing. My cooperation is a sign that the other prisoner is also cooperating, and that is good news.' However, it is less widely recognized that the classic case of evidential reasoning in Newcomb's Problem, and some (but not all) other examples of supposed evidential reasoning, can be interpreted in terms of collective activity (as I have argued elsewhere; see Hurley, 1989, ch. 4, and Hurley, 1991, 1994). Some cases of supposedly evidential reasoning have intuitive appeal, such as Newcomb's Problem[6] and Quattrone and Tversky's voting result, while others have none, such as the smoking gene case. Since the availability of evidential reasoning is constant across these cases, it cannot explain why the supposedly 'evidential' choice is attractive in some cases and not others. Rather, the possibility of collective activity varies, and explains why intuitions differ, across these cases. That is, the choice supposedly supported by 'evidential' reasoning is intuitively attractive in just the cases where collective activity is possible, and intuitively unattractive in cases where there is no possibility of collective activity.

The psychological naturalness and explanatory power of collective activity are illustrated by Quattrone and Tversky's (1984) voting experiment. In this experiment, all subjects are told that they support Party A in the coming election and that voting is relatively costly; they are asked whether they would bother to vote. They are also all told that the electorate consists of four million Party A supporters, four million Party B supporters, and four million non-aligned voters. They are divided into two groups, who are given different theories about what will determine the result of the election. According to the Non-Aligned Theory, supporters of Party A and of Party B will vote in equal numbers, and the non-aligned voters who turn out will swing the election. According to the Party Supporters Theory, the non-aligned voters will split evenly, and the number of party supporters who turn out will determine the result of the election.

The result of the experiment is that subjects given the Party Supporters Theory have a greater tendency to vote than those given the Non-Aligned Theory, even though the effect of an individual's vote considered separately would be the same both cases. If we presuppose individual units, the two cases cannot be distinguished; yet subjects distinguish them. Are they irrational to do so? A counter example to individualism about rationality is provided if the rationality of voting can differ in two different social contexts, even though the consequences of an act of voting considered individually are the same in the two contexts.

There are two hypotheses that could explain the greater tendency to vote on the part of subjects given the Party Supporters Theory (related rival hypotheses could explain the choice of the one-box strategy in Newcomb's Problem). One is the diagnostic hypothesis: subjects given the Party Supporters Theory are more likely to vote because their own votes are a sign of a favourable outcome, are 'good news', while the votes of subjects given the Non-Aligned Theory are not. This interpretation regards the differential tendency to vote given the Party Supporters Theory as irrational. The other is the cooperative hypothesis: subjects given the Party Supporters Theory are more likely to vote because their voting counts as participation in collective activity, while voting by subjects given the Non-Aligned Theory does not. Those who receive the Party Supporters Theory, but not those who receive the Non-Aligned Theory, can readily conceive of their act as part of collective activity by Party A members, the consequences of which are evaluated against a background of what non-aligned voters are expected to do. If participation in collective activity can be rational, then the differential tendency to vote given the Party Supporters Theory is not necessarily irrational, given the cooperative interpretation of this result.

I argue that the diagnostic hypothesis is less plausible than the cooperative hypothesis, for the following reason (see Hurley, 1991, 1994, for further details). In other cases, such as the smoking gene case, diagnostic reasoning is equally available but cooperative reasoning is not: if a gene causes both smoking and lung cancer, then refraining from smoking is good news, but it is no part of any collective activity. The diagnostic value of refraining from smoking is strong, even if it does not here depend on any belief about other players (there are none here) reasoning in the same way I do. If the diagnostic explanation of the voting result were correct, it would predict that the choice to refrain from smoking because that would count as good news should be just as appealing as the choice to vote under the Party Supporters Theory. This prediction is not supported: the choice to refrain from smoking in this case has little intuitive appeal. On the other hand, the cooperative explanation of the voting result would predict that the choice to refrain from smoking under the smoking gene theory would be less appealing than the choice to vote under the Party Supporters Theory, since the former involves no collective activity. This prediction is supported.

Thus, the possibility of flexible units and collective activity has explanatory power. The assumption of a fixed individual unit of activity is not readily justified on instrumental, theoretical, psychological, or explanatory grounds. To summarize: Individual units are not required by instrumental evaluation of consequences; various units of activity are possible; the unit of activity need not match the source of evaluation of consequences; different units may have different causal powers, so that participation in collective units can be rational; such participation can also be psychologically natural and can explain behaviour.

9.2 The formation of collective units of activity: local vs. global processes

I suggest that the theory of rationality should drop its naïve assumption of a fixed individual unit of activity, and begin the business of endogenizing questions about units of activity. Such questions include: If the boundaries of units are not exogenously fixed, how are they determined? How are units formed and selected? Does this require centralized information or control, or can units emerge as needed as a result of local interactions? What kinds of information do individuals need about one another in order to operate together in collective units? At what points are unit formation and selection subject to rational assessment? Before reaching normative issues about which units of activity should operate, it is helpful to consider the processes by which collective units of activity can be formed, which is my focus in the rest of this chapter.

It is useful to distinguish between global and local processes by which units of activity might form. Donald Regan's account (1980) of collective activity in coordination games such as Hi-Lo requires cooperators first to identify the class of those intending to cooperate with whomever else is cooperating, next to determine what collective activity by that group would have the best consequences, given what noncooperators are expected to do, and finally to play their part in that collective activity. This procedure is *global*, in the sense that cooperators have to type-check the *whole class* of potential cooperators in order to determine which individuals are cooperators and thus to identify the class of cooperators, before they can determine which activity by that group would have best consequences. This extensive procedure could well be prohibitive in the absence of central coordination, and there may be regress worries about identifying members of the self-referential class of those intending to cooperate with others who have such intentions (worries that Regan addresses). However, such worries are reduced if the identities of cooperators have been pre-established for certain purposes, say, as a result of its members facing a common problem, so that preformed groups are in effect ready for action (see and cf. Bacharach, 1999). Moreover, the procedure doesn't need to be foolproof to be useful or adaptive.

A different approach would be to look for *local* procedures from which potent collective units of activity emerge. Flexible self-organization can result from local applications of simple rules, with no central coordination. The slime mould, for example, spends most of its life as separate single-celled units, but under the right conditions these cells come together and coalesce into a single larger organism; the slime mould opportunistically oscillates between one unit and many units. No headquarters or global view coordinates this process; rather, each cell follows simple local rules about the release and tracking of pheromone trails. An ant colony can also be regarded as a unit of activity governed by various local chemical signals that determine the behaviour of individual ants (see Holldobler and Wilson, 1990). More attention is needed in the study of collective activity to principles of emergent self-organization found in biology and elsewhere.

John Howard's (1988) Mirror Strategy for one-off Prisoner's Dilemmas has the advantage of allowing groups of cooperators to self-organize as a result of following a simple if self-referential local rule: cooperate with any others you encounter who act on this very same rule. This rule outperforms defection even in one-off games where the same players need not meet repeatedly; that is, it does not depend on reputation effects in repeated prisoner's dilemmas (in which various strategies, such as Tit-for-Tat, can outperform Defection, as is well known). Howard has implemented the Mirror Strategy computationally, thus allaying worries that mutual identification must somehow fall foul of a computational regress. Moreover, if every individual cooperates just with its copies, there may be no need to identify and scan the whole group for cooperativeness; the collective activity can emerge from decentralized encounters governed by this simple rule. That is, a collective unit of cooperative activity emerges, embracing all those players who act on the mirror strategy, from decentralized pair-wise encounters. Evidently, rules of cooperation that permit groups to self-organize locally have significant pragmatic advantages.

Notice a striking fact about both Regan's global procedure and Howard's local procedure. Both Regan's and Howard's cooperators need to detect the way one another think – that is, their methods of choice or intentions or mental states or programs, the underlying causes of their behaviour – not just to observe their behaviour. Which choices their cooperators should make are not determined until it is known whether relevant other persons are cooperators, so cooperation must be conditioned not on the choices of others but on their methods of choice.

However, if methods of choice can be used without perfect reliability, cooperators may need to be circumspect in their assessment of others' methods, and allow for the possibility of lapses (Bacharach, 1999). Moreover, it may be difficult to detect methods of choice with perfect reliability, especially given incentives to obtain the benefits of cooperation without paying the costs by deceptive mimicry of the signals by which cooperators identify one another. Such imitative free riding could be expected in turn to prompt more sophisticated and insightful capacities to detect the true methods of choice behind possibly deceptive behavioural signals, in an arms race between insightful recognition of true methods of choice and deceptive mimicry of behaviour patterns associated with methods of choice, as I shall explain.

9.3   The role of mind-reading in collective activity

In the last section I distinguished global and local processes by which collective units of activity might form and operate. In this section I examine a different distinction, the distinction between information about behaviour and information about the underlying causes of behaviour, or mental states such as intentions. I will compare the possibilities for collective activity when individuals act on the basis of information about the behaviour of other individuals and when they act on the basis of information about the underlying mental causes of other individual's behaviour. That is, I will compare behaviour-reading and 'mind-reading' as a basis for collective activity.

I use 'mind-reading' here in a way that will be familiar to students of philosophy of psychology, not in the popular sense of telepathy but as shorthand for understanding of the mental states of others. Mind readers do not merely keep track of the behaviour of other agents, but also understand other agents in terms of their mental states. Mind readers can attribute intentions to others even when their acts do not carry out their intentions, or attempt to do so but fail (Tomasello and Carpenter, 2004); mind readers can attribute beliefs to others even when those beliefs differ from their own or are false. Mind-reading is something that human children only learn to do gradually; children under four do not generally attribute false beliefs to others, for example. Moreover, the capacity for mind-reading is characteristically (even if not exclusively) human. Evidence for mind-reading in non-human animals is scarce and highly controversial; even if some animals have some limited mind-reading abilities, they lack the natural and sophisticated human talent for it. (For some of the large body of literature on these claims, see Davies and Stone, 1995a, b; Carruthers and Smith, 1996; Tomasello and Call, 1997, part II; Tomasello, 1999; Heyes, 1998; Hare et al., 2000, 2001; Hare, 2001; Nudds and Hurley, forthcoming, especially the chapters by Povinelli and Vonk, and by Tomasello and Call; Tomasello and Carpenter, 2004; etc.)

My focus in this section is on the relationship between, on the one hand, the capacity for mind-reading, for understanding and identifying with others mentally, and, on the other hand, the processes by which collective units form and operate, the capacity to identify with others as part of a collective unit of activity. However, in the background is a more general issue. Psychologists ask: what is the functional difference between genuine mind-reading and smart behaviour-reading (Whiten, 1996; Heyes, 1998; Povinelli and Vonk, forthcoming)? Many of the social problems animals face can be solved merely in terms of behaviour-circumstance correlations and corresponding behavioural predictions, without the need to postulate mediating mental states (see and cf. Heyes and Dickinson, 1993; Povinelli, 1996; Call and Tomasello, 1999; Hurley, 2003a).[7] And after all, it might be said, all we ever 'really observe' is behaviour in environments; we infer mental states from these. What problem-solving pressures are addressed by going beyond merely tracking behaviour-circumstance correlations, by attributing mental states to explain observed behaviour?[8] My focus on the role of mind-reading in collective activity will also shed light on this more general issue.

Recall first the striking property, noted above, of the solutions to collective action problems proposed by Howard and by Regan. Their proposals turn on the capacity of cooperators to identify the methods of choice others employ, not simply to track or predict the behaviour of others. In effect, their cooperators must understand and identify with other cooperators mentally, in terms of the mental states that lead to their behaviour, such as intentions to cooperate with other cooperators. Their cooperators need to know whether others have the mental processes of a cooperator before they can determine what cooperators should or will do. Howard's and Regan's cooperators must thus rely on more than unmediated associations between circumstances and behaviour – on mind-reading rather than mere behaviour-reading. Moreover, participants in such collective activity would have not just to be mind readers, but also to be able to identify, more or less reliably, other mind readers. Of course, mind-reading would not have to be foolproof to be beneficial in the context of collective activity; the degree of benefit obtained from collective activity based on mind-reading would vary with the accuracy of mind-reading.

Howard and Regan in effect show how mind-reading can provide solutions to collective action problems. Now compare activity based on behaviour-reading. Suppose a group of cooperators develops shared behaviours by means of which members identify one another as cooperators and exclude noncooperators from free riding. Noncooperators could then selectively imitate such behaviours in order to induce cooperative behaviour from group members, and then fail to return cooperative behaviour, thus deceptively obtaining the benefits of cooperation without paying the costs.[9] Freeriding through deceptive mimicry limits the advantages to be obtained through collective activity based on behaviour-reading.

An arms race could be expected to result, between deceptive mimicry and the processes by which cooperators recognize one another. In order to counter the invasion of collective cooperative units by ever more sophisticated deceptive mimics, the processes by which cooperators recognize one another would be driven progressively further away from the detection of surface behaviour-circumstance correlations toward the detection of the underlying mental causes of behaviour: would be driven away from mere behaviour-reading toward mind-reading. Capacities for mimicry might in turn be expected to become more subtle and mentalistic.[10] Such an arms race could result in the development of capacities for mind-reading and intersubjective identification.[11] Collective activity could then be based on mind-reading rather than merely on behaviour-reading. Again, mind-reading would not have to be foolproof to be beneficial in the context of collective activity; the degree of benefit obtained from collective activity based on mind-reading would vary with the accuracy of mind-reading.

Let me bring together the pieces of argument I have set out so far in this section. First, at least some solutions to collective action problems depend on mind-reading. Second, deceptive mimicry sets up pressure for the recognition of cooperators to be based on mind-reading rather than merely behaviour-reading. Groups that develop this ability, at any rate, will have advantages over groups that do not, in obtaining the benefits of co-operation and coordination in the presence of deceptive mimicry. Pressure toward mind-reading on this hypothesis would be a function of the importance of flexible cooperation. Finally, light is shed on the general background question of what functional difference there is between mind-reading and mere behaviour-reading: mind-reading can function to enable collective activity, and can have advantages over behaviour-reading in this respect.

I have argued so far that mind-reading can function to enable the solution of problems of coordination and cooperation, and that this differentiates it from smart behaviour-reading that merely tracks and predicts behaviour-circumstance correlations. I want now to extend these reflections to differentiate several hypotheses about the functions of mind-reading.

Compare the different pressures governing attributions of mental states, on the one hand, to nonhuman animals that are not mind readers, and on the other hand, to other people who are themselves also in the business of attributing mental states. How does whether a creature is a mind reader or merely a behaviour reader bear on whether that creature itself is a rational agent? In my view, a creature does not necessarily have to be a mind reader in order to be a rational agent. I do not rule out any attributions of mental states or rational agency to animals as unjustified anthropomorphism. Moreover, I suspect that making sense of animals by attributing mental states to them has often had practical functions for human beings, who have lived and interacted with animals in critically important ways for millennia (Hurley, 2003b).

Nevertheless, there are important differences between the functions of mind-reading applied to animals and to people (whether familiar people or strange people). It is true that our power over animals or our distance from them may attenuate the practical benefits of attributing mental states to them. But that could be true of oppressed or far away people also; the differences go deeper than that. Deeper differences in the functions of understanding animal and human minds would arise if, as most current evidence suggests, nonhuman animals are not full-fledged mind readers themselves.

These deeper differences follow from my considerations earlier in this section. To see why, note that the demands of rationality when I play against nature, which is a-rational though not necessarily random, are quite different from the demands of rationality when I play against other rational agents, who are simultaneously playing against me and who understand me as a rational agent. The latter, strategic situations can require that I try to understand the beliefs that the other will have about what I will do, which in turn will depend on the beliefs it has about my beliefs about it will do, and so on. Or, on a less individualistic conception of rationality, they can require that I try to ascertain whether the other has the general intentions and mental states of cooperator. But nature does not have beliefs about what I will do or about my mental states. And if I am not a mind reader, then I do not regard other animals as having beliefs about these things either. While I may play against their behaviour as part of nature, I cannot play against them as other rational agents. While I may be instrumentally rational in the sense of decision theory, I cannot be strategically rational in the sense of game theory, or engage in collective activity of the kinds Howard and Regan describe. Whether one believes that rationality in strategic contexts requires individualism or admits of collective activity, it requires some level of mind-reading ability. Lack of mind-reading ability limits solutions to game theoretic problems to relatively inflexible, genetically encoded solutions. Mind-reading may evolve when the pressure to cooperate flexibly, across a range of circumstances that does not lend itself to genetic encoding, becomes great enough.[12]

Thus, animals who are not mind readers cannot play in strategically rational ways against others understood also to be rational players and to be simultaneously playing against them; nor can they rationally participate in collective activity. Game-theoretic issues of strategic rationality and mutual mind-reading do not get a grip on them. But this does not rule out the possibility that non mind readers can play in instrumentally rational ways against nature, where nature includes the behaviour of other animals but that behaviour is not understood as itself animated by rationality.[13] Indeed, given the interdeterminacies of mutual prediction that plague game theory, mere instrumental, non-strategic rationality may be more predictive than strategic rationality.

Let's now distinguish two categories. One is the broad category of rational agents. Another is the subset category of mind readers, rational agents who make it their business to understand others as rational agents.[14] Arguably, the capacity to understand rational agency makes an explanatorily important difference: the acquisition of mind-reading abilities may be an evolutionary watershed; it may mark the beginning of culture; it may be profoundly enabling in various ways (for one version of this story, see Tomasello, 1999). But it would not follow that rational agency itself makes an explanatorily important difference, even though this is what interests mind readers. It depends on *why* mind-reading makes such a difference.

One possibility is that understanding the minds of other agents has important evolutionary and cultural differences because what is understood – rational agency – itself has important consequences, regardless of whether the agents so understood are themselves mind readers. If rational agency makes big differences in a creature's capacity to deal with his natural and social environment, then the ability to recognize and track rational agency may also have important consequences. On this view, unilateral mind-reading is adaptive. A second possibility is that mind-reading has important evolutionary and cultural consequences because *mutual* mind-reading has such consequences, in facilitating cooperation and coordination, even though understanding of the minds of non mind readers makes very little difference. Even if agency alone is inconsequential, so that recognizing and tracking agency unilaterally makes little difference, the onset of mutual mind-reading of agents by agents might have important evolutionary and cultural consequences. On this view, it is mutual mind-reading that is adaptive. A third possibility seems to me the most plausible: rational agency has important consequences even if agents are not also mind readers, so that recognizing and tracking rational agency unilaterally also has important consequences; while mutual mind-reading has further, probably even more important consequences, in opening up possibilities of flexible coordination and cooperation on which human culture can build. On this view, mutual mind-reading is a functional by-product or exaptation of adaptive unilateral mind-reading.

I thus suggest that mutual mind-reading can be viewed as an exaptation that enables the formation of collective units of activity and hence makes available at least some of the potential benefits of coordination and cooperation.

9.4   Conclusion

Individualism about rationality fixes the unit of activity at the individual, giving rise to problems exemplified in Hi-Lo and Prisoner's Dilemma games. But I have argued that the instrumental evaluation of consequences does not require a fixed individual unit. Units of activity can vary and overlap, coalesce and dissolve, with various consequences; the question of which unit *should* operate arises. The assumption of a fixed individual unit is hard to justify: acting as part of a group rather than as an individual is often psychologically natural and can be instrumentally rational. More attention is needed to how units of activity are formed and selected. Collective units of activity can be formed by global or local processes. I have suggested moreover that mind-reading plays an important role in these processes, hence in making available the potential benefits of coordination and cooperation.

Acknowledgements

Thanks to Michael Bratman, Andrew Colman, Natalie Gold, Philipp Beckmann, Hannes Rakoczy, Christopher Woodard, and members of various audiences for discussion of earlier drafts of this material.

Notes

1. To denote the generic topic of understanding other minds, I prefer the term 'mind-reading' to 'theory of mind'. Since the two main substantive theories of

understanding other minds are theory and simulation theory, it is confusing to use 'theory of mind' as the generic term as well.

2. See Hurley, 1989, 153–154, for an example that involves voting strategy in a corrupt electoral system; see also Colman, 2003, 145 for a response to another tempting but unsuccessful way to avoid the Hi-Lo problem.

3. Roughly, a tendency to give too much weight to initial evidence, and not to correct sufficiently in light of later evidence that points another way.

4. Here, I disagree with Colman's response (2003) to my commentary (2003); he assumes that collective activity depends on preference aggregation and thus faces the obstacle of social choice results. But on my view, collective activity can serve non-aggregated individual preferences and goals, as in Howard's Mirror Strategy for Prisoner's Dilemma, described below, which does not depend on preference aggregation.

5. I am here alluding to Elster's metaphor for pre-emptive strategies, in *Ulysses and the Sirens*.

6. In Newcomb's problem, an agent faces a transparent box containing a thousand dollars and an opaque box containing either a million dollars or nothing. She can choose to take either the opaque box only, or both boxes. She has been told, and believes, that a highly reliable predictor of human behaviour has already put a million dollars into the opaque box if and only if it has predicted that she will take only the opaque box. Taking the opaque box has a better expected utility than taking both boxes, and it is also good news, since it indicates that you are the type of person who takes one box, which the predictor is likely to have predicted; but taking both is a dominant strategy since it yields an extra thousand dollars whether or not a million has already been put in the opaque box. For references and further discussion see Hurley, 1991, 1994.

7. See and cf. Heyes, 1998; Povinelli, 1996; forthcoming, Heyes and Dickinson, 1993; Call and Tomasello, 1999.

8. See and cf. Davies and Stone, 1995a, b; Carruthers and Smith, 1996; Heyes, 1998; Hare et al., 2000, 2001; Povinelli, forthcoming; Tomasello and Call, forthcoming.

9. So-called *greenbeard genes* could produce genetically determined analogues of such imitative free riding (see Dawkins, 1982, 149). But the evolution of a general capacity for selective imitation would make it possible to get the advantages of free riding without the need to evolve genes for specific behaviours. In this way the ability to turn imitation on and off would be a Machiavellian social advantage; on Machiavellian intelligence, see Bryne and White, 1988; Whiten and Byrne, 1997.

10. As in Dijksterhuis's 'high road' to imitation, 2004, which involves copying general patterns of behaviour associated with character traits and stereotypes found in one's social environment, rather than copying specific observed behaviours; see also Gambetta, 2004.

11. See Hurley, forthcoming, 2005 for an extended version of this argument; see also Hurley, 2003b.

12. Note that some of the most compelling recent evidence for some limited mind-reading abilities in apes relates to competitive rather than cooperative contexts; see Hare et al., 2000, 2001; Hare, 2001; Tomasello and Call, forthcoming. Perhaps our own ancestors faced especially intense pressures to achieve flexible cooperation across a range of circumstances not amenable to genetic solutions.

13. In Hurley, 2003a, b, I defend the pointfulness of understanding as rational agents animals who do not in turn attribute rational agency to others.

14. I am focusing here on early mind-reading skills, which involve attributing agency, rather than more advanced mind-reading skills, which involve for example attributing false beliefs to others where appropriate.

References

Arrow, K. (1963) *Social Choice and Individual Values*, 2nd edn (New Haven and London: Yale University Press).

Bacharach, M. (1999) 'Interactive Team Reasoning: a Contribution to the Theory of Co-operation', *Research in Economics*, 53, 117–147.

Byrne, R. and Whiten, A. (eds) (1988) *Machiavellian Intelligence* (Oxford: Clarendon Press).

Call, J. and Tomasello, M. (1999) 'A Nonverbal Theory of Mind Test: the Performance of Children and Apes', *Child Development*, 70, 381–395.

Carruthers, P. and Smith, P. K. (1996) *Theories of Theories of Mind* (Cambridge: Cambridge University Press).

Colman, A. (2003) 'Cooperation, psychological game theory, and limitations of rationality in social interaction', *Behavioral and Brain Sciences*, 26(2), 139–153/198.

Davies, M. and Stone, T. (1995a) *Folk Psychology* (Oxford: Blackwell).

Davies, M. and Stone, T. (1995b) *Mental Simulation* (Oxford: Blackwell).

Dawkins, R. (1982) *The Extended Phenotype* (Oxford: Oxford University Press).

Dijksterhuis, A. (2004) 'Why we are Social Animals: The High Road to Imitation as Social Glue' in S. Hurley and N. Chater (eds) *Perspectives on Imitation: From Neuroscience to Social Science* (Cambridge: MIT Press).

Elster, J. (1979) *Ulysses and the Sirens : Studies in Rationality and Irrationality* (Cambridge: Cambridge University Press).

Gambetta, D. (2004) 'Deceptive Mimicry in Humans' in S. Hurley and N. Chater (eds) *Perspectives on Imitation: From Neuroscience to Social Science* (Cambridge: MIT Press).

Hare, B. (2001) 'Can competitive paradigms increase the validity of experiments on primate social cognition?', *Animal Cognition*, 4, 269–280.

Hare, B., Call, J., Agnetta, B. and Tomasello, M. (2000) 'Chimpanzees know what conspecifics do and do not see', *Animal Behavior*, 59, 771–785.

Hare, B., Call, J. and Tomasello, M. (2001) 'Do chimpanzees know what conspecifics know?', *Animal Behaviour*, 61, 139–151.

Heyes, C. (1998) 'Theory of mind in nonhuman primates', *Behavioral and Brain Sciences*, 21, 101–148.

Heyes, C. and Dickinson, A. (1993) 'The intentionality of animal action' in M. Davies and G. Humphreys (eds) *Consciousness* (Oxford: Blackwell).

Holldobler, B. and Wilson, E. O. (1990) *The Ants* (Cambridge: Belknap Press).

Howard, J. (1988) 'Cooperation in the prisoner's dilemma', *Theory and Decision*, 24, 203–213.

Hurley, S. (1989) *Natural Reasons* (New York: Oxford University Press).

Hurley, S. (1991) 'Newcomb's problem, prisoners' dilemma, and collective action', *Synthese*, 86, 173–196.

Hurley, S. (1994) 'A new take from Nozick on Newcomb's problem and prisoners' dilemma', *Analysis*, 54, 65–72.

Hurley, S. (2003a) 'Animal action in the space of reasons', *Mind and Language*, 18(3) 231–256.

Hurley, S. (2003b) 'Making sense of animals: architecture vs. interpretation', *Mind and Language*, 18(3), 273–280.

Hurley, S. (2003c) 'The limits of individualism are not the limits of rationality', *Behavioral and Brain Sciences*, 26(2), 164–165.

Hurley, S. (forthcoming, 2005) 'Active perception and perceiving action: the shared circuits hypothesis' in T. Gendler and J. Hawthorne (eds) *Perceptual Experience*. (New York: Oxford University Press).

Hurley, S. and Chater, N. (2004) *Perspectives on Imitation: From Neuroscience to Social Science* vols. 1 and 2 (Cambridge: MIT Press).

Hutchins, E. (1995) *Cognition in the Wild* (Cambridge: MIT Press).

Parfit, D. (1984) *Reasons and Persons* (Oxford: Oxford University Press).

Povinelli, D. (1996) 'Chimpanzee theory of mind?' in P. Carruthers and P. K. Smith (eds) *Theories of Theories of Mind.* Cambridge, UK: Cambridge University Press, 293–329.

Povinelli, D. and Vonk, J. (forthcoming) 'We don't need a microscope to explore the chimpanzee's mind' in M. Nudds and S. Hurley (eds) *Rational Animals?* (Oxford: Oxford University Press).

Quattrone, G. and Tversky, A. (1984) 'Causal versus diagnostic contingencies: on self-deception and the voter's illusion', *Journal of Personality and Social Psychology*, 46, 237–248.

Regan, D. (1980) *Utilitarianism and Co-operation* (Oxford: Clarendon Press).

Tomasello, M. (1999) *The Cultural Origins of Human Cognition* (Cambridge: Harvard University Press).

Tomasello, M. and Call, J. (1997) *Primate Cognition* (Oxford: Oxford University Press).

Tomasello, M. and Call, J. (forthcoming) 'Do chimpanzees know what others see – or only what they are looking at?' in M. Nudds and S. Hurley (eds) *Rational Animals?* (Oxford: Oxford University Press).

Tomasello, M. and Carpenter, M. (2004) 'Intention reading and imitation learning' in S. Hurley and N. Chater (eds) *Perspectives on Imitation: From Neuroscience to Social Science*, vol. 2. (Cambridge: MIT Press).

Sen, A. (1970) *Collective Choice and Social Welfare* (San Francisco: Holden-Day).

Sen, A. (1982) *Choice, Welfare, and Measurement* (Oxford: Blackwell).

Whiten, A. (1996) 'When does smart behaviour-reading become mind-reading?' in P. Carruthers and P. K. Smith *Theories of Theories of Mind* Cambridge: Cambridge University Press, 277–292.

Whiten, A. and Byrne, R. (eds) (1997) *Machiavellian Intelligence II: Extensions and Evaluations* (Cambridge: Cambridge University Press).

10
Evolution of Cooperation Without Awareness in Minimal Social Situations

Andrew M. Colman

A surprising prediction from a simple evolutionary game-theoretic model, based on meagre assumptions, is that a form of cooperation can evolve among agents acting without any deliberate intention to cooperate. There are circumstances in which agents can learn to behave cooperatively without even becoming aware of their strategic interdependence. This phenomenon occurs in what are called *minimal social situations*, through an unconscious mechanism of adaptive learning in pairs or groups of agents lacking any deliberate intention to cooperate.[1] Whether or not it is reasonable to interpret this as a form of teamwork is debatable. The argument pivots on what are considered to be the essential or prototypic features of teamwork, and other contributors to this volume are better qualified than I to analyze this conceptual issue. But what seems uncontroversial is that minimal social situations represent special or limiting cases that should interest people who study teamwork and may help to throw light on more complex forms of teamwork. Minimal social situations are curiosities, outside the mainstream of evolutionary game theory, but the underlying theory is intrinsically interesting and may turn out to have some utility in explaining the evolution of social behaviour in conditions of incomplete information.

The increasing popularity of evolutionary games, from the closing decades of the second millennium onwards, has been fuelled by a growing suspicion that orthodox game theory, based on ideally rational players, may be irredeemably indeterminate. Orthodox game theory seeks to specify the strategies that would be chosen by rational players – rational in the sense of invariably acting to maximize their expected utilities relative to their knowledge and beliefs. It is easy to prove, via the celebrated Indirect Argument[2] of von Neumann and Morgenstern (1944, pp. 146–148), that if a game has a *uniquely* rational solution, then that solution necessarily comprises a profile of strategies that we now call a *Nash equilibrium* in which each strategy is a utility-maximizing best reply to the combined strategies of the remaining players. But most interesting games, apart from those that are strictly competitive (finite, two-person, zero-sum), have multiple Nash equilibria that are neither equivalent nor interchangeable, and this implies that rational players, having identified the equilibria of a game, are left with a problem of equilibrium selection. It is in this sense that classical game theory, based on Nash equilibrium, is indeterminate.

Evolutionary game theory came into its own following the partial eclipse of the purely rational and normative approach set out by the founding game theorists.[3] It deals with non-rational strategic interaction driven by mindless adaptive processes based on trial and error. It can be traced to a passage in John Nash's doctoral thesis, completed in 1950 but not published in full until more than half a century later (Nash, 2002). Evolutionary game models are designed to explore the behaviour of goal-directed automata in simulated strategic interactions (Hofbauer and Sigmund, 1998; Weibull, 1995). In some models, based on adaptive learning mechanisms, individual automata adjust their strategy choices in response to the payoffs they receive in simulated interactions; in others, based on replicator dynamics, the relative proportions of different types of automata in the population change in response to payoffs. In either case, the interacting automata are programmed to maximize their individual payoffs, even though their strategy choices are made without conscious thought or deliberate choice. Evolutionary models generally converge to the vicinity of evolutionarily stable strategies,[4] which are invulnerable to evolutionary invasion by alternative strategies and (it turns out) are invariably Nash equilibria, and this process can mimic rational interactive choice analogously to the way in which biological evolution often mimics intelligent design. Minimal social situations provide vivid examples of this.

In the paragraphs that follow, I shall explain the fundamental ideas behind two-person and multi-person minimal social situations and provide some intuitive background to the evolution of cooperation without awareness. I shall then outline a formal theory designed to explain these process in both dyads and larger groups and review some admittedly sparse empirical evidence from experiments with human decision makers in artificially contrived minimal social situations. Finally, I shall attempt to draw the threads together and discuss the implications of cooperation without awareness.[5]

10.1 Two-person minimal social situation

The minimal social situation (MSS) was first described by the US psychologist Joseph Sidowski in his doctoral dissertation and in articles based on it (Sidowski, 1957; Sidowski, Wyckoff and Tabory, 1956). The two-person or dyadic MSS is a game of incomplete information in which both players know their own strategy sets but neither knows the co-player's strategy set nor either player's payoff function. In its most extreme form, both players suffer from a profound and debilitating kind of ignorance: they are oblivious not only of the nature of their strategic interdependence but even of the fact that their decisions are choices in a game of strategy.

The payoff matrix of the game generally used to study the minimal social situation, named *Mutual Fate Control* by Thibaut and Kelley (1959, ch. 7), is displayed in Figure 10.1. Player I chooses between row *C* and row *D*, Player II simultaneously (or, what amounts to the same thing, independently) chooses between columns *C* and *D*, and the pair of symbols in each cell are the payoffs to Player I and Player II in that order. There is no need to attach numerical utilities to the payoffs; we assume merely that an outcome is either positive (+) or negative (–) for each player. If both players choose the cooperative strategy *C*, then the outcome is shown in the upper-left cell, and both players receive positive payoffs. If both choose *D*, then both suffer negative payoffs. If one chooses *C* and the other *D*, then the co-operator receives a negative payoff and the defector a positive payoff.

The Mutual Fate Control game can be interpreted as an impoverished Prisoner's Dilemma game, in which the level of measurement in the payoff functions is reduced to a binary scale (Sozański, 1992, p. 110). This is clarified in Figure 10.2. But the Prisoner's Dilemma game differs from the Mutual Fate Control game in important ways. In the Prisoner's Dilemma game, there is a unique (pure-strategy, strict) Nash equilibrium at (*D*, *D*),

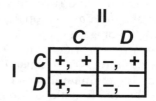

Figure 10.1   Mutual Fate Control game

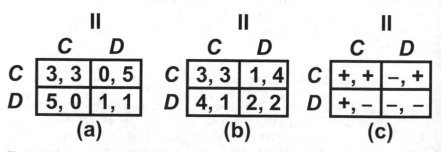

Figure 10.2   (a) Canonical Prisoner's Dilemma, with payoffs used by Axelrod (1994, 1997) and many other researchers. (b) Ordinal Prisoner's Dilemma, using ordinal payoffs 1, 2, 3, 4. (c) Mutual Fate Control, using binary payoffs.

representing joint defection. Furthermore, for each player, D yields a strictly higher payoff than C irrespective of the strategy chosen by the co-player, so that D is a strongly *dominant strategy*. In the Mutual Fate Control game, on the other hand, all four outcomes (C, C), (C, D), (D, C), (D, D) are (pure-strategy, weak) Nash equilibria, and there is no strongly dominant strategy. The characteristic feature of the Mutual Fate Control game, as its name suggests, is that the players' payoffs are unaffected by their own actions and are entirely in the hands of their co-players – another feature not shared by the Prisoner's Dilemma game.

10.2 Intuitive background

Could a Mutual Fate Control game arise in a naturally occurring situation? Leaving aside the incomplete information that is characteristic of the MSS, there is no doubt that the Mutual Fate Control payoff structure is easily realized in everyday social interactions. Kelley and Thibaut (1978, pp. 5–13) discussed at some length an example taken from Tolstoy's novella, *Family Happiness*. Here is a simpler example of my own. A kidnapper has seized a wealthy industrialist's daughter and is threatening to kill her unless the industrialist pays a modest ransom. Let us assume that the kidnapper's strategy set consists of two actions: *cooperate* (C) by sparing the hostage, or *defect* (D) by killing her. The industrialist can cooperate by paying the ransom (C), or defect by withholding it (D). Assume also that the kidnapper prefers the ransom to be paid but is sufficiently ruthless to be indifferent as to whether the hostage is spared or killed, and that the industrialist prefers his daughter to be spared but is sufficiently wealthy or well-insured to be indifferent as to whether the ransom is paid or withheld. With these assumptions, the payoff structure evidently corresponds to the Mutual Fate Control game matrix shown in Figure 10.1.

The game may even arise in symbiotic relationships between nonhuman species. An obvious example from evolutionary biology is the symbiosis between a honeybee, which evolved (but might not have evolved) a strategy of transferring pollen from a flowering plant, and the plant, which evolved (but might not have evolved) a strategy of supplying nectar to the bee. If we make the admittedly strong simplifying assumption that the plant's marginal cost of producing nectar and the honeybee's marginal cost of carrying pollen are negligible in relation to the payoffs of the symbiosis, measured in units of Darwinian fitness (reproductive success), then this too is a Mutual Fate Control game.

It is more difficult to think of lifelike examples of the MSS in which the players are human and the necessary conditions of incomplete information are met. The following slightly artificial example of the cross-wired train is taken from Colman (1982a, pp. 289–291; 1995, pp. 40–50).[6] Two people commute to work on the same train every weekday, always sitting in adjacent compartments. During the winter months, both compartments are uncomfortably cold. Each compartment has a lever marked 'heater', but there is nothing to indicate whether turning it to the left or to the right increases the temperature. (Up to this point, the story is hardly far-fetched – old British Rail rolling stock used to have heaters just like this.) Because of a fault in the electrical wiring of the train, moving either lever to the left increases the temperature, and moving it to the right decreases the temperature, in the *adjacent* compartment. The two commuters obviously have no direct control over the temperature in their own compartments. Their comfort is entirely in each other's hands, although neither of them knows this. But they would nonetheless both benefit if both turned their levers to the left at the beginning of every journey.

The following intriguing question arises: Can the commuters in the cross-wired train learn to cooperate by turning each other's heaters on in spite of being ignorant of their mutual dependence or even of each other's existence? More generally, can players learn to cooperate in a repeated MSS? If so, then cooperative behaviour, defined minimally as joint *C*-choosing, can evolve without conscious intention or awareness. Kelley (1968) named this phenomenon *interpersonal accommodation*, and if it is not itself a special form of teamwork, then it may at least help to understand some genuine forms of teamwork.

10.3 Experimental findings

The earliest MSS experiments (Sidowski, 1957; Sidowski, Wyckoff and Tabory, 1956) predated the rise of evolutionary game theory by three decades. They were based on a methodology and incentive scheme that seem slightly strange by contemporary standards. Pairs of players were seated in separate rooms, unaware of each other's existence, and electrodes were attached to their left hands. Each player was provided with a pair of buttons for choosing strategies and a digital display showing the cumulative number of points scored. The game was repeated many times, and on every round (repetition), each player pressed one of the buttons with the twin goals of earning a reward (point) and avoiding a punishment (painful electric shock). The experimental apparatus was arranged so that the rewards and punishments corresponded to the Mutual Fate Control payoff structure shown in Figure 10.1. Thus, pressing the left-hand button (labelled *C* in Figure 10.1) caused the co-player to be rewarded with points, and pressing the right-hand button (*D* in Figure 10.1) caused the co-player to be punished with electric shock (the functions of the left-hand and right-hand buttons were reversed for half the players).[7]

The findings showed that players generally learned to coordinate on the efficient (*C*, *C*) Nash equilibrium, even when they were unaware of their strategic interdependence. After approximately 200 repetitions, the relative frequency of *C*-choosing approached 75–80 per cent. Sidowski (1957) ran some of his players in a non-MSS treatment condition in which they were informed that 'there is another *S* in another room who controls the number of shocks and the number of scores that you will receive. You in turn control the number of shocks and scores which the other *S* receives' (p. 320). The results showed that this additional information did not lead to any increase in the relative frequency of cooperative choices (p. 324). This suggests that whatever accounts for the evolution of cooperation in the MSS may also explain cooperation in more general strategic interactions calling for cooperation and teamwork. Under MSS conditions of incomplete information, players assumed that their payoffs were determined in some way by their own choices, but they tended to choose *C* with increasing frequency over repetitions nonetheless. In the long run, some pairs of players settled down to choosing *C* on every round. Players behaved as if they were learning to cooperate, although in the uninformed MSS treatment condition the situation was, from their point of view, non-interactive, and they did not know (and did not guess) that they had co-players with whom to cooperate. This behaviour arguably represents the learning of a form of cooperation without awareness.

Following these early experiments, several further investigations of the MSS, using human and occasionally animal players, were published, with broadly similar findings (Bertilson and Lien, 1982; Bertilson, Wonderlich and Blum, 1983, 1984; Boren, 1966; Crawford and Sidowski, 1964; Delepoulle, Preux and Darcheville, 2000; Kelley, Thibaut, Radloff and Mundy, 1962; Molm, 1981; Rabinowitz, Kelley and Rosenblatt, 1966; Sidowski and Smith, 1961). The structural properties of variations of the Mutual Fate Control game have been analyzed mathematically and classified into equivalence classes and isomorphisms (Sozański, 1992), and computational studies have been undertaken of the performance of various stochastic learning models in the MSS (Arickx and Van Avermaet, 1981; Delepoulle, Preux and Darcheville, 2000).

How can the experimental findings be explained? Kelley, Thibaut, Radloff and Mundy (1962) proposed that players tend to adopt a myopic *win-stay, lose-change* (WSLC) strategy. This strategy is applicable to any repeated game based on a one-shot stage game with binary strategy sets – in which each player chooses from just two strategies on each round. Mutual Fate Control falls into this category. A player using the WSLC strategy repeats a stage-game strategy whenever it yields a positive payoff (above a specified aspiration level) and switches to the alternative stage-game strategy after receiving a negative payoff (below the aspiration level). In the Mutual Fate Control game, the aspiration level defines itself, because every payoff is obviously either positive (+) or negative (–); thus a player repeats the strategy chosen on the preceding round if it yielded a positive payoff and switches to the alternative strategy after receiving a negative payoff. Rapoport and Chammah (1965, pp. 73–74) rediscovered WSLC in a study of the repeated Prisoner's Dilemma game and called it *Simpleton*. Nowak and Sigmund (1993) rediscovered it again in their evolutionary research into repeated Prisoner's Dilemma games and called it *Pavlov*.[8] Nothing quite like the Pavlov strategy was included in the computational studies mentioned at the end of the previous paragraph. The name *Pavlov* has caught on in the literature on evolutionary games, so I shall adopt it here. It turns out that this simple strategy leads to rapid evolution of cooperation in the MSS, as I shall now show.

10.4   Formalization of dyadic MSS

We can represent the outcomes on successive rounds of the MSS by a sequence of ordered pairs whose elements correspond to the choices of Player I and Player II respectively. For reasons of mathematical convenience that will emerge later, it will be useful to use the symbol 0 to represent C and 1 to represent D. Let us assume that the game is repeated an indefinite number of times, and that the players' initial choices are arbitrary, but that on all subsequent rounds they use the Pavlov strategy. Assume first that both players initially choose 0 (cooperate). Because payoffs are positive, neither player will switch to the alternative strategy:

$$(0, 0) \rightarrow (0, 0) \rightarrow (0, 0) \rightarrow \ldots$$

Next, assume that both players initially choose 1 (defect). In this case, both will receive negative payoffs, which will cause them to switch to 0 on the following round, after which they will repeat these 0 choices on all subsequent rounds, as already shown above. Thus:

$$(1, 1) \rightarrow (0, 0) \rightarrow (0, 0) \rightarrow \ldots$$

Last, if one player initially chooses 0 and the other 1, then the 0-chooser will receive a negative payoff and will therefore switch to 1 on the following round, and the 1-chooser will receive a positive payoff and will therefore stay with 1. On the second round, both players will therefore choose 1, followed (as shown above) by 0 on all subsequent rounds:

$$(0, 1) \rightarrow (1, 1) \rightarrow (0, 0) \rightarrow (0, 0) \rightarrow \ldots$$
$$(1, 0) \rightarrow (1, 1) \rightarrow (0, 0) \rightarrow (0, 0) \rightarrow \ldots$$

It is clear from this analysis that players who use the Pavlov strategy learn to cooperate – to choose mutually rewarding strategies – by the third round at the latest, and continue to cooperate indefinitely after that. Thus, if the commuters travelling on the cross-wired train discussed earlier were to adopt the Pavlov strategy, they would travel in comfort from the third journey onwards.

The Pavlov strategy is essentially a formalization of Thorndike's (1898, 1911) law of effect. Behaviour approximating it is observed widely in nature (Nowak and Sigmund, 1993), and it is the linchpin of Skinnerian learning theory; therefore it not only provides an explanation of the experimental findings but comes with a respectable theoretical and empirical pedigree in experimental psychology. Pavlov also has several properties that Axelrod (1984, 1997) identified as being characteristic of strategies that were most successful in his evolutionarily Prisoner's Dilemma tournaments. In particular, Pavlov is *nice* (never being the first to defect), *forgiving* (willing to cooperate at some point after the co-player has defected, if the co-player later cooperates, for example), and *provocable* (willing to retaliate in response to the co-player's defection). The experimental evidence is consistent with the hypothesis that human players implement the Pavlov strategy, or something resembling it, but not strictly (Burnstein, 1969; Crawford and Sidowski, 1964; Rabinowitz, Kelley and Rosenblatt, 1966; Sidowski, 1957; Sidowski, Wyckoff and Tabory, 1956; Sidowski and Smith, 1961). Cooperative choices usually begin to exceed chance frequency after a few rounds and continue to increase in frequency to about 75 per cent after 200 rounds. According to the Pavlov strategy, 100 per cent cooperation should occur after three rounds.

This suggests that if players use the Pavlov strategy, then they implement it imperfectly. Nonetheless, in the light of evidence from the psychology of learning (e.g. Mackintosh, 1994), it seems highly likely that they are governed to a large extent by the law of effect, even if imperfectly. The formal analysis above is deterministic, but in other areas of evolutionary game theory, models often incorporate a stochastic element that has the effect of introducing noise into the process. The simplest method of introducing noise would be by assuming that there is a small probability ε associated with each decision, causing a player to respond to a positive payoff by switching strategies, instead of repeating the same stage-game strategy, and to respond to a negative payoff by repeating strategies instead of switching. Introducing a stochastic element would not undermine the fundamental conclusion that the Pavlov strategy leads to the evolution of joint cooperation, but neither would it facilitate the adaptive process in this simple two-person model, though a special form of randomness can facilitate cooperation in the multi-person model, as I shall show later. For the two-person case, Delepoulle, Preux and Darcheville (2000) showed that a more complex stochastic learning model developed by Staddon and Zhang (1991) yields results that most closely resemble the experimental data from human players in the MSS.

10.5   Multi-person MMSS

The *multi-person minimal social situation* (MMSS) is a generalization of the MSS to an arbitrary number of players (Coleman, Colman and Thomas, 1990). The set of $n \geq 2$ players, each with a uniquely designated predecessor and successor, may be represented by a cyclic graph of valency 2. To visualize this structure, it is useful to imagine the n players seated round a table. It is then intuitively obvious that Player 1's predecessor is Player n and that Player n's successor is Player 1. Each player has a choice of two strategies, 0 and 1, hence the choices of the n players on each repetition of the stage game can be represented by an n-vector of zeros and ones called a *configuration*. As in the two-person model discussed earlier, whenever a player chooses 0, that player's successor receives a positive payoff, and whenever a player chooses 1, that player's successor receives a negative payoff.

According to the Pavlov strategy, any player who receives a positive payoff will repeat the same strategy on the following round, and any player who receives a negative payoff will switch strategies on the following round. Every configuration therefore has a uniquely specified configuration that follows it according to the Pavlov strategy. It is obvious that a jointly cooperative configuration consisting entirely of zeros will be repeated on all subsequent rounds. Any configuration that leads ultimately to this zero configuration is called a *cooperative configuration*. The two-person MSS is a special case of the generalized MMSS, and the analysis of the MSS presented earlier shows that all configurations are cooperative in the dyadic case. However, I shall now show that is not true in general, by examining two illustrative configurations in the six-person MMSS (see Table 10.1).

The configuration (1, 0, 1, 0, 1, 0) is followed by (1, 1, 1, 1, 1, 1), and then by (0, 0, 0, 0, 0, 0), which is repeated indefinitely. The initial configuration (1, 0, 1, 0, 1, 0) is therefore a cooperative configuration. The configuration (1, 1, 0, 0, 1, 1), on the other hand, generates the following sequence: (1, 1, 0, 0, 1, 1) → (0, 0, 1, 0, 1, 0) → (0, 0, 1, 1, 1, 1) → (1, 0, 1, 0, 0, 0) → (1, 1, 1, 1, 0, 0) → (1, 0, 0, 0, 1, 0) → (1, 1, 0, 0, 1, 1), returning to the starting point. This sequence will evidently cycle for ever, never reaching (0, 0, 0, 0, 0, 0). This shows that the initial configuration is not cooperative – and neither is any of the other configurations in the cycle.

An arbitrary configuration in an n-person MMSS can be represented by the vector

$$(x_1, x_2, \ldots, x_n),$$

where $x_i \in \{0, 1\}$. It is helpful to consider 0 and 1 as elements of the Galois field GF(2) of integers modulo 2. A Galois field is a finite set of elements,

	Round 1	Round 2	Round 3	Round 4	Round 5	Round 6	Round 7
Configurations	(1, 0, 1, 0, 1, 0)	(1, 1, 1, 1, 1, 1)	(0, 0, 0, 0, 0, 0)				
Payoff vectors	(+, −, +, −, +, −)	(−, −, −, −, −, −)	(+, +, +, +, +, +)				
Configurations	(1, 1, 0, 0, 1, 1)	(0, 0, 1, 0, 1, 0)	(0, 0, 1, 1, 1, 1)	(1, 0, 1, 0, 0, 0)	(1, 1, 1, 1, 0, 0)	(1, 0, 0, 0, 1, 0)	(1, 1, 0, 0, 1, 1)
Payoff vectors	(−, −, +, +, −, −)	(+, +, −, +, −, −)	(−, +, +, −, −, −)	(+, −, +, −, +, +)	(+, −, −, −, −, +)	(+, −, +, +, +, −)	(−, −, −, +, +, −)

Table 10.1 Configurations (strategy vectors) and payoff vectors in a repeated six-player MMSS starting from two different initial configurations

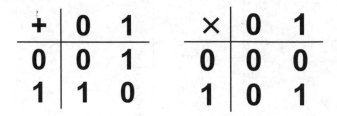

Figure 10.3   Addition and multiplication in the Galois field GF(2)

together with operations of addition and multiplication satisfying axioms that govern addition and multiplication of rational numbers in conventional arithmetic. The binary Galois field GF(2), having just two elements labelled 0 and 1, and operations of addition and multiplication defined as in Figure 10.3, satisfies the axioms. GF(2) provides a convenient structure for modelling the MMSS, because it enables the transition from one configuration to the next under the Pavlov strategy to be expressed as a simple linear transformation.

In the MMSS under Pavlov, the configuration $(y_1, ..., y_n)$ immediately following $(x_1, ..., x_n)$ is defined as follows:

$$y_i = \begin{cases} x_i & \text{if } x_{i-1} = 0 \\ x_{i+1} & \text{if } x_{i-1} = 1 \end{cases}$$

where the subscripts are reduced modulo n. Since in GF(2) $0 + 0 = 1 + 1 = 0$, and $0 + 1 = 1 + 0 = 1$,

$$y_i = x_{i-1} + x_i \ (i = 1, ..., n).$$

The configuration immediately following $(x_1, ..., x_n)$ is therefore obtained by applying the linear transformation

$$T: (x_1, ..., x_n)' \rightarrow (x_n + x_1, x_1 + x_2, ..., x_{n-1} + x_n)'$$

where x' denotes the transpose of the row vector x. The transformation matrix T is shown below:

$$T = \begin{pmatrix} 1 & 0 & 0 & 0 & ... & 1 \\ 1 & 1 & 0 & 0 & ... & 0 \\ 0 & 1 & 1 & 0 & ... & 0 \\ \vdots & & & & & \\ 0 & 0 & ... & 0 & 1 & 1 \end{pmatrix}$$

In this transformation matrix $T = [t_{ij}]$, $t_{ij} = 1$ if $i = j$ or $i = j + 1$ (mod n), and $t_{ij} = 0$ otherwise. If the initial configuration is $x = (x_1, ..., x_n)$, then the sequence of configurations (represented by transposed row vectors) on subsequent rounds will be Tx', T^2x', T^3x', and so on. An initial configuration is cooperative if $x = (x_1, ..., x_n)$ lies in the kernel of the linear transformation T^k for some k, that is, if for some k, $T^kx' = (0, 0, ..., 0)'$.

What follows is a summary of some theorems regarding the MMSS under Pavlov, with proofs supplied in an appendix.

Theorem 1. *If the configuration* $(x_1, ..., x_n)$ *is followed immediately by* $(0, 0, ..., 0)$, *then either* $(x_1, ..., x_n) = (0, 0, ..., 0)$ *or* $(x_1, ..., x_n) = (1, 1, ..., 1)$.

This theorem establishes that only configurations in which all players make the same choice as one another are immediately followed by joint cooperation. In any MMSS, joint cooperation is always preceded either by joint cooperation or by joint defection. This implies that unless the players all cooperate from the start, they must all defect on the same round before joint cooperation can occur.

Theorem 2. *If n is odd, then the only cooperative configurations are* $(0, 0, ..., 0)$ *and* $(1, 1, ..., 1)$.

This implies that if the number of players is odd, then joint cooperation is achieved only if all players make the same initial choice, whether this is joint cooperation or joint defection, and it results after two rounds at most. The following two theorems are based on established properties of Galois fields.

Theorem 3. *If* $j = 2^p$, $p \in Z^+$ *(where* Z^+ *is the set of non-negative integers) then* T^j: $(x_1, ..., x_n)$ $\rangle$ $(x_{1-j} + x_1, ..., x_{n-j} + x_n)$, *where the subscripts are expressed modulo n.*

This means that if j is any number that is a power of 2, then j repetitions of the transformation T take each component x_i of the configuration x into $x_{i-j} + x_i$. In other words, after 2 repetitions, the value of the component x_i will be equal to $x_{i-2} + x_i$, bearing in mind that addition is modulo 2, so that $0 + 0 = 1 + 1 = 0$, and $0 + 1 = 1 + 0 = 1$. Similarly, after 4 repetitions, x_i will be equal to $x_{i-4} + x_i$, after 8 repetitions, x_i will be equal to $x_{i-8} + x_i$, and so on for any power of 2.

Theorem 4. *A configuration* $(x_1, ..., x_n)$ *is a cooperative configuration iff* $x_i = x_{i-k}$ *for all i, where* $n = bk$, $k = 2^a$, $a, b \in Z^+$ *(the set of non-negative integers), and b is odd.*

This theorem allows us to characterize the cooperative configurations of an n-person MMSS as follows. If n is odd, then the cooperative configurations are $(x_1, ..., x_n)$ such that $x_i = x_{i+1}$ for all i (mod n). These are just the jointly cooperative and jointly defecting configurations $(0, 0, ..., 0)$ and $(1, 1, ..., 1)$ respectively. If n is even, and if k is the highest power of 2 that divides n evenly, then the cooperative configurations are $(x_1, ..., x_n)$ such that $x_i = x_{i-k}$ for all i (mod n). This means that, in an

n-person MMSS, if k is the highest power of 2 that divides n evenly, then for the configuration to be cooperative, once the strategy choices of k players have been specified, the choices of the remaining players are strictly determined. It follows that the number of cooperative configurations for the corresponding group size is 2^k. In the two-person minimal situation, in which $k = 2$, the number of cooperative configurations is 4, confirming the analysis performed by enumeration for the dyadic case above. In larger MMSSs, however, cooperation evolves only in special cases.

Theorem 5. *In a stochastic modification of the Pavlov strategy in which a player chooses 0 whenever a deterministic Pavlov player would choose 0, and chooses 1 with probability p ($0 < p < 1$) whenever a deterministic Pavlov player would choose 1 with certainty, play converges in probability towards joint cooperation over repetitions in every MMSS.*

The main conclusion of Theorem 4 was that, unless the number of players is a power of 2, iterated play using the Pavlov strategy does not converge to joint cooperation except from special initial configurations. That conclusion was derived from a purely deterministic model in which players implement the Pavlov strategy mechanically. Here I consider a stochastic modification[9] called *Optimistic Pavlov* in which a player who should, according to the deterministic Pavlov strategy, choose 1 (defect) with certainty defects with probability p ($0 < p < 1$). Intuitively, this models a Pavlov-like player who prefers one of the strategies (0) to the other, and who follows the deterministic Pavlov strategy whenever it mandates a cooperative (0) choice, but chooses 1 with positive probability strictly less than unity when a deterministic Pavlov player would choose 1 with certainty. It is called Optimistic Pavlov because it mirrors the behaviour of a player with complete information who is generally cooperative and sanguine about the eventual evolution of joint cooperation and is somewhat reluctant to defect when deterministic Pavlov mandates defection. Theorem 5 establishes that Optimistic Pavlov play converges in probability towards joint cooperation in any MMSS, including an odd-sized MMSS.

10.6 Predictions and conclusions

The deterministic Pavlov theory yields predictions that are not obvious but are nevertheless empirically testable. First, although the relative frequencies of cooperative choices and joint cooperation tend to increase over repetitions in the two-person MSS, the theory predicts no such increases in odd-sized groups. Second, any even-sized MMSS in which the number of players is a power of two should behave like the two-person MSS: irrespective of the initial strategy choices, there should be progress toward joint cooperation when the game is repeated. Third, if the number of players is even but not a power of two, so that some initial configurations are cooperative according to the theory and others are not, then only the cooperative configurations should progress toward joint cooperation. Finally, in MMSSs of different sizes, proportions of cooperative choices and joint cooperative outcomes after many repetitions should correlate with the proportions of configurations that are cooperative according to the theory. Optimistic Pavlov theory, on the other hand, predicts that play will converge in probability towards joint cooperation in every MMSS.

It is difficult to perform the necessary experiments to test these predictions because of the large number of participants consumed in the course of experimental MMSS research. For statistical purposes, the unit of analysis has to be the group, because individual actions within groups are not independent, and this means that the number of participants required to study MSSSs increases rapidly with the number of players. This generates an associated problem of funding adequate incentives, which are considered necessary in contemporary experimental gaming. Furthermore, the players should ideally be isolated from one another and linked to an experimenter (but not to one another) by interactive computer terminals, which creates logistical problems. I have carried out some preliminary experiments, without monetary incentives or proper isolation. These were really only pilot studies with small numbers of groups. The results are interesting, however.

I found significantly smaller proportions of cooperative choices and joint cooperative outcomes in three groups playing the three-person MMSS than in three dyads playing the two-person MSS over 40 repetitions. Simple comparisons between the proportions of joint cooperative outcomes in MMSSs of different sizes can be misleading, because in the three-person MMSS there is one joint cooperative configuration out of eight, whereas the two-person MSS has one joint cooperative configuration out of only four, hence joint cooperation has a higher a priori probability of occurrence in smaller groups. However, cooperative individual choices increased markedly over four trial blocks of ten rounds each in the two-person MSS but not in the three-person MMSS, and that is in line with deterministic Pavlov theory.

I investigated three groups in the four-person MMSS over 40 repetitions. Very few joint cooperative outcomes occurred. The repetitions were divided into four trial blocks of ten rounds each. In three of the groups, as predicted by both Pavlov and Optimistic Pavlov theory, significant increases in cooperative choices were observed, most of the increase appearing to occur between the first and second trial block. In one of the groups, the increase occurred only between the first and second trial block.

In groups of 2, 4, 8, 16, and so on, cooperation should invariably evolve. In groups of 6, 10, 12, 14, and so on, deterministic Pavlov theory predicts that cooperation should evolve from certain (identifiable) initial configurations and not from others, but these predictions are not necessarily robust in the presence of noise, because a single aberrant choice can take an MMSS into or out of a non-cooperative cycle. According to Optimistic Pavlov theory, cooperation should evolve in all these groups. The relevant data have yet to be collected. If any of the predictions are refuted by clear empirical evidence, then one or other of the theories will have to be rejected. In particular, the assumption that players approximate Pavlov or Optimistic Pavlov strategies will have to be abandoned.

The type of accommodative behaviour that evolves without awareness in the MMSS is arguably a form of cooperative teamwork meriting further attention. The introduction of a stochastic element into the Pavlov strategy seems to allow cooperation to evolve in groups of all sizes, provided that there is a reservoir of confidence causing players to be at least slightly reluctant to switch strategies after receiving negative payoffs. If this interpretation is correct, then cooperation should evolve without awareness in any group, among players who are more sanguine or tolerant than strict Pavlov players.

Appendix

Proofs of Theorems 1 to 4 were given in Coleman, Colman and Thomas (1990) and are reproduced here for convenience. Theorem 5 is new.

Theorem 1. *If the configuration* $(x_1, ..., x_n)$ *is followed immediately by* $(0, 0, ..., 0)$, *then either* $(x_1, ..., x_n) = (0, 0, ..., 0)$ *or* $(x_1, ..., x_n) = (1, 1, ..., 1)$.

Proof. If $x_i = 0$, then $x_{i-1} = 0$, otherwise the ith component of the transformed vector Tx' would be 1. Similarly, bearing in mind that $1 + 1 = 0$ in GF(2), if $x_i = 1$, then $x_{i-1} = 1$, otherwise the ith component of the transformed vector would be 1.

Theorem 2. *If n is odd, then the only cooperative configurations are* $(0, 0, ..., 0)$ *and* $(1, 1, ..., 1)$.

Proof. If $Tx' = (0, 0, ..., 0)'$, then it follows from Theorem 1 that either $x = (0, 0, ..., 0)$ or $x = (1, 1, ..., 1)$, and if $(0, 0, ..., 0)$ is not the initial configuration, then it must be preceded by $(1, 1, ..., 1)$. Suppose that $(1, 1, ..., 1)$ is also not the initial configuration. Then $Tw' = (1, 1, ..., 1)'$ for some w. Now if $w_i = 0$, then $w_{i-1} = 1$, otherwise the ith component of Tw' would be zero. For the same reason, if $w_i = 1$, then $w_{i-1} = 0$. Therefore, $w_{i-2} = w_i$. Consider the vector component w_n. Because n is odd, $w_n = w_{n-2} = ... = w_1$. This implies that if $w_1 = 0$, then $w_{1-1} = w_n = 0$, and that if $w_1 = 1$, then $w_{1-1} = w_n = 1$, which yields a contradiction.

Theorem 3. *If* $j = 2^p$, $p \in Z^+$ *(where* Z^+ *is the set of non-negative integers) then* $T^j : (x_1, ..., x_n) \rightarrow (x_{1-j} + x_1, ..., x_{n-j} + x_n)$, *where the subscripts are expressed modulo n.*

Proof. Assume that the result is true for some p. Then, if $q = 2^p$, T^q: $(x_1, ..., x_n) \to (x_{1-q} + x_1, ..., x_{n-q} + x_n)$. The proof proceeds by induction on p. For $p + 1$, $2^{p+1} = 2q$, and $T^{2q} = T^q T^q$. Now

$$T^{2q} = T^q T^q: (x_1, ..., x_n) \to (y_1, ..., y_n),$$

where $y_i = (x_{i-2q} + x_{i-q}) + (x_{i-q} + x_i) = x_{i-2q} + x_i$, because, whether $x_{i-q} = 0$ or 1, $x_{i-q} + x_{i-q} = 0$. Thus,

$$T^{2q}: (x_1, ..., x_n) \to (x_{1-2q} + x_1, ..., x_{n-2q} + x_n).$$

We have proved that if the result holds for same p then it holds for $p + 1$. The final step is to show that it holds for $p = 0$. In that case, $q = 2^0 = 1$, and $T^1 = T$ is the basic transformation

$$T: (x_1, ..., x_n) \to (x_n + x_1, x_1 + x_2, ..., x_{n-1} + x_n),$$

for which the result holds. We have therefore proved that if j is any number that is a power of 2, then j repetitions of the transformation T take each component x_i of the configuration x into $x_{i-j} + x_i$.

Theorem 4. *A configuration* $(x_1, ..., x_n)$ *is a cooperative configuration iff* $x_i = x_{i-k}$ *for all i, where* $n = bk$, $k = 2^a$, $a, b \in Z^+$ *(the set of non-negative integers), and b is odd.*
   Proof. Theorem 3 established that

$$T: (x_1, ..., x_n) \to (x_{1\,j} + x_1, ..., x_{n\,j} + x_n),$$

where $j = 2^p$, $p \in Z^+$. Hence the kernel of T^j is

$$\ker T^j = \{(x_1, ..., x_n) \mid x_{1-j} + x_1 = ... = x_{n-j} + x_n = 0\} = \{(x_1, ..., x_n) \mid x_i = x_{i+j} \text{ for all } i\}.$$

Because $\ker T^p$ is a subset of $\ker T^{p+1}$ for all $p \in N$ (the set of natural numbers), the set of cooperative configurations is $\ker T^p$ if $\ker T^p = \ker T^m$ for $p < m$. A constructive proof of this begins by establishing that if $k = 2^a$, $m = 2k = 2^{a+1}$, then $\ker T^k = \ker T^m = \ker T^{2k}$.
   Let $c = (b + 1)/2$. Then $b = 2c - 1$, and $kb = k(2c - 1)$. Hence $2ck \equiv k \pmod{kb}$, that is,

$$cm \equiv k \pmod{n}.$$

It now follows that if $x \in \ker T^m$, then $x_i = x_{i+m}$ for all $i \pmod{n}$, and hence that $x_{i+m} = x_{i+2m} = x_{i+3m} = ...$, and hence, because $c \in Z^+$,

$$x_i = x_{i+cm} \text{ for all } i \pmod{n}.$$

Because $cm \equiv k \pmod{n}$

$x_i = x_{i+k}$ for all $i \pmod{n}$,

and this shows that $x \in ker\ T^k$, and hence that $ker\ T^m$ is a subset of $ker\ T^k$. Furthermore, because $k < m$,

$ker\ T^k = ker\ T^m$.

This completes the proof.

Theorem 5. *In a stochastic modification of the Pavlov strategy in which a player chooses 0 whenever a deterministic Pavlov player would choose 0, and chooses 1 with probability p $(0 < p < 1)$ whenever a deterministic Pavlov player would choose 1 with certainty, play converges in probability towards joint cooperation over repetitions in every MMSS.*

Proof. If Player $i - 1$ chooses x_{i-1} and Player i chooses x_i in Round 0, then in Round 1 the probability $p(x_i^1 = 1)$ that Player i defects (chooses 1) is $p(x_i^1 = 1) = p(x_{i-1}^0 + x_i^0)$, and in general

$$p\ (x_i^k = 1) = p\ (x_{i-1}^{k-1} + x_i^{k-1}) \quad (i = 1, ..., n),$$

where x_i^k is the strategy choice of Player i in Round k, addition is mod 2 (with $1 + 1 = 0$), and subscripts are reduced mod n (with $i - i = 0 = n$). Because $x_{i-1}^{k-1} + x_i^{k-1} \in \{0, 1\}$, it follows that $p\ (x_i^k = 1) \in \{0, p\}$, and $p\ (x_i^k = 1) = p$ iff $x_{i-1}^{k-1} + x_i^{k-1} = 1$. If $p\ (x_i^k = 1) = p$ then, on subsequent rounds, $p\ (x_i^{k+1} = 1) = p^2$, $p\ (x_i^{k-2} = 1) = p^3$, and so on. Furthermore, $0 < p < 1$, hence p^r tends to zero as r increases. Therefore, $p\ (x_i^k = 1) = p^r$ unless on any round $k - 1$ the value of x_{i-1}^{k-1} changes, in which case $p\ (x_i^k = 1) = 0$. It follows that, over r repetitions of the MMSS, $p\ (x_i^r = 1)$ tends to zero for all x_i and therefore that the outcome configuration converges in probability towards joint cooperation. This completes the proof.

Notes

1. For a general discussion of interpersonal accommodation with and without awareness and communication in various types of interactions, including dyadic minimal social situations, see Kelley (1968).
2. For a simple proof, see Luce and Raiffa (1957, pp. 63–65), the most frequently cited version of von Neumann and Morgenstern's (1944, pp. 146–148) important result. The gist of the argument is that each player, knowing that the co-players are rational, expects them to choose strategies corresponding to the uniquely rational solution, and in turn chooses a utility-maximizing response to the co-players' strategies; hence every player chooses a utility-maximizing reply to the strategies of the co-players, yielding a Nash equilibrium by definition.
3. See von Neumann (1928, p. 295) and von Neumann and Morgenstern (1944, pp. 31–33). More than a decade after the appearance of von Neumann and

Morgenstern's book, the authors of the leading textbook of game theory wrote: 'We feel that it is crucial that the social scientist recognize that game theory is not *descriptive*, but rather (conditionally) *normative*. It states neither how people do behave nor how they should behave in an absolute sense, but how they should behave if they wish to achieve certain ends' (Luce and Raiffa, 1957, p. 63, italics in original).

4. An evolutionarily stable strategy (ESS) is one with the property that if most members of a population adopt it, then no mutant strategy can invade the population by natural selection, and it is therefore the strategy that we should expect to see commonly in nature. Although an ESS is invariably a Nash equilibrium, the converse does not hold: a Nash equilibrium is not necessarily an ESS (Hofbauer and Sigmund, 1998, pp. 62–65; Weibull, 1995, pp. 48–50).

5. The preparation of this chapter was supported, in part, by Grant No. RES-000-23-0154 from the Economic and Social Research Council of the UK. I am grateful for helpful comments on an earlier version from participants at the Teamwork workshop and from my colleague Ali al-Nowaihi. This chapter draws heavily on the work reported in Coleman, Colman and Thomas (1990) and the discussion in Colman (1995, pp. 40–50).

6. For a completely different lifelike example, see Colman (1982b, pp. 37–44).

7. In later experiments with human players, the electric shocks were dispensed with, and the usual procedure was simply (and merely) to award points for positive payoffs and to deduct points for negative payoffs. Another peculiarity (and weakness) of the early experiments was that players made their choices as and when they wished, and the payoffs were delivered immediately.

8. The name *Pavlov* alludes to the strategy's reflex-like character. Nowak and Sigmund were unaware of the earlier publications of Kelley et al. and Rapoport and Chammah (Martin Nowak, personal communication). It is a striking indication of the gulf between game theorists and experimental psychologists that the name *Pavlov* continued to be used for many years in the literature of evolutionary games without anyone commenting that the strategy already had a name. It seems that the name *win-stay, lose-change* (WSLC) was not an evolutionarily stable meme, because *Pavlov* has largely supplanted it in the literature.

9. I am indebted to Ali al-Nowaihi for this interesting refinement.

References

M. Arickx and E. Van Avermaet (1981) 'Interdependent Learning in a Minimal Social Situation', *Behavioral Science*, 26, 229–242.

R. Axelrod (1984) *The Evolution of Cooperation* (New York: Basic Books).

R. Axelrod (1997) *The Complexity of Cooperation: Agent-based Models of Competition and Collaboration* (Princeton, NJ: Princeton University Press).

H. S. Bertilson and S. K. Lien (1982) 'Comparison of Reaction Time and Interpersonal Communication Tasks to Test Effectiveness of a Matching Strategy in Reducing Attack-instigated Aggression', *Perceptual and Motor Skills*, 55, 659–665.

H. S. Bertilson, S. A. Wonderlich and M. W. Blum (1983) 'Withdrawal, Matching, Withdrawal-matching, and Variable-matching Strategies in Reducing Attack-instigated Aggression', *Aggressive Behavior*, 9, 1–11.

H. S. Bertilson, S. A. Wonderlich and M. W. Blum (1984) 'Withdrawal and Matching Strategies in Reducing Attack-instigated Aggression', *Psychological Reports*, 55, 823–828.

J. J. Boren (1966) 'An Experimental Social Relation Between Two Monkeys', *Journal of the Experimental Analysis of Behavior*, 9, 691–700.

E. Burnstein (1969) 'The role of reward and punishment in the development of behavioral interdependence', in J. Mills (ed.), *Experimental Social psychology* (London: Macmillan), pp. 341–405.

A. A. Coleman, A. M. Colman and R. M. Thomas (1990) 'Cooperation Without Awareness: A Multiperson Generalization of the Minimal Social Situation', *Behavioral Science*, 35, 115–121.

A. M. Colman (ed.) (1982a) *Cooperation and Competition in Humans and Animals* (Wokingham: Van Nostrand Reinhold).

A. M. Colman (1982b) *Game Theory and Experimental Games: The Study of Strategic Interaction* (Oxford: Pergamon).

A. M. Colman (1995) *Game Theory and Its Applications in the Social and Biological Sciences* (2nd edn, London: Routledge).

T. Crawford and J. B. Sidowski (1964) 'Monetary Incentive and Cooperation/ Competition Instructions in a Minimal Social Situation', *Psychological Reports*, 15, 233–234.

S. Delepoulle, P. Preux and J.-C. Darcheville (2000) 'Evolution of Cooperation Within a Behavior-based Perspective: Confronting Nature and Animats', *Artificial Evolution Lecture Notes in Computer Science*, 18291, 204–216.

J. Hofbauer and K. Sigmund (1998) *Evolutionary Games and Population Dynamics* (Cambridge: Cambridge University Press).

H. H. Kelley (1968) 'Interpersonal accommodation', *American Psychologist*, 23, 399–410.

H. H. Kelley and J. W. Thibaut (1978) *Interpersonal Relations: A Theory of Interdependence* (New York: Wiley).

H. H. Kelley, J. W. Thibaut, R. Radloff and D. Mundy (1962) 'The Development of Cooperation in the 'Minimal Social Situation'', *Psychological Monographs*, 76, Whole No. 19.

R. D. Luce and H. Raiffa (1957) *Games and Decisions: Introduction and Critical Survey* (New York: Wiley).

N. J. Mackintosh (ed.) (1994) *Animal Learning and Cognition: Handbook of Perception and Cognition* (2nd edn, San Diego, CA: Academic Press).

L. D. Molm (1981) 'A Contingency Change Analysis of the Disruption and Recovery of Social Exchange and Cooperation', *Social Forces*, 59, 729–751.

J. F. Nash (2002) 'Non-cooperative Games', in H. W. Kuhn and S. Nasar (eds), *The Essential John Nash* (Princeton, NJ: Princeton University Press) pp. 51–84.

M. A. Nowak and K. Sigmund (1993) 'A Strategy of Win-stay, Lose-shift that Outperforms Tit-for-Tat in the Prisoner's Dilemma Game', *Nature*, 364, 56–58.

L. Rabinowitz, H. H. Kelley and R. M. Rosenblatt (1966) 'Effects of Different Types of Interdependence and Response Conditions in the Minimal Social Situation', *Journal of Experimental Social Psychology*, 2, 169–197.

A. Rapoport and A. M. Chammah (1965) *Prisoner's Dilemma: A Study in Conflict and Cooperation* (Ann Arbor, MI: University of Michigan Press).

J. B. Sidowski (1957) 'Reward and Punishment in the Minimal Social Situation', *Journal of Experimental Psychology*, 54, 318–326.

J. B. Sidowski and M. Smith (1961) 'Sex and Game Instruction Variables in a Minimal Social Situation', *Psychological Reports*, 8, 393–397.

J. B. Sidowski, L. B. Wyckoff and L. Tabory (1956) 'The Influence of Reinforcement and Punishment in a Minimal Social Situation', *Journal of Abnormal and Social Psychology*, 52, 115–119.

T. Sozański (1992) 'A Combinatorial Theory of Minimal Social Situations', *Journal of Mathematical Sociology*, 17, 105–125.

J. E. R. Staddon and Y. Zhang (1991) 'On the assignment-of-credit problem in operand learning', in M. L. Commons, S. Grossberg and J. E. R. Staddon (eds), *Neural Network Model of Conditioning and Action: The XIIth Harvard Symposium* (Hillsdale, NJ: Erlbaum) pp. 279–293.

J. W. Thibaut and H. H. Kelley (1959) *The Social Psychology of Groups* (New York: Wiley).

E. L. Thorndike (1898) 'Animal Intelligence: An Experimental Study of the Associative Processes in Animals', *Psychological Review Monograph Supplement*, 2(4), Whole No. 8.

R. L. Thorndike (1911) *Animal Intelligence: Experimental Studies* (New York: Macmillan).

J. von Neumann (1928) 'Zur Theorie der Gesellschaftsspiele', *Mathematische Annalen*, 100, 295–320.

J. von Neumann and O. Morgenstern (1944) *Theory of Games and Economic Behavior.* (Princeton, NJ: Princeton University Press).

J. W. Weibull (1995) *Evolutionary Game Theory* (Cambridge, MA: MIT Press).

11
Learning in Robot Teams

Jeremy Wyatt, Yoshiyuki Matsumura and Matthew Todd

Robots are most likely to be useful to us when they can work with both humans and other robots. Robots that work in teams pose many challenges for engineers. How should robots communicate with one another and with humans; how can they represent and share beliefs about an uncertain and changing world, or indeed about the beliefs of other agents; how should tasks be divided among team members; how much information about the actions of other team members do robots need to act usefully within the team?

The question we are particularly interested in is 'how can we build teams of robots that can learn to cooperate?' This chapter describes some high level results of our experimental work in the form of two studies. In the first we will describe robot teams that are capable of learning to cooperate. In particular we will describe teams of simulated robots that learn to play football, learning the different roles required for a successful team without being explicitly told what these roles are. We will also present some results from our efforts to evolve pairs of simulated robots that carry objects co-operatively. These show that sometimes we can achieve better results by rewarding team members for being selfish than by rewarding team members equally. This sort of work ties in to what is known as evolutionary game theory, originally suggested by evolutionary biologists (Maynard-Smith, 1982) to explain some of the effects of natural selection. Thus there is a scientific motivation for our work as well as an engineering challenge.

It should be emphasized that the learning problems to be tackled are non-trivial. Indeed for many people studying algorithms that learn, a field called *machine learning* (Mitchell, 1997), it is rather surprising that we can learn some of the behaviours described here at all. Machine learning methods are in their infancy, and often fail on an apparently simple problem, while succeeding on another that to the naïve human eye looks much harder. We don't yet understand why.

Both the robot teams described here learn from a weak form of feedback called *reward* or *fitness*. The first is similar in some respects to the rewards used in psychological studies of animal learning, particularly behaviourist approaches to stimulus-response learning, also known as reinforcement learning. The second is similar to the idea of fitness in evolutionary biology, except that here the selection is artificial, not natural. These weak forms of feedback are surprisingly powerful given enough time, as we shall see. The paper is composed of two case studies, which we now describe in turn, before turning to the issues they raise.

11.1   Learning to play robot football

Robot football is one of the most popular domains in which to study robot teams. The ostensible goal is to build a team of humanoid robots that will play competently against a team of human footballers by the year 2050. Whether or not this is achieved the effect of the regular competitions between teams from different universities, schools and corporations, has been to focus much research effort in robotics on this one task. The task works as an experimental benchmark, with a clear set of rules making comparison of teams easy. There are a number of different leagues for different types of robots, including simulated robots, miniature robots, humanoid robots, and even robot dogs. Most work on learning is applied to the simulated league. This is due to the thousands of hours of computing time needed to learn appropriate behaviour. We include a shot from a typical simulator league game in Figure 11.1.

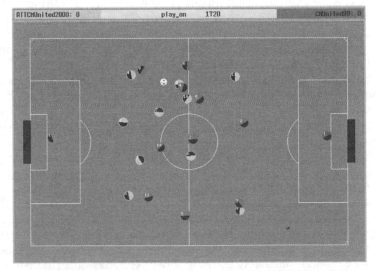

Figure 11.1   Shot from a typical Robocup soccer simulator league match

11.1.1 Learning to play football from rewards

The challenge we set ourselves was to see if a team of robots could learn to play football just using goal scoring as the form of feedback. Each goal scored by the team is regarded as a reward, and each goal scored by the opposing team as a punishment. The learning algorithm uses an extension of mathematical models of operant and classical conditioning from psychology (Sutton and Barto, 1990), and will be outlined below. While each player learns separately, all players are rewarded or punished equally. Players learn behaviours that lead the team to high rewards, and avoid behaviours leading to low rewards. To do this each learner must acquire an estimate of both the long- and short-term consequences of its actions. Imagine a defender who passes the ball forward to one its teammates in free space. This is usually a better action than passing the ball across its team's goalmouth; it may, or may not be better than dribbling the ball up the pitch. Whatever the best answer the robot must learn to assess the best course of action by watching the sequence of rewards that follows. It may take many steps after the beginning of a move for a goal to be scored and a reward obtained. This delay makes learning hard and is known as the problem of learning from delayed rewards. It is an ability rarely, if ever, encountered in animals.

Each player in the simulation has limited perception. It can 'see' only a certain distance, and cannot for example know exactly where it is on the pitch. The players do not have to perform any visual processing. Instead each one has direct access to imperfect information about the relative positions of nearby objects and players. The relative positions of other objects and players are expressed in terms of polar coordinates (heading and distance). Other objects players can see are corner flags, the goalmouths, and the ball. The information available to each player will be updated automatically many times a second. Each robot can only see in front of it, in an arc of about 90 degrees. There are various kinds of uncertainty in the robots' sensing. It may be possible to identify which team a nearby player is on, for example, but not the team of a player far away. The estimates of objects' positions are also increasingly inaccurate with distance. The number of possible situations or *states* that the game may be in is enormous, since the simulator gives angles in units of $1/10^{th}$ of a degree, and because the unit of distance is small. In principle there are $22^{1,000,000,000}$ different states for the game, composed of 1,000,000,000 situations each player can distinguish. There are also four different actions: *dash*, *kick*, *turn* and *stay*. These must also be parameterized by distance, angle and power to yield many thousands of possible responses at each decision point.

This is clearly far too large to deal with directly. Therefore our learning task is broken down in part by the designer. Each player has a number of hand designed, or separately learned, low level behaviours that will often be needed. These include behaviours such as move to an object, move to the ball, shoot, dribble, pass, clear, get behind the ball, and face an object. There are 14 low level behaviours in all. The perceptual information available to low level behaviours is also hand selected. The learning task then is for each player to decide which of the 14 behaviours it should perform at any time. This choice of which behaviour to perform is made by a coordinating controller, which is commonly referred to as a coordinating behaviour. In order to make this feasible the perceptual information available to the coordinating behaviour must also be simplified. Instead of representing all 1,000,000,000 situations it has access to nine imperfect variables or features. These are described in Table 11.1. Since each feature has only two values, *true* or *false*, the number of distinguishable situations for each robot is reduced to $2^9 = 1,024$.

11.1.2 The reinforcement learning algorithm

We now describe how each robot learns to identify the best behaviour to perform in each of the 1,024 states we have identified. The robot tries an action each time step, and identifies the resulting situation. Time steps are short enough that it can complete this cycle several times a second. Occasionally it receives rewards. The robot learns to estimate how much

Ball_kickable	The ball is deemed kickable if the distance from the client to the ball is less than 1.88 units.
Ball_near	If the ball is within 12 units, then it is considered to be near.
Own_player_near	This is true if a player who can be identified as one your team members, is within passing distance (20 units).
Opposition_player_near	True if an opposition player is within 20 units of the client.
Nearest_team_player_to_ball	The robot constructs a list of players and estimates how far away they are from the ball and then looks at its own distance. If its distance is lowest then it is nearest to the ball.
Near_own_goal	True if the distance to the player's goal is less than 20 units.
Near_opposition_goal	True if the distance to the opposition goal is less than 20 units.
Facing_own_goal	True if the player can see its goalmouth at all.
Facing_opposition_goal	True if the player can see the opposition goalmouth.

Table 11.1 The perceptual features available to each robot's coordinating behaviour

reward it will pick up in the long term on average. It does this by trying each behaviour many times in each possible situation. It thereby learns a separate estimate of the goodness of each behaviour in each one of the 1,024 situations it can distinguish. We will explain exactly how below. The core of the algorithm is a type of reinforcement learning algorithm called Q-learning (Sutton and Barto, 1998).

We give all robots in a team a reward of 1 in the time step immediately after the team scored a goal, −1 if the opposing team scored a goal, and 0 on all other time steps. Let us denote the situation the player perceives at time t as s_t; the behaviour the player performs at time t as a_t, and the situation it ends up in the following time step as s_{t+1}. Let us denote the reward picked up at any time t as r_t.

Now each player learns the estimated long-term cumulative reward it will pick up. The estimates are indexed by behaviours and states in a table. Since there are 1,024 different states and 14 different behaviours there are $14 \times 1,024 = 14,336$ different estimates. The estimate for some situation s and action a is denoted, for simplicity, by $Q(s,a)$. We will call this a situation-behaviour value or utility, and it denotes the estimated quality of the behaviour a when initiated in the situation s. It turns out that we can obtain good estimates of quality simply by taking any initial guess, say zero for every one, and then every time we take a decision updating our guess using the following rule:

$$Q_{t+1}\,(s_t,\,a_t) = (1 - \alpha)\,Q_t\,(s_t,\,a_t) + \alpha\,(r_{t+1} + \max_b\{Q_t\,(s_{t+1},\,b)\})$$

This effectively tells a learner: take some of your current estimate of the situation-behaviour value for the behaviour you just performed, $Q_t(s_t,\,a_t)$, and add some of the reward, r_{t+1} you just picked up, and some of your estimate of the best looking behaviour you could perform in the new situation you are in. Use the result to replace the current estimate of the situation-behaviour value for the action you just performed. The number α determines how much 'some' is, and must be between 0 and 1. If $\alpha = 1$ then learning is quick and dirty and as it moves nearer to 0 learning becomes slower, but the long-term results are more accurate. There are many other details of the learning method (Sutton and Barto, 1998), but most can be ignored for our purposes. One important point is that a behaviour may in fact run for many steps before it terminates, and the estimates of utility are revised. Another is that there is a proof that the learning will eventually converge on the right estimates of quality if a number of conditions hold. Finally, we should ask how the learner should act while it is learning, and when it has learned. This is easy. When it has learned the quality estimates with confidence, the best strategy is to always take the behaviour with the highest estimated quality. While it is learning the learner can usually act according to that strategy, but it also needs to experiment occasionally, by selecting an action at random. Having detailed the essence of learning in an individual we now turn to the problems of applying it to learning in a team.

11.1.3 Learning in a team

In our learning team each player has a separate version of the learning mechanism described above. Players do not share their learning experiences by sharing their situation-behaviour values, or even their experiences. The only form of sharing that occurs is that the reward for a goal is delivered to the whole team, regardless of what each player was doing at the time the goal was scored. Learning in the team occurs by playing against a hand designed team. We set up each learning episode so that it had no time limit but lasted until 1 goal had been scored. Each team takes about 1,500 learning episodes to learn to play football. This is a figure that we have arrived at by experiment and little improvement seems to occur in the rewards generated, or the behaviours discovered after this number of episodes. Some of the early episodes may be very long however. Every 500 episodes learning was halted and we tested the progress of the team against the hand designed team in a longer game. These games lasted until 20 goals had been scored.

We tried three different learning strategies to see if the simplest form of learning could be improved on (Todd, 1999). These were:

(1) Tabula rasa learning: the team members learned some low-level behaviours while learning the coordinating behaviour. There was no feedback other than the goals scored.
(2) Learning with set plays: we pre-trained the team using set plays that encouraged them to learn to shoot when near their opponents' goal; to clear the ball when it was near their own goal; and how to kick off. Each set play was tried 50 times, and then 1,500 normal episodes were run.
(3) Learning with progress indicators: we defined some rewards for situations other than goal scoring, e.g. if you are surrounded by opposition players then that is likely to be bad so the reward is –0.1. They also learned some low-level behaviours at the same time.

11.1.4 The results

The results for strategies 1, 2 and 3 are shown in Figures 11.2, 11.3 and 11.4 respectively. It can be seen that even after 1,500 learning episodes learning strategy 1 leads to a team that scores about half the number of goals of its hand designed opponent. Strategies 2 and 3 do rather better, with both nearly equal to the hand designed team. We hypothesize that the set plays speed the learning by allowing the robots to learn quickly on a more constrained task. In learning strategy 3 we hypothesize that the progress

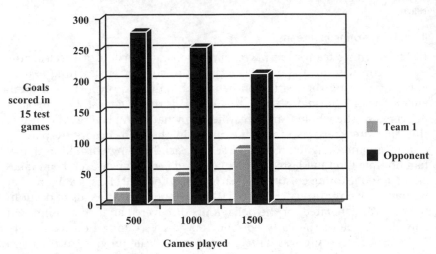

Figure 11.2   Results for learning strategy 1

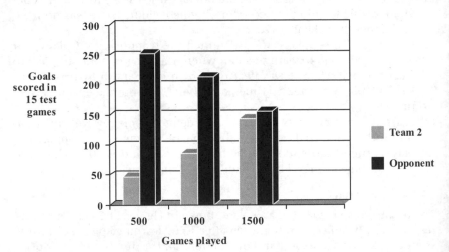

Figure 11.3   Results for learning strategy 2

Performance of Learning Team 3

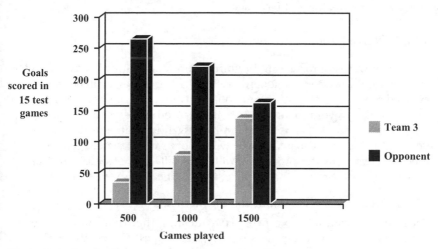

Figure 11.4   Results for learning strategy 3

indicators work by providing a richer feedback signal from which to learn in the unconstrained task.

We also tested these teams against the then world champion team, CMUnited (Stone, 2000), which employed a number of sophisticated, hand designed control techniques. While the learning teams were heavily beaten – they scored an average of 1 goal a game against CMUnited's 19 goals – this is actually a rather impressive performance, as there is no record of any other team ever scoring any goals against CMUnited in that particular competition year. This shows that even a crude learning mechanism with weak feedback can achieve a reasonable level of performance against much more carefully engineered solutions.

What is important for this paper, however, is not the level of performance achieved, but the kinds of team behaviour learned. Initially all the players move around randomly, but after 500 episodes they learn to dribble, pass and shoot; while still following the ball around the pitch. By 1,000 learning episodes the players have begun to specialize into different roles, with some players learning to stay in parts of the pitch, and some learned to stay near the opponents' goal waiting for the ball to be passed to them. After 1,500 games most players stayed in one area, and were able to pass the ball up the field to the opponents' goal.

The key result of relevance here is that teams of initially homogenous agents were able to automatically diversify under a learning scheme that rewards the whole team, and rewards all team members equally. We have also noticed that learning schemes in which only the goal scorer is rewarded do not achieve this level of diversification. It is intriguing that we can observe this phenomenon with such a simple learning mechanism and using such a weak form of feedback.

11.2 Evolving robot partners for carrying objects

We now turn to approaches to building teams automatically based on ideas from natural selection (Goldberg, 1989). In this series of experiments we evolved robot controllers that can cooperatively carry objects toward a goal. The idea of the evolutionary process is that we initially generate a random population of robots; select the fittest robots (those that perform best on the task); and then breed pairs of selected robots so that a new generation of robots is created. By this process we will eventually move toward a population in which there are robots that perform the task nearly as well as possible.

11.2.1 The task and the fitness sharing method

Because our evolutionary process is artificial, rather than natural, we can manipulate the way the fitness of the phenotypes (the creatures that are the expression of the genetic code or genotype) is used to drive selection and breeding. Our interest here is in how different ways of sharing the fitness of the individual robots affects our ability to evolve good teams. Here we will see the effect of three different fitness sharing schemes that we refer to as *cooperative, competitive,* and *symbiotic.* We will see exactly how each of these work shortly.

First we will describe the task, and the robots involved; then to the calculation of fitness; and finally to the mechanisms used to control the

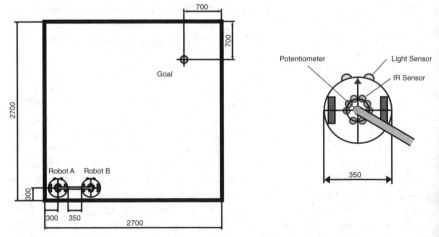

Figure 11.5 The task and environment are shown on the left, and some details of the robots' sensing and action are detailed on the right.

robots. The robots are simulated and each is equipped with light and distance sensors (IR or Infrared sensors sense the distance to objects). Each robot is circular, can turn on the spot or travel forward in the direction it is facing, and is attached in the centre to a pivot on the end of a bar (Figure 11.5). The task of the robots is to carry the bar towards the delivery area marked by the light source in its lower left-hand corner. The distance sensors tell a robot the proximity of not just the arena walls but also of the other robot. The robots cannot communicate directly with one another, but must still cooperate with one another to succeed in their task.

To perform artificial selection we will need a measure of the performance of the robots. The basic metric is depicted in Figure 11.6. The performance of a robot is measured by calculating its cumulative distance from the goal area through time. We do this by measuring the straight-line distance from the centre of the robot to the goal area at time t, d_t. Then we sum the values of d_t over the time for which the robot runs. This will produce a measure that is better the smaller it is. For convenience we wish to make bigger values correspond to better performance. We therefore pick a large constant K, and apply the following formula to calculate the performance of the robot, which we denote $f(.)$:

$$f(robot) = K - \sum_{t=0}^{N} d_t$$

The life of each robot finishes when the goal area is reached, or when the available lifespan, N, is exhausted. The performance of each robot is then

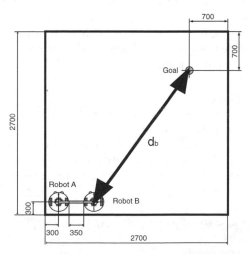

Figure 11.6 The raw performance of each robot at each time step is determined by measuring the distance d between the robot and the goal area. The distance is summed over all time steps to calculate the overall performance.

used to calculate the fitness of the robots in various ways. This is where the fitness sharing schemes mentioned come into play. We now describe each of these in turn.

(i) Cooperative scheme
In this scheme the fitness of each robot is dependent not only on its own performance, but also on that of its companion:

Fitness (robot A)   = Fitness (robot B)
                       = f (robot A) + f (robot B)

In this scheme a robot will perform only as well as the team of which it is a member. To understand this scheme it is also worth noting that for testing purposes a robot is drawn randomly from the population and paired with another randomly selected robot from the same population.

(ii) Competitive scheme
In this scheme each robot is rewarded purely for how well it does. Thus the performance of the robot is exactly the same as its fitness:

Fitness (robot) = f (robot)

In this scheme robots are again paired randomly with one another for evaluation, and while the fitness strictly depends on the robot itself, there will be a correlation between the fitness of the robots since they are joined by the bar, and cannot escape one another. Nevertheless robots are rewarded for their individual performance, and not directly for being good team members. This can lead to selfish behaviour in some systems that causes lower fitness over the whole population.

(iii) Symbiotic scheme
In the final scheme the two robots are for evolutionary purposes regarded as one creature. In other words their genetic information is joined together and they are selected for evaluation as single unit, not as two separate randomly generated individuals. Thus the fitness of the compound creature is the combined fitness of the two robots in the team. Here the team is essentially treated as an individual:

Fitness (robot A and robot B) = f (robot A) + f (robot B)

11.2.2 The robot controllers

We now turn to the method by which the robots decide how to act in their world. Both robots are controlled by simple brains, which are termed artificial neural networks. It is important to understand that these artificial neural networks bear only the vaguest resemblance to a biological neural network. The neurons shown in Figure 11.7 transform the sensory input into a pair of motor outputs.

We do not have space here to give the details of how the network performs this transformation, which is often called a *forward pass*. The typical way the forward pass is carried out is described in (Gurney, 1997), and our specific method in (Matsumura et al., 2002). It is sufficient for our purpose to understand that the behaviour the network implements is completely determined by a vector of numbers that specify the synaptic strengths between the neurons. If we imagine a network with three such weights then we can see that it is also a three-dimensional vector, i.e. a point within a three-dimensional space. If we assume that the possible weights all have the same size limits we can think of the space of all the possible networks as forming a 3-d shape, which is in fact simply a cube. In our case the vector needed to specify the network we use has more than three synapses and so is of a higher dimension than three. Thus the networks are points within what we call a hyper-cube. A square is simply a hyper-cube of dimension two, and a cube is a hyper-cube of dimension three. It is quite hard, of course, to visualize hyper-cubes of dimension greater than three!

We can think of our vector of synaptic strengths as being a grossly simplified chromosome, and of our robot creature as having just one of these chromosomes. This vector or chromosome is the genotype, the structure on which we will perform the mechanisms associated with reproduction. The robot controlled by the corresponding network corresponds to the phenotype, the entity or creature which will be assessed for its fitness in order to carry out artificial selection.

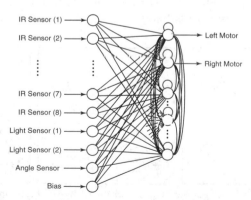

Figure 11.7 The artificial neural network used to control the robot. The diagram does not show any of the strengths of the synaptic connections, or the way in which the neurons transform their input signal into an output signal.

Initially we must create a population of robots to tackle the task. To do this we randomly generate (or guess) the networks that control them. We can think of this as randomly generating points within our hyper-cube, or equivalently possible chromosomes. Then we select some of the corresponding networks: those that produce highly fit robots, and then we artificially reproduce them. Here we typically breed networks only by mutation, not by swapping over some of the genetic material between individuals. In our scheme each individual also captures in its genotype the rules by which the genotype itself will be mutated.

Thus we can think of our evolutionary process as being a randomized search by a population of individuals through a high dimensional space. Successful individuals correspond to points in the space that are reproduced (with some alterations caused by mutation), and unsuccessful individuals are eliminated from the space altogether.

11.2.3 The results

The qualitative results are quite clear in that the cooperative scheme does very badly while the competitive and symbiotic schemes essentially solve the problem. In fact the cooperative scheme never improves on the random individuals created for the first generation. This result seems to run counter to what we learned from the robot football case study. In that instance learning of diverse roles depended on all team members being rewarded equally, regardless of who scored the goal. We hypothesize that the answer lies partly in the evolutionary dynamics and partly in the nature of the task. In the cooperative scheme better individuals are paired with worse individuals, and the team-based fitness function means that there is no selective pressure to differentiate between them. The good and the bad individual within the team are always rated equally. Thus the only individuals that will do better than average, and who will produce proportionately more offspring than others, are those who happen to be selected

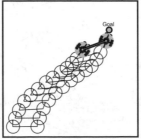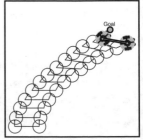

Figure 11.8 Archetypal behaviours exhibited by the best robots at the end of the evolutionary process under each fitness sharing scheme. The best team evolved using the cooperative scheme is on left; the competitive scheme is in the middle and the symbiotic scheme is on the right.

with another better than average team-mate. It is presumably unlikely in this case that two better than average individuals are selected together. The task also has some impact on the effectiveness of the competitive scheme. This is because a good behaviour for any team member is the same as the greedy behaviour for the individual, and because the good behaviour for any team member is always pretty much the same. Both robots need to head towards the light as fast as possible. The better robots benefit in the competitive scheme, while still being hampered by their less competent partners. While their movement is restricted the fitness they gain for any move toward the goal is theirs alone. It is not drowned out by averaging that fitness with that of the weaker partner. This seems to provide a significant enough selective pressure that evolution occurs.

The symbiotic fitness scheme removes most of the interesting effects of co-evolution. Indeed, in that scheme we are effectively evolving a single creature. This, while successful, avoids rather than confronts the issue of how cooperation emerges in evolutionary games.

11.3   Discussion

We have seen two apparently contrasting case studies, and have tried to explain, in qualitative terms, the significance of the differences. In the first case study we showed that cooperative and specialized team members emerged when the team was rewarded globally for its behaviour. This use of homogenous rewards to induce diversity in teams is a common approach in branches of computer science such as Artificial Intelligence and Artificial Life. In the second case study we saw that if the evolutionary dynamics are wrong then a competitive approach can produce good teams where the team members do not need to be diverse. Each robot has its own fitness function, but the best robot teams are composed of homogenous robots. It is sensible to hypothesize that heterogeneity in the fitness scheme may *only* work where good teams are homogenous. This seems like a nice inversion of the previous case, but it is certainly unlikely to be universal and depends on a number of properties of the task and the fitness scheme. Although the fitness scheme is referred to as *competitive*, the robot learns only from its *own* performance, with no reference to the comparative performance of the other robot. So it could be seen as an *individualist* rather than a *competitive* scheme.

Second, it is interesting to examine the structure of the bar carrying task. Whatever the behaviour of the other robot a good strategy for either robot is to move toward the light, since that will maximize its fitness by reducing its average distance from the goal. The best behaviour, and thus neural network, will vary with the behaviour of the other robot, but the alteration to the robot's movement imposed by the bar and the movement of the other robot probably does not make finding good strategies too hard. In other words there is likely to be a smooth and easily climbed slope in the fitness landscape for the evolutionary algorithm to ascend that improves the behaviour of one robot regardless of the behaviour of the other. Crudely put, moving toward the goal is what game theorists call a dominant behaviour or strategy (Myerson, 1991). In many co-evolutionary systems, however, such dominant strategies do not exist and we see oscillations in the behaviour of the members of the co-evolutionary system. This phenomenon has been observed in co-evolutionary systems composed of robots (Floreano et al., 1998).

Which of the fitness schemes in the co-evolutionary scenario is most similar to the global reward scheme in the reinforcement learning of football scenario? On the face of it the cooperative scheme seems most similar. The rewards for the individuals in the football team are determined by the outcomes of the whole team's behaviour. The individuals in the football team then optimize their own behaviour in order to maximize this global performance. The same is true in the cooperative fitness scheme in the evolutionary robotics example. In that scheme, however, we also select partners randomly from the two populations. It is probably this random regrouping that prevents an improvement in behaviour beyond that present in the initial generation. This phenomenon is also seen elsewhere. The literature on group-selection suggests that, for cooperation to evolve, random re-grouping is not sufficient to evolve cooperative behaviour. For this to emerge there needs to be *assortative re-grouping*, i.e. correlation between the types that are paired together (Sober and Wilson, 1998).

So is the team-based reinforcement learning more like the symbiotic scheme? It is in so far as the team members are not swapped between teams within a population: there is only *one* learning team. So as in the symbiotic scheme there is no regrouping. But there are differences between the symbiotic and the team-based reinforcement learning scheme. In the symbiotic case the search process operates on the genetic representation of the whole team. In the reinforcement learning case the team members learn by conducting their own individual searches through the space of possible behaviours. The other team members are also performing their own searches, and the outcome of each of these depends on the current behaviour of the other team members. The individual, however, will only select changes in behaviour that improve the performance of the team on average. In this sense the team-based reinforcement learning is like the symbiotic scheme even if the search process is distributed across the team members.

References

Dario Floreano, Stefano Nolfi and Francesco Mondada (1998) 'Competitive Co-evolutionary robotics: from theory to practice' in R. Pfeifer (ed.) *From Animals to Animats V: Proceedings of the Fifth International Conference on Simulation of Adaptive Behavior* (Cambridge, Ma.: MIT Press-Bradford Books).

David Goldberg (1989) *Genetic Algorithms in Search, Optimisation and Machine Learning* (Reading Ma.: Addison Wesley).

Kevin Gurney (1997) *Introduction to Neural Networks* (London: UCL Press).

Yoshiyuki Matsumura, Kazuhiro Ohkura and Kanji Ueda (2002) 'Robust Evolutionary Programming Applied to Artificial Neural Networks' *Proceedings of 4th Asia Pacific Conference on Simulated Evolution and Learning (SEAL 02)*, pp. 345–349.

John Maynard Smith (1982) *Evolution and the Theory of Games* (Cambridge: Cambridge University Press).

Tom Mitchell (1997) *Machine Learning* (New York: McGraw Hill).

R. B. Myerson (1991) *Game Theory: Analysis of Conflict* (Cambridge, Ma.: Harvard University Press).

Elliott Sober and David Sloan Wilson (1998) *Unto Others: The Evolution and Psychology of Unselfish Behaviour* (Cambridge Ma.: Harvard University Press).

Richard Sutton and Andrew Barto (1990) 'Time Derivative Models of Pavlovian Reinforcement' in M. Gabriel and J. Moore (eds) *Learning and Computational Neuroscience: Foundations of Adaptive Networks*, pp. 497–537 (Cambridge Ma.: MIT Press).

Richard Sutton and Andrew Barto (1998) *Reinforcement Learning: An Introduction* (Cambridge, Ma.: MIT Press/Bradford Books).

Peter Stone (2000) *Layered Learning in Multiagent Systems: A Winning Approach to Robotic Soccer* (Cambridge, Ma.: MIT Press).

Matthew Todd (1999) Multi-agent Learning, unpublished BSc Thesis, School of Computer Science, University of Birmingham.

Index